Alexander
the Great

PROBLEMS IN EUROPEAN CIVILIZATION SERIES

Alexander the Great: Ancient and Modern Perspectives

Edited and with an introduction by
Joseph Roisman
Colby College

D. C. HEATH AND COMPANY
Lexington, Massachusetts Toronto

Address editorial correspondence to

D. C. Heath and Company
125 Spring Street
Lexington, MA 02173

Acquisitions Editor: James Miller
Developmental Editor: Lauren Johnson
Production Editor: Heather L. Garrison
Designer: Alwyn R. Velásquez
Photo Researcher: Martha Shethar
Production Coordinator: Charles Dutton
Permissions Editor: Margaret Roll

Cover: Bust of Alexander the Great

Copyright © 1995 by D. C. Heath and Company

All rights reserved. No part of this publication may be
reproduced or transmitted in any form or by any means,
electronic or mechanical, including photocopy, recording,
or any information storage or retrieval system, without
permission in writing from the publisher.

Published simultaneously in Canada.

Printed in the United States of America.

International Standard Book Number: 0–669–34501–6

Library of Congress Catalog Number: 94–76933

10 9 8 7 6 5 4 3 2

*To my family
near and far*

Preface

In recent years historians of Alexander have debated the question of how best to tell the man's story: through the genre of biography, or through a history of his time? This collection is neither a biography of the king nor a detailed history of his world, but uses elements of both approaches, comprising documents and essays pertinent to what I see as the main problems and issues surrounding Alexander and his career. The book contains eight parts that discuss the sources on Alexander, the Macedonian state and the death of his father Philip II, Alexander's relationship with the Greeks, his aims, Alexander's army and the Battle of Issus, his relationship with his Macedonian generals, Alexander's divinity, and his policy of integrating victors and vanquished. Each part includes the most relevant ancient sources, followed by modern interpretations of the evidence. The choice of modern interpretations for this collection was based on their contributions to our understanding of Alexander's history and their accessibility to readers who are not experts in the field. The combination of ancient testimonies and modern analyses distinguishes this collection from other anthologies on Alexander. Such a format will introduce readers to diverse interpretations and, I hope, will both encourage them to form their own opinions and stimulate class discussion.

Both documents and essays are abridged and edited in order to meet the constraints of space, but not at the expense of the main thesis, arguments, and significant information. To achieve consistency, names are transliterated in their Latin form. I wish to thank my former instructor, Wolfgang Z. Rubinsohn, who introduced me to Alexander studies and whose methods inspired this collection. I am grateful to Colby College for allowing me time to work on this anthology, to senior editor James Miller of D. C. Heath for initiating the project, and to Lauren Johnson, developmental editor at D. C. Heath, for her careful, conscientious, and yet amiable assistance. Thanks, also, to the reviewers who commented on the manuscript: Winthrop Lindsay Adams, University of Utah; Ernst Badian, Harvard University; Jack Martin Balcer, Ohio State University; Eugene Borza, Pennsylvania State University; Drew Harrington, Western Kentucky University; Frank Romer, University of Arizona; Barry Strauss, Cornell University; and Allen Ward, University of Connecticut.

J. R.

Contents

Alexander's Reign— A Chronology

Owing to the nature of the evidence, there is no agreement among scholars on the dates of certain events of Alexander's reign. The following dates seem to be least in dispute. All dates are B.C.E. (Before the Common Era).

359–336	The reign of Philip II.
338–336	Philip II establishes Macedonian hegemony in Greece after the battle of Chaeronea and sends Attalus and Parmenio with an army to Asia Minor.
336	Philip II is assassinated; Alexander accedes to the throne.
335	Alexander campaigns in the northern Balkans; Thebes falls.
334	The invasion of Asia; the Battle of Granicus; the capture of the western coast of Asia Minor.
333	Alexander winters at Gordium, takes Cilicia, and defeats Darius in the Battle of Issus.
332	The sieges of Tyre and Gaza.
331	Alexander in Egypt: visits Siwah and founds Alexandria; the Mesopotamia campaign and the Battle of Gaugamela.
330	The sack of Persepolis; the campaign in Media; Darius's death; campaigns in Hyrcania, Areia,

and Drangiana; the Philotas affair; arrival at
Arachosia.

329   The crossing of the Hindu Kush; capture of
Bessus; arrival at the Jaxartes; insurrections of
Bactrians and Sogdianians; winter at Bactra.

328   Campaigns in Bactra and Sogdiana; the murder of
Clitus.

327   Alexander's marriage to Roxane; campaigns
against Bactrians; the *proskynesis* affair and the
Pages' conspiracy; the march to India.

326   Arrival at Taxila; crossing of the Indus; Battle of
the Hydaspes; the mutiny on the Hyphasis; return
to the Hydaspes, and the sail down the river.

325   Campaign against the Malli; Craterus's march to
Carmania with part of the army; Alexander
reaches the Indian Ocean; the fleet under
Nearchus departs to Carmania; Alexander
marches through the Gedrosian desert and re-
unites with Craterus at Carmania.

324   Alexander's meeting with Nearchus and travel to
Persis; the Susa marriages; the Opis mutiny;
Hephaestion's death; the exiles' decree.

323   Alexander at Babylon; plans for a campaign in
Arabia; Alexander's death (June 10).

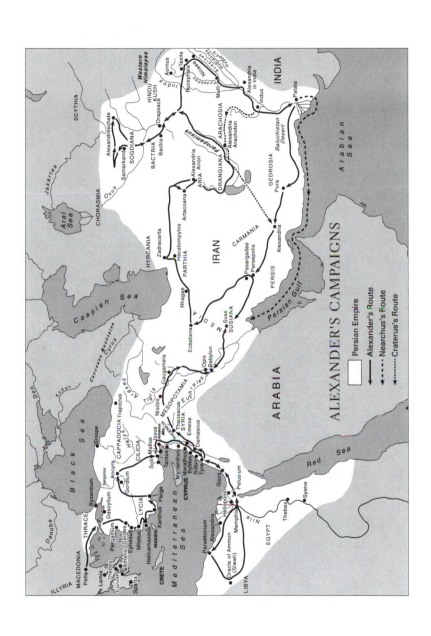

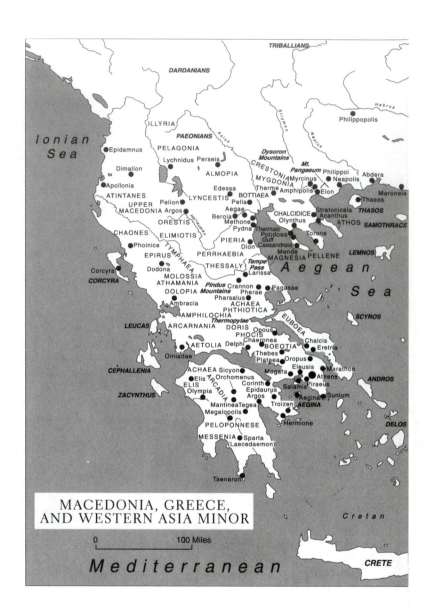

TRIBALLIANS

DARDANIANS

*Ionian
Sea*

ILLYRIA

Epidamnus

PAEONIANS

PELAGONIA

Lychnidus Perseis

Dimallon

ALMOPIA

Apollonia

ATINTANES

UPPER
MACEDONIA

Pelion

Edessa

LYNCESTIS

Argos

ORESTIS

Aegae

Beroia

Methone

CHAONES

ELIMIOTIS

Pydna

Phoinice

TYMPHAEA

PERRHAEBIA

EPIRUS

PIERIA

Dion

Corcyra

Dodona

MOLOSSIA

THESSALY

CORCYRA

ATHAMANIA

*Pindus
Mountains*

Crannon

Pagasae

DOLOPIA

Pherae

Pharsalus

Ambracia

ACHAEA
PHTHIOTICA

AMPHILOCHIA

Thermopylae

LEUCAS

ARCARNANIA

DORIS

Opous

PHOCIS

Chaeronea

AETOLIA

Delphi

BOEOTIA

Oiniadae

Thebes

Plataea

CEPHALLENIA

ACHAEA

Sicyon

Orchomenus

Megara

Elis

ARCADIA

Corinth

ELIS

Epidaurus

ZACYNTHUS

Olympia

Argos

Mantinea Tegea

Megalopolis

PELOPONNESE

Hermione

MESSENIA

Sparta
(Laecedaemon)

Taenaron

DYSORON
Mountains

CRESTONIA

Axius

Strymon

Mt.
Pangaeum

MYGDONIA

Myrcinus

Therme

Amphipolis

Eion

BOTTIAEA

Pella

Thermaic
Gulf

Potidaea

Cassandreia

Mende

CHALCIDICE

Olynthus

Torone

MAGNESIA

*Tempe
Pass*

Larissa

Hebrus

Nestus

Philippopolis

Philippoi

Neapolis

Abdera

Maronea

Thasos

THASOS

Stratonicea

Acanthus

ATHOS

SAMOTHRACE

PELLENE

LEMNOS

A e g e a n

S e a

SCYROS

EUBOEA

Chalcis

Eretria

Oropus

Eleusis

Marathon

Athens

Salamis

Piraeus

Aegina

Sunium

Troizen

AEGINA

ANDROS

DELOS

Cretan

MACEDONIA, GREECE,
AND WESTERN ASIA MINOR

0   100 Miles

M e d i t e r r a n e a n

CRETE

Abbreviations and Frequently Cited Authors

The abbreviations and authors listed below are used throughout the book.

Arr.	Arrian, *Anabasis*
Athen.	Athenaeus, *Deipnosophistae*
B.C. and B.C.E.	Before the Common Era
C.E. (or A.D.)	The Common Era
Curt.	Quintus Curtius Rufus, *History of Alexander the Great*
Dem.	Demosthenes, *Orations*
Diod.	Diodorus of Sicily, *Universal History*
Il.	Homer, *Iliad*
Ind.	Arrian, *Indica*
Isoc.	Isocrates, *Orations*
Justin	Justin, *Abridgment of Pompeius Trogus' Historiae Philippicae*
Moral.	Plutarch, *Moralia*
Plut.	Plutarch, *Alexander*
Polybius	Polybius, *History*
Strabo	Strabo, *Geography*

Principal Proper Names*

Craterus:	a Macedonian nobleman and one of Alexander's chief marshals
Cyrus the Great:	founder of the Persian Empire (550–530)
Darius III:	king of Persia during Alexander's campaign
Heracles:	a Greek hero, son of Zeus and a mortal woman, who was believed to have been Alexander's ancestor on his father's side
Hephaestion:	a Macedonian nobleman and Alexander's closest friend who died in 324
Olympias:	Alexander's mother, from Epirus
Parmenio:	a veteran Macedonian marshal and Alexander's second in command until his execution in 330
Perdiccas:	Alexander's marshal and friend, who became the regent of the empire after the king's death
Perseus:	a Greek hero, son of Zeus and a mortal woman, who was believed to have been Alexander's ancestor on his mother's side
Philip II:	king of Macedonia (359–336) and Alexander's father
Philotas:	Parmenio's son and the commander of the cavalry until his execution in 330
Polybius:	ca. 200–118, a Greek historian of Rome's conquest of the Mediterranean
Xerxes:	king of Persia whose invasion of Greece in 480–479 ended in defeat

*All dates are B.C.E.

Introduction

In 1926 the British historian William Woodthorpe Tarn wrote that Alexander the Great inspired two lines of sociopolitical thought: despotism by the grace of God and brotherhood of mankind. Will Cuppy, the American journalist and humorist, wrote not long after Tarn that Alexander was known by the title "the Great" because he killed more people of more kinds than any other man of his time. It is likely that both authors were wrong. Their differing assessments, however, demonstrate that every person has an Alexander of his or her own, and that our view of the past is strongly shaped by our own circumstances and experiences. Such contrasting evaluations also show the risk of designating one account or perception of the Macedonian king more authoritative than others.

Alexander the Great's fame crossed so many territorial and cultural boundaries that historians, even in ancient times, have found it difficult to reconstruct his story from the diverse traditions about him. Some of Alexander's contemporaries, companions of his Asian campaign, recorded his story, but even their accounts, now lost, were not necessarily complete or free of errors or bias. Indeed, the difficulties of telling Alexander's story have proved so great that some prominent modern historians of Alexander have expressed reservations about writing a history or a biography of him.

In one sense this book reflects such concerns. It is not a history or biography of Alexander but a collection of studies on what may constitute major problems of his reign. The approach is thematic more than chronological, because Alexander was occupied with the topics discussed here throughout his career. Each part includes the most relevant ancient evidence about the subject at hand, as well as one or more modern studies. Our knowledge of Alexander's career comes from the ancient sources, and it is hoped that this format will provide readers with evidence to compare and correlate with the modern interpretations. The purpose of this collection is thus to evoke interest in the subject rather than to serve as the voice of authority.

The first part introduces the reader to perceptions of Alexander by some leading historians of the modern era. Eugene N. Borza's survey of major contributions to Alexander's historiography seems to justify the observation of the Italian historian Benedetto Croce that the historian of the past is the child of his or her age. Because modern views of Alexander are so diverse, it is important to examine the ancient evidence about the king; hence the inclusion of passages illustrating the methods and motives of the extant sources on Alexander. These ancient texts are followed by Peter A. Brunt's discussion of the nature of this ancient literary evidence.

Recently, more and more scholars have come to recognize Alexander's great debt to his father, Philip II, and the impact of the Macedonian political, social, and cultural environment on Alexander's conduct and thoughts. Part II includes A. B. Bosworth's survey of historical developments in Macedonia before Alexander's accession to the throne. Alexander became king following the assassination of his father. The story of Philip's murder is intriguing, and the possibility of Alexander's involvement generated ancient speculations. Stanley M. Burstein discusses Philip's death and the persons involved by supplementing the literary accounts with archaeological evidence from what has been identified as Philip's tomb.

Alexander's relationship with the Greeks constituted a major and ongoing challenge of his career. The Macedonian king was steeped in Greek culture and, officially, led a campaign of revenge and liberation against Persia in which the Greeks served as his independent allies. In reality, he was the Greeks' master and did not always respect their autonomy or interests. Part III offers citations from the text of a treaty between Alexander and the Greeks, but it also includes a description of his destruction of the rebellious city of Thebes in 335

B.C.E. and his controversial order in 324 B.C.E. that the Greek states allow their exiles to return home. A. J. Heisserer and Bosworth look at how Alexander and the Greeks regulated their relationship and how they reacted when their wishes and interests collided.

The magnitude of Alexander's achievements makes the question of his aims and motives especially interesting. Although goals and motivation are hard to uncover in any given period, both ancient and modern historians of Alexander have always asked questions about his motives: for example, did Alexander intend to take the entire Persian Empire as early as the beginning of his campaign? What were his plans once he mastered the empire? Part IV introduces Peter A. Brunt's view concerning the history of Alexander's ambitions and plans, which are important to understanding his campaign as well as his personality.

Alexander owes his fame to his military success, and historians, who normally differ in their assessments of him, are in unusual agreement about the outstanding performance of the king and his forces in battle. In Part V, Nicholas G. L. Hammond examines the special relationship that existed between king and army in Macedonia and how the army was organized. He shows the soldiers and their commander in action at Issus, one of the great set-piece battles of the campaign.

Macedonian nobles and Alexander's friends were those closest to the king in the chain of military and political command. Philotas was a senior officer in the army and a son of Parmenio, Alexander's second in command. One of the most severe crises to reshape Alexander's court occurred when Philotas was charged with a conspiracy against the king and consequently was put to death with his father. In Part VI, Ernst Badian and Waldemar Heckel look at the careers of those involved in the plot and ask who benefited from the affair. Their answers differ. Badian asserts that the charges against Philotas were concocted in order to destroy the old marshal through his son, whereas Heckel sees in the conspiracy the culmination of a power struggle between coalitions of Macedonians in the army and the court.

Another question that divided Alexander's court centered on his quest for superhuman status. Both ancient and modern admirers of Alexander have felt uneasy about Alexander's assertion that he was the son of the god Zeus Ammon and his request that people prostrate themselves before him. In Part VII, Lowell Edmunds discusses Alexander's religious beliefs in an effort to understand his quest for divine status. Badian examines the evidence for Alexander's deification and tries to explicate the king's perception of his own status by assessing its cultural and political contexts.

In the last part, Tarn links Alexander's divine aspirations with what he believes to have been the king's vision of a harmonious world in which race, origin, and faith would lose their divisive powers. Bosworth challenges the historicity of such a vision and argues that no real integration or sharing of power existed between conquerors and conquered in Alexander's empire.

The themes discussed above recur throughout Alexander's story. Questions regarding Alexander's personality, the organization of the empire, the relationship between king and subjects, encounters among cultures, and so on, are raised in every part of this anthology even when they are not directly addressed. It is the complex fabric of issues surrounding Alexander that makes his story so fascinating. Invincibility in battle may have given rise to his wide and lasting reputation, but successful generalship was not the sum of his person nor of his age.

Variety of Opinion

Alexander the Great opened a new era in the history of the world, and by his lifework determined its development for many centuries. He is conspicuous among the great men of history. . . .   —*U. Wilcken*

Instead of Hellenizing Asia, he was tending to asiatise Macedonia and Hellas.   —*G. Grote*

In this matter [promotion of Greek culture in Asia], as in others, Alexander was guided by practical considerations, not by a consciousness of possessing a "mission."   —*J. R. Hamilton*

Born in a half-world between Greece and Europe, he lived above all for the ideal of a distant past, striving to realize an age [of mythical heroes] which he had been too late to share.   —*R. Lane Fox*

But on the personal level, the story of Alexander the Great appears to us an almost embarassingly perfect illustration of the man who conquered the world only to lose his soul. After fighting, scheming and murdering in pursuit of the secure tenure of absolute power, he found himself at last on a lonely pinnacle over an abyss, with no use for his power and security unattainable.   —*E. Badian*

His achievements in warfare and prowess have not been surpassed by any commander.   —*N. G. L. Hammond*

His achievements in his lifetime were soon forgotten and the world shaped by his conquests had few tangible memorials of him. What remained was and is *folie de grandeur.*   —A. B. *Bosworth*

Everyone uses him as a projection of their own private truth, their own dreams and aspirations, fears and power-fantasies.   —P. *Green*

A marble herm portrait of Alexander, now in the Louvre, Paris. It is a second century C. E. Roman copy of what was probably an original portrait of the king made by the court sculptor, Lysippus. (Réunion des Musées Nationaux)

Alexander the Great: Ancient Sources and Modern Studies

Studies on Alexander

Eugene N. Borza

An Introduction to Alexander Studies

Eugene N. Borza is a professor of history at Pennsylvania State University. His works include *In the Shadow of Olympus: The Emergence of Macedon* (Princeton University Press, 1990). In this section, Borza describes the portraits of Alexander as drawn by major historians of the king in Europe and America.

"An Introduction to Alexander Studies" by Eugene N. Borza from *Alexander the Great*, pp. ix–xxi, by Ulrich Wilcken, translated by G. C. Richards, is reprinted with the permission of W. W. Norton and Company, Inc. Copyright © 1967 by W. W. Norton and Company, Inc.

In Search of Alexander

Ever since he emerged from a somewhat backward Macedonian nation to claim much of Greece and Asia as his own, Alexander the Great has exercised a secure hold on the human imagination. The nature of this attraction is a complex phenomenon. It is enough to say that there are many Alexanders, perhaps as many as there are those who profess a serious interest in him. The multifarious nature of Alexander requires a brief inquiry into a dilemma in which the modern student frequently finds himself.

One soon comes to recognize that he is really dealing with three Alexanders or, rather, Alexander on three sometimes distinct, sometimes not clearly separable planes. The first of these is the mythological-romantic Alexander. He is an Alexander who is said to appear in the literature of eighty nations ranging from the British Isles to the Malay Peninsula. . . .

According to the many legends he was a king, a hero, a god, a conqueror, a philosopher, a scientist, a prophet, a statesman, and a visionary whose ideals of universal brotherhood are said to have laid the basis for Stoic thought and predated Christianity by three centuries. He was also a drunkard, a parricide, a thief, and a butcher. He has been accused of depravities base enough to offend the sensibilities of all the ages. In short, he is a giant in literature and folk tradition, and his name and exploits, fanciful or true, are probably more widely known than those of anyone until modern times.

The second Alexander is the historical Alexander. We know that with his father, Philip of Macedon, he subdued and organized the quarrelsome lot of Greek cities now past the prime of their Golden Age. Succeeding Philip, he crossed from Europe to Asia, and on the field of battle brought to an end the ancient but tottering majesty of the Persian Empire. Having fulfilled his role as the leader of a holy war against the traditional enemy, Alexander took an army to the Indus, the edge of the known world, and returned to expire in Babylon in his thirty-third year. Of this incredible expedition we know only the bare outlines, with an imperfect chronology. That he changed a part of the world through which he marched is certain, having laid the basis for the eventual introduction of Greek civilization into a vast area of Western Asia. . . . He ranks historically among the most important men who ever lived purely on the basis of his accomplishments and the change which he wrought on the history of that part of the world.

The third Alexander is Alexander the man. What makes an understanding of the real man difficult is the constant conflict between the mythological and historical figures. For Alexander became a legend virtually in his own era, and that legend, extended and corrupted throughout antiquity, has made him an enigma, affecting as it did every piece of serious or foolish writing about him.

Thus each man who approaches the study of Alexander is confronted with the mythological and historical figures. What he makes out of these is for him the real Alexander, an interpretation which becomes personal. The problems confronting the biographer of Alexander, although not unique, are nevertheless compounded by the poor state of the evidence. . . .

The startlingly dissimilar portraits of Alexander which issue from modern historians can be attributed at least as much to the psychological predilections of the scholar as to the state of the evidence itself. Ulrich Wilcken clearly recognized that the problem was personal in his preface where he suggests that "every student has an Alexander of his own." One of the most perceptive scholars working on Alexander in recent years put the case more strongly when he wrote, "We all interpret the great drama of Alexander in terms of our experience and our dreams." This recalls what Theodor Mommsen once wrote in an only slightly different context: "Those who have lived through historical events, as I have, begin to see that history is neither written nor made without love or hate."

Modern Studies

It may be said that modern Alexander scholarship began in 1833 with the initial publication of a biography by Johann Gustav Droysen [*Geschichte Alexanders des Grossen*]. Droysen was a product of a nineteenth-century school of German historiography which had developed the principles of modern critical historical method. But more important, Droysen was deeply moved by the historical events of his own era. He saw Prussia emerge as a powerful German state, and throughout his life he pressed for the unification of the German peoples under Prussian leadership. Droysen was especially optimistic in 1848, and entering politics (in an era in which historians were not reluctant to participate in making history), he became a member of Parliament. His hopes for German unity were soon crushed, and, except for another brief return to the political arena in 1859, he spent the remaining years of his life in retirement, reworking his material on ancient history, and writing vigorously on Prussia and German unity.

In the light of his own historical experience and political orientation as a Prussian nationalist and fervent monarchist, Droysen's conception of Alexander should come as no surprise. The intricate problems of the Greek city-states in the Classical period, with their almost constant strife and internecine conflicts, were of little interest to Droysen. The Greeks had managed to keep the Persian menace away from the Greek mainland but just barely, and had not yet begun to fulfill what Droysen later conceived as their historical mission. Eventually, however, Philip of Macedon appeared. For Droysen, Philip is the great unifier of Greece, and his son, Alexander, the agent of the diffusion of Greek civilization. Alexander is the world figure, the historical hero who ended one era and began a new and more glorious one. Here the nation and the great national leader emerge as dominant historical themes. The roles of Philip and Alexander as unifier and innovator respectively reflect Droysen's own experience in mid-nineteenth-century Germany. Moreover, it was Droysen who vigorously expounded the notion of Hellenism, that is, the fusion of Greek and Oriental cultures which Alexander wrought and which influenced the course of Mediterranean civilization throughout the rest of antiquity. Droysen's conceptions were propounded so forcefully that they have conditioned virtually all subsequent scholarship on the subject. For most of Droysen's successors Alexander remained a world-mover, although opinions have varied widely on his personal motives and the exact extent of his achievement.

Serious biographical investigations of Alexander were not a pronounced feature of classical studies of the late nineteenth and early twentieth centuries. This period saw the introduction of increasingly sophisticated techniques of historical study, and especially the development of a number of ancillary disciplines such as papyrology, paleography, numismatics, and epigraphy. . . .

Twentieth-century Alexander biography took a new turn with the appearance of the sixth volume of the *Cambridge Ancient History* in which W. W. Tarn contributed an extensive account of the young Macedonian monarch. Tarn, who remains the great Hellenistic historian of this century, had produced some short studies on Alexander earlier in which he developed ideas that were destined to make his Alexander the most debated, if not the most famous, of the modern era. In effect, Tarn took the basic Droysen conception of Alexander as world-mover and added to it the dimension of a new social philosophy. Aristotle had taught that Greeks were fit to rule and aliens only to be ruled. But

> when [Alexander] prayed for a union of hearts and a joint common-wealth of Macedonians and Persians, he proclaimed for the first time, through a brotherhood of peoples, the brotherhood of man. . . . Alexander inspired Zeno's vision of a world in which all men should be members one of another, citizens of one State without distinction of race or institutions, subject only to and in harmony with the Common Law immanent in the Universe, and united in one social life not by compulsion but only by their own willing consent or (as he put it) by Love.

When Tarn's critics attacked his Alexander as being too idealistic, he replied in a paper that Alexander was indeed the first to contemplate the unity of mankind. He described this unity (using the Greek term *homonoia*) as one of the great revolutions in human thought. Tarn was a lawyer by training, and the extraordinary attention he paid to evidence in order to support his case shows an acute mind at work. Poor health forced him to retire from the Bar in 1905, and he was thus enabled to devote the rest of his life to historical pursuits. Tarn was a man of some means and did not find it necessary to seek a university position as a means of support. Ensconced on his Scottish estate, with occasional trips to London to gather material, he lived the "good" life of the British upper class. One critic has referred to "the gentlemanly and sporting Alexander of Tarn," credited "with the extreme views toward life and death and honor, and temperance in love and wine which are associated with the English gentry." Tarn's idealistic Alexander became the dominant portrait. . . .

Partly in response to the criticism leveled at him, and surely in defense of a commitment to his hero, Tarn published in 1948 his *Alexander the Great* in two volumes. The first volume is a short biography of Alexander, substantially a little-revised version of his earlier chapters in the *Cambridge Ancient History* in which the main theses about Alexander's motives and conceptions were stated with great vigor. Volume II, subtitled *Sources and Studies,* is an inspired and highly technical series of studies on the main problems in Alexander scholarship as well as a detailed consideration of the source problem. Whatever disagreements scholars were later to have with Tarn's views and conclusions, it is generally agreed that this single work marks a large step forward in the progress of modern Alexander scholarship, manifesting as it does the careful work and erudition with which the author built his portrait. . . .

In 1949, F. Schachermeyr published his *Alexander der Grosse, Ingenium und Macht,* and introduced an Alexander who, according to one reviewer, was a "conception which would have been impossible before Hitler and World War II." Schachermeyr's Alexander was a brilliant, though ruthless, man of ambition who found the framework of Macedon too restrictive and so set out to expand his personal world as well as his kingdom. Possessed of an awesome ego and a seemingly limitless capacity to act decisively, this Alexander successfully threw off the strictures of the Macedonian feudal nobility and emerged in Asia as a Titan of the first rank. Ruthless, forceful and mystical, he destroyed an old order and established a new world state centered on his own personality. Behaving "like a young Nazi let loose in the Alps," he showed himself capable of dreaming the dream of world conquest and achieving it. Such is Schachermeyr's conception, conditioned in part by a tradition begun by Droysen, but certainly more recently intensified by the author's own experience in Germany. Schachermeyr finally pleads that the world has seen enough Titans, let us be spared another.

In recent years the work of Ernst Badian has contributed much to our understanding of Alexander by bringing to bear upon the work of Tarn and others a most perceptive kind of criticism. Badian has taken a portion of Schachermeyr's view that Alexander was seeking horizons larger than the kingdom of Macedon. Raised to the throne by nobles who expected to rule through him, Alexander soon recognized that he had to assert his independence from the various Macedonian factions for whom he was a puppet. As success piled upon success on the battlefields of Asia, Alexander began to replace the older Macedonians with his own men; he purged others from his court and in doing so emerged as a king in his own right. The price he paid for his freedom, however, was a barrier erected between himself and his European traditions, for as Alexander dissociated himself from his background he began to assume many of the trappings of an Oriental despot. He was never able to return from the summit of power which was also a peak of loneliness. Badian has not produced a full biographical treatment (one eagerly hopes that he will), but the Alexander who has begun to emerge from a series of technical and popular articles is a man who reaches the pinnacle of success only to find himself alone, cut off from his own traditions, and made ruthless by insecurity. Badian's Alexander is essentially a pragmatist, unpossessed of the philosophical worldview attributed to him by Tarn, but perfectly willing from time to time to exploit any convenient myth to reach his goal. This is an amoral Alexander, concerned almost entirely with the struggle to secure his position as absolute ruler. In the course of achieving this end, and abetted by his own enormous talents, he ended one era and began another. It is still the picture of the world-mover, albeit one whose motives are intimately connected with his own ambition and design for survival.

The Ancient Sources

The following selections from the extant ancient sources present these authors' views of Alexander and their reasons for writing his story. It is worth remembering that these authors did not always abide by the rules that they set for themselves in writing about Alexander. The sources for Alexander's reign are then discussed by Brunt.

Strabo

On Callisthenes as a Primary Source

Strabo (ca. 64 B.C.E.–19 C.E.) was a Greek geographer and antiquarian. His book *Geography* is based largely on information taken from earlier accounts. In this passage, he uses Callisthenes, Alexander's court

From Strabo, *Geography*, 17.1.43, vol. 8, trans. H. L. Jones (Cambridge, Mass.: Harvard University Press, 1982).

historian (see Brunt below) to compare oracles of Strabo's own days and earlier ones. The passage indicates the tone of the first written account of Alexander's campaign. (See Part VII for Alexander's visit to Ammon.)

Now that I have already said much about Ammon, I wish to add only this: Among the ancients both divination in general and oracles were held in greater honour, but now great neglect of them prevails, since the Romans are satisfied with the oracles of Sibylla [prophetess of Apollo] and with the [Etruscan] prophecies obtained by means of the entrails of animals, flight of birds, and omens from the sky; and on this account, also, the oracle at Ammon has been almost abandoned, though it was held in honour in earlier times; and this fact is most clearly shown by those who have recorded the deeds of Alexander, since, although they add numerous forms of mere flattery, yet they do indicate some things that are worthy of belief. At any rate, Callisthenes says that Alexander conceived a very great ambition to go inland to the oracle, since he had heard that Perseus, as also Heracles, had done so in earlier times; and that he started from Paraetonium, although the south winds had set in, and forced his way; and that when he lost his way because of the thick dust, he was saved by rainfalls and by the guidance of two crows. But this last assertion is flattery and so are the next: that the priest permitted the king alone to pass into the temple in his usual dress, but the rest changed their clothes; that all heard the oracles from outside except Alexander, but he inside; that the oracular responses were not, as at Delphi and among the Branchidae [priests at Didyma, Asia Minor], given in words, but mostly by nods and tokens, as in Homer, "[Zeus] spoke and nodded assent with his dark brows" — the prophet having assumed the role of Zeus; that, however, the fellow expressly told the king that he, Alexander, was son of Zeus. And to this statement Callisthenes dramatically adds that, although the oracle of Apollo among the Branchidae had ceased to speak from the time the temple had been robbed by the Branchidae, who sided with the Persians in the time of Xerxes, and although the spring also had ceased to flow, yet at Alexander's arrival the spring began to flow again and that many oracles were carried by the Milesian ambassadors to Memphis concerning

Alexander's descent from Zeus, his future victory in the neighbour-
hood of Arbela, the death of Darius, and the revolutionary attempts in Lacedaemon. And he says that the Erythraean Athenaïs
also gave out an utterance concerning Alexander's high descent;
for, he adds, this woman was like the ancient Erythraean Sibylla.
Such, then, are the accounts of the historians.

Arrian

On Ptolemy
and Aristobulus
as Primary Sources

Lucius (?) Flavius Arrianus (ca. 95–180 C.E.) was a Greek from Bithynia
in Asia Minor whose successful career under the emperor Hadrian included a consulship (129) and a governorship of the province Cappadocia (132–137). A prolific author whose works include philosophical
treatises and the history of Alexander (the *Anabasis*), Arrian wrote histories of Alexander's successors and of his own native land as well.

Wherever Ptolemy son of Lagus and Aristobulus son of Aristobulus
have both given the same accounts of Alexander son of Philip, it is my
practice to record what they say as completely true, but where they
differ, to select the version I regard as more trustworthy and also better worth telling. In fact other writers have given a variety of accounts
of Alexander, nor is there any other figure of whom there are more
historians who are more contradictory of each other, but in my view
Ptolemy and Aristobulus are more trustworthy in their narrative,

Reprinted by permission of the publishers and the Loeb Classical Library from
Arrian: *History of Alexander*, Preface, vol. 1, translated by Peter A. Brunt,
Cambridge, Mass.: Harvard University Press, 1976.

since Aristobulus took part in king Alexander's expedition, and Ptolemy not only did the same, but as he himself was a king, mendacity would have been more dishonourable for him than for anyone else; again, both wrote when Alexander was dead and neither was under any constraint or hope of gain to make him set down anything but what actually happened. However, I have also recorded some statements made in other accounts of others, when I thought them worth mention and not entirely untrustworthy, but only as tales told of Alexander. Anyone who is surprised that with so many historians already in the field it should have occurred to me too to compose this history should express his surprise only after perusing all their works and then reading mine.

Quintus Curtius Rufus

On the Character of Alexander and Accounts of Him

Quintus Curtius Rufus was a Roman whose only extant work is a history of Alexander. Because of the loss of the first two books of the work, his identity as well as his professed goal in writing the history cannot be securely established. Nevertheless, many scholars date his history to the early first century C.E. See Brunt below for additional information.

Alexander captured the royal Persian family after the battle of Issus (333). In the description of Alexander's visit to the family, Curtius characterizes the king.

From *The History of Alexander*, 3.12.18–23, 7.8.10–11, 9.1.34, 9.5.21, 10.10.5–6, by Quintus Curtius Rufus, trans. by John Yardley, Penguin Books, 1984, pp. 46, 168, 214, 224, 256. Translation copyright © 1984, John Yardley. Reproduced by permission of Penguin Books Ltd.

Had he been able to maintain this degree of moderation to the end of his life, I would certainly consider him to have enjoyed more good fortune than appeared to be his when he was emulating Father Liber's [Dionysus's] triumph on his victorious march through all the nations from the Hellespont right to the Ocean. For then he would surely have overcome the defects he failed to overcome, his pride and his temper; he would have stopped short of killing his friends at dinner, and he would have been reluctant to execute without trial men who had distinguished themselves in battle and had conquered so many nations along with him. But good fortune had not as yet overwhelmed him: while it was on the increase, he bore it with self-restraint and abstinence, but eventually he failed to control it when it reached its peak. At this particular time, certainly, his actions were such that he outshone all previous kings in self-control and clemency. The unmarried princesses, who were extremely beautiful, he treated with as much respect as if they were his own sisters. As for Darius' wife, who was surpassed by none of her generation in beauty, Alexander was so far from offering her violence that he took the utmost care to prevent anyone from taking advantage of her while she was in captivity. He gave orders for all their finery to be returned to the women, and as captives they lacked none of the magnificence of their former state — only their self-esteem. . . .

[The following passages from Curtius indicate his historiographical methods and his attitudes toward his sources.]

The Scythians [nomadic people in Central Asia] differ from other barbarians, however, in not being intellectually backward and unrefined — some of them are even said to have a capacity for philosophy (as far as is possible for a race perpetually under arms). What they are reported to have said before the king is perhaps foreign to our way of thinking and our character, since we have enjoyed more cultivated times and intellects but, though their oratory could be criticized, my accurate reporting should not. I shall relate without alteration the account as it has been passed down to us. . . .

Personally, I report more than I believe, for, while I cannot bear to declare as fact matters of which I am uncertain, I also cannot omit what I have been told. . . .

According to Clitarchus and Timagenes,* Ptolemy (who was subsequently a king) took part in this battle [against a city in India]. Ptolemy himself, however, certainly from no desire to detract from his own reputation, records that he was not there, since he had been sent on an expedition. Such was the carelessness of the compilers of the older histories or, an equally reprehensible shortcoming, their gullibility. . . .

Some have believed that the distribution of the provinces was prescribed by Alexander's will, but I have ascertained that this report, though transmitted by our sources, is without foundation. In fact, after the division of the empire, it seems they would have all individually established their own dominions — if a boundary could ever stand in the way of unbridled ambition. . . .

Plutarch

On Writing Biography

Plutarch (ca. 46– ca. 120 C.E.) was a Greek biographer and author. His biography of Alexander was published in a series of pairs of biographies of Greeks and Romans. In addition, Plutarch wrote two rhetorical compositions on the king (*On Alexander the Great: Virtue or Fortune*), which are included in a collection of his literary works entitled *Moralia*.

My subject in this book is the life of Alexander, the king, and of Julius Caesar, the conqueror of Pompey. The careers of these men embrace such a multitude of events that my preamble shall consist

*For Clitarchus, see Brunt below. Timagenes was a historian from Alexandria (first century B.C.E.)

From Plutarch, *Alexander*, Preface, in The Age of Alexander, by Plutarch, trans. by Ian Scott-Kilvert, Penguin Classics, 1973, p. 252. Copyright © 1973, Ian Scott-Kilvert. Reproduced by permission of Penguin Books Ltd.

of nothing more than this one plea: if I do not record all their most celebrated achievements or describe any of them exhaustively, but merely summarize for the most part what they accomplished, I ask my readers not to regard this as a fault. For I am writing biography, not history, and the truth is that the most brilliant exploits often tell us nothing of the virtues or vices of the men who performed them, while on the other hand a chance remark or a joke may reveal far more of a man's character than the mere feat of winning battles in which thousands fall, or of marshalling great armies, or laying siege to cities. When a portrait painter sets out to create a likeness, he relies above all upon the face and the expression of the eyes and pays less attention to the other parts of the body: in the same way it is my task to dwell upon those actions which illuminate the workings of the soul, and by this means to create a portrait of each man's life. I leave the story of his greatest struggles and achievements to be told by others.

Peter A. Brunt

The Sources for the
History of Alexander

Peter A. Brunt was the Camden Professor of ancient history at Brasenose College, Oxford. Among his works is *Studies in Greek History and Thought* (Clarendon Press, 1992). In this selection, Brunt discusses the nature of the primary sources for Alexander's history and their relationship to the extant ancient histories of the king.

Archaeology, inscriptions and coins tell us little of Alexander: we have to rely mainly on literary sources, and of the many contemporary accounts of his reign, none survives; all [of the following] ex-

"Introduction." Reprinted by permission of the publishers and the Loeb Classical Library from Arrian: *History of Alexander,* Vol. 1, translated by Peter A. Brunt, Cambridge, Mass.: Harvard University Press, 1976.

tant narratives are rather late. In the mid first century B.C. Diodorus the Sicilian composed a *Universal History* in Greek, of which book 16 deals with Philip, 17 with Alexander (there is a long [part missing,] and only a table of contents shows what he recounted between winter 330/29 and summer 327), and 18–20 with Alexander's successors. Between 29 B.C. and A.D. 226, and almost certainly in the first century A.D., Quintus Curtius Rufus wrote a Latin history of Alexander in ten books, of which the first two which went down to spring 333 are lost; there are also some later gaps. Early in the second century A.D. Plutarch included Alexander in his *Parallel Lives*. A lost Latin Universal History written by Pompeius Trogus under [the emperor] Augustus was epitomized probably in the third century A.D. by Justin; his work is of small value. There are of course allusions in other writers, notably the scholarly *Geography* by Strabo (ca. A.D. 1), whose lost historical work also contained something on Alexander.

Naturally there must have been many other treatments of Alexander written in antiquity after Alexander's own time. . . . [The most important account was written by] Lucius (or Aulus) Flavius Arrianus . . . from a family at Nicomedia, a Hellenized city in Bithynia. . . . From his name, most fully recorded in a recently found inscription, we can see that he was a Roman citizen; . . . He was governor of Cappadocia from ca. A.D. 132 to 137; he had previously been consul, probably in 129. If he reached this office at the normal age, he would have been born not later than 89. . . .

Before his public career began, Arrian had attended the classes of the Stoic teacher, Epictetus, . . . [and] wrote down extensive notes of his master's lectures or sermons. . . . Years later, he published these *Discourses* in eight books. . . .

Early in his tenure of the province Arrian inspected the forts on the Black Sea coast; he reported officially to Hadrian [the Roman emperor] in Latin, but also presented him with a little literary work in Greek called "The Voyage Round the Black Sea" (*Periplous Euxini*). . . . Later he was confronted with a serious danger of an invasion [of the nomadic Alans from southeast Russia], and again wrote a short description of his preparations to repel it (*Ectaxis contra Alanos*). . . . He was still governor when he wrote a third treatise in 136–137 on *Tactics*; . . .

There is no evidence that Arrian was employed again by Rome. He presently retired to Athens, where he was a citizen and became *archon* (chief magistrate) in 148–149. . . . He is said to have lived into the reign of Marcus Aurelius (161–180), but was dead when Lucian [the Greek author of satiric dialogues] wrote his *Alexander the False Prophet* shortly after 180. Most of his writings doubtless date from his retirement. . . .

Arrian was a prolific writer, though apart from the works mentioned above and those comprised in this edition, his essay on *Hunting (Cynegeticus)* is the only one to survive. Mere fragments, or summaries by the ninth-century Byzantine scholar, Photius, attest his *History of Affairs after Alexander* in ten books (presumably a sequel to the *Anabasis*) which ended so abruptly in 321 B.C. that it must have been left unfinished, a *History of Parthia* in 17 books, which had reached [the emperor] Trajan's Parthian war in the 8th, and a *History of Bithynia* from mythical times to its annexation by Rome in 74 B.C. in eight books. His preface to this work (known from Photius) referred to lost biographies of [the Syracusan rulers] Dion and Timoleon and implied that these lives, as well as the *Anabasis*, were exercises in historiography, preparing him for his great life-work of recording the story of his own fatherland; . . .

The connecting link between many of these varied productions may be found in Arrian's admiration for Xenophon, who also ranked both as philosopher and historian. . . .

Clearly the evidentiary value of all [the] non-contemporary historians, including Arrian himself, rests on their ability to obtain and transmit reliable contemporary information. Even if it had been the practice of classical historians to search out documentary records for the past, they could not have found much to their purpose, and at best they had to turn to contemporary narratives. Their proper course was to examine and collate such narratives, written by eyewitnesses or at least by men who had themselves been able to question eyewitnesses. (Even a companion of Alexander could not have seen and heard for himself more than a little of what occurred.) But some of them simply paraphrased, summarized or expanded existing works by authors who themselves depended directly or indirectly on the primary authorities; the possibilities of error were thus multiplied at every stage, as careless or wilful omissions and additions might occur. Thus it is clear that whatever sources Curtius used he embellished what he found with all the arts of Silver Latin rhetoric, and any later writer who trusted him implicitly would be to that extent further from the truth. Still, all accounts of Alexander which are not mere fiction . . . must ultimately go back to contemporary sources. . . .

There were many contemporary accounts of Alexander; I name only the most notable. Callisthenes of Olynthus, Aristotle's kinsman and pupil, already an accredited historian, was taken with him by Alexander to commemorate his deeds; he perished at Alexander's hands in 327, but his narrative went down to 331 and perhaps to 329. Anaximenes of Lampsacus continued his history of Philip with a work on Alexander that is cited only twice. Chares of Mitylene, an usher in Alexander's court, is credited with at least ten books which *may* have comprised no more than a series of reminiscences and anecdotes of court life. A work by the Cynic philosopher, Onesicritus of Astypalaea, a pilot in Alexander's Indus flotilla and in [the fleet led by Alexander's chief admiral, Nearchus], is cited mainly for geographical descriptions and marvels, and treated by Arrian with contempt (Arr. 6.2.3; *Indica* 3.6), but it may have had a far wider scope and certainly ranged further than the memoir of his voyage by Nearchus himself, which was Arrian's chief source in the *Indica*. Clitarchus of Alexandria wrote at least twelve books on Alexander; though he may not have actually served on the expedition, the suggestion that he was not a contemporary has been refuted, and he must surely have published before Ptolemy. A somewhat older friend of Alexander, Ptolemy played a part of growing importance in the campaigns and became [governor] of Egypt on Alexander's death; here he made himself an independent ruler and assumed the royal title in 304, founding a dynasty which lasted till the death of Cleopatra in 30; he more or less retired in 285, three years before his death. Since Arrian refers to him as king, it is commonly assumed that he did not write his history until after 304, and perhaps not until his years of leisure and extreme old age. These assumptions seem to me unwarranted. Naturally Arrian knew that he became king, whether or not he was so described on Arrian's copy, and Arrian's point is perhaps that the man with the qualities of a king would not tell lies; this point, if valid at all, would hold good at whatever date the "kingly man" was writing. Moreover, even if Arrian supposed that he wrote when king, we do not know that the supposition was justified by anything in Ptolemy's text. And we have only to think of Caesar to see that the claims of government and warfare do not exclude literary composition. Finally, Aristobulus too accompanied Alexander, and was employed to repair the tomb of Cyrus (Arr. 6.29); we do not know what professional expertise he had, nor where he came from, but he ultimately became a citizen of Cassandria in Macedon, founded in 316; he was writing after the battle of Ipsus in 306 (Arr. 7.18.5; cf. 22.5), and allegedly began only when he was eighty-three; this, if true, tells us little, as the date of his birth is not on record.

The "fragments" of these writers are collected in Jacoby's *Fragmente der griechischen Historiker* and have been translated by C. A. Robinson (*The History of Alexander the Great,* 1953). The term "fragments" is misleading. Very seldom do we have their actual words as distinct from summaries or mere allusions. . . . Moreover, the fragments, such as they are, may give us a very imperfect idea of the scope and importance of their works. If Arrian's *Anabasis* were lost, only three or four uninformative fragments of Ptolemy would survive, and while we should know more of Aristobulus through Strabo, we might have supposed that he was primarily interested in geographical descriptions, whereas Arrian uses him for other matters as well, and in fact gives little space to geography in the *Anabasis,* as distinct from the *Indica.* . . .

Callisthenes alone is *known* to have been actually writing during the course of the campaigns. By contrast Aristobulus composed his work not less than 20 to 30 years after the events he described, and it is generally but rashly assumed that Ptolemy too wrote after a long lapse of time. Callisthenes, it is true, need not have been the only historian actually engaged in writing in Alexander's lifetime, and others may have made contemporary notes. A historian who did neither must, when at last he came to compose, have relied on works previously published by others, on documentary evidence, on his own and others' recollections, or on all these kinds of information. Now it is a marked feature of Arrian's work that he gives very detailed reports of a dry factual kind; he tells who commanded particular regiments, who were given particular provincial appointments at particular times, how many days the army took to reach a specified place or how many stades it covered. Similar information is also found in Curtius, and even in Diodorus; though the brevity of his account compels him generally to omit such data, there is enough to show that they appeared in his source. All this suggests that some of the contemporary historians, including the sources of Curtius and Diodorus as well as Arrian, disposed of documentary material.

Both Arrian (7.25) and Plutarch (*Alexander* 76) purport to describe Alexander's last days from "the royal journals," to which there are a few other references elsewhere, all concerned with his spending days drinking and sleeping! We are also told that the journals were "written up" by Eumenes, the royal secretary (who was to play a turbulent part in the struggles after Alexander's death), in collaboration with one Diodotus. It has commonly been supposed that the journals in fact recorded all important decisions made by Alexander and all notable events reported to him, as well as an account of his own actions day by day; . . . It is further assumed that a copy of Alexander's journals came into the possession of Ptolemy, presumably in 321 on the death of Perdiccas [the regent of the empire after Alexander's death], and that he used them for his history. This hypothesis is not proved, nor probable. The journals are cited only for Alexander's personal habits and particularly for his last days, not for any military or political measures; for instance Plutarch (55.3) seeks to show the innocence of Callisthenes from a royal letter, not from the journals, and Arrian cannot resolve his doubts about Callisthenes' fate (Arr. 4.14.3) from the journals. If Ptolemy used them here and elsewhere, he certainly never made this plain to Arrian. It is far from clear from Arr. 7.26.3 that even for Alexander's last days Arrian obtained his knowledge of the journals from Ptolemy (or Aristobulus) rather than directly, but it is certain that the version he knew was materially different from that known to Plutarch; neither was necessarily authentic. If Arrian's "documentary" material comes from the journals through Ptolemy, we must ask how some such material also reached Diodorus and Curtius; evidently part of it was in their common source, and that source is usually taken to be Clitarchus, who must be supposed to have written before Ptolemy (Curt. 9.5.21). It seems to me clear that the so-called journals were of limited scope and circulated in different versions, which were literary compositions. Various theories have been proposed by scholars who do not accept the orthodox but (in my judgement) incorrect dogma that official journals underlie Ptolemy's history. On one view, the fact that they are not attested except for Alexander's final residence at Babylon can be readily explained: it was at Babylon that local records were kept under the old kings, as later under the [Hellenistic kings of Syria], narrating all the doings of the king; such records could have been the basis for literary compositions. Alternatively an alleged "record" of Alexander's last days was circulated by Eumenes himself (or perhaps rather in his name) to show that there was no truth in the stories that Alexander had been poisoned at the instance of Antipater or others, and this "record" might in turn have been altered by various hands for propagandist purposes. . . . In any event the notion that Ptolemy's history was specially reliable because he had access, and perhaps sole access, to the king's own journals, should be given up.

Plutarch and others often cite the letters of Alexander and other figures of his time. Some are undeniably spurious, as they contain manifest absurdities. Others make statements which are or might be true. Scholars commonly hold that each must be treated on its merits. Unfortunately, we do not possess any unquestionably authentic letters, which would make stylistic tests possible. Moreover, a forger would obviously draw on histories of Alexander, and might use true information by this method. Hence we cannot properly infer that a letter must be genuine, if its statements are correct. Now it seems that all those used by Plutarch (and others) came from one collection, and it is hard to see how genuine letters would have been mixed up with spurious letters or in what circumstances genuine private letters would have been published at all. In my judgement all should be rejected.

One kind of documentary material does seem to have been available to the historians of Alexander, viz. the reports of "bematists" [surveyors] on marches and distances. . . .

From all this it follows that historians like Aristobulus who wrote some time after the events had to rely on their own and others' recollections, on contemporary notes and on already published accounts which had come their way. Callisthenes' official record, so far as it went, must therefore have been of great value to all his successors. But we do not know that it was the only truly contemporaneous version of events. And the difficulty of understanding how minute details could be given for the period Callisthenes certainly did not cover will be mitigated by the assumption that later writers, including Clitarchus and Ptolemy, composed their stories much sooner after Alexander's death than is often assumed, or that (whenever they wrote) they could refer to their own notes made at the time.

Callisthenes was censured in antiquity for his rhetoric, his adulation of Alexander and (by [the Greek historian] Polybius, quite unjustly) for incompetence in military matters. Clitarchus, the only other contemporary historian who is known to have been read widely for a long period, was thought to be clever but mendacious. Strabo, who often cites Onesicritus, Nearchus and Aristobulus, was contemptuous of the way in which all the historians who accompanied Alexander "toyed with facts," glorifying Alexander, imposing fables on the credulity of their readers and contradicting each other on matters of which, as eyewitnesses, they should have been able to give true and uniform reports. He had in mind their geographical descriptions, but his criticisms have a wider relevance. Onesicritus, whom he once characterizes as the arch-liar (Strabo 15.1.28), had the audacity to tell how Alexander cohabited with the queen of the Amazons; so did Clitarchus, though he (unlike Onesicritus) was perhaps not with the army at the time. Even Ptolemy and Aristobulus did not eschew the fabulous in recounting Alexander's visit to Siwah (Arr. 3.3). It is less surprising that in the end an "Alexander-Romance" was fashioned, perhaps by the first century B.C., which bears as little relation to the historic king as the *Chanson de Roland* to Charlemagne. In his preface Arrian himself speaks with contempt of the current histories of Alexander (cf. 6.11), and with an emphasis unique in ancient historiography proclaims his reliance on the more trustworthy accounts of Ptolemy and Aristobulus. . . .

Arrian . . . undertakes to record as facts what Ptolemy and Aristobulus agreed in recording and, where they differed, to select what he thinks most credible and memorable. Although he sometimes notes discrepancies between them, that is certainly not his invariable practice, nor did he promise to follow such a practice. One divergence gravely disturbed him (Ar. 4.14.4), and it seems likely that if they had often *disagreed* he would have lost confidence in one, if not in both. I suppose, therefore, that the differences he has in mind arose mainly when one provided information that the other did not give; in such circumstances Arrian could reasonably have treated their stories as complementary. In fact neither is often cited specifically, nor when either or both are cited, is it always easy to see why; there seems to be an element of caprice. . . . However, Arrian's preface seems to promise that all statements of fact will come from Ptolemy or Aristobulus or both, whereas what he derives from other sources will be given as mere "tales." His actual practice is not quite so simple. On the one hand, some parts of the "factual" narrative in books 6 and 7 seem to come from Nearchus, his chief source for the *Indica,* whom he regarded as no less reliable than Ptolemy and Aristobulus, and with good reason; on the other hand, there are occasions, registered in the notes, in which "tales" can be shown to have been told by one or both of his main authorities.

Most scholars assume that he normally relied more on Ptolemy than on Aristobulus. This may be true, though it is usually taken too much for granted. Certainly, as an old friend of Alexander (3.6) and a high ranking officer in his army, Ptolemy should have been better placed to know the truth than Aristobulus, and his military and political experience might well have given him more insight into matters of war and statecraft. But though these considerations have had much weight with the moderns, they do not seem to have occurred to Arrian. If he shows some preference for Ptolemy in the preface, it is on the ludicrous ground that as a king he could not have lied without special dishonour. It is also clear from comparison of Arrian's narrative with "fragments" of Aristobulus preserved elsewhere that Arrian omitted much that Aristobulus told, particularly geographical descriptions. Unfortunately Ptolemy is so seldom cited elsewhere that we have virtually no independent check on Arrian's use of his work, and cannot tell how much he omitted from it, or whether he at times silently rejected Ptolemy in favour of Aristobulus; it would have been perfectly in accord with his own preface if he had done so, whenever he found Aristobulus' account more credible or memorable. . . . On the common view that Ptolemy was his preferred source, these omissions may well be from Ptolemy's history, and we certainly ought not to assume that even if Arrian is mainly Ptolemy, Ptolemy is mostly in Arrian. . . . The importance of Aristobulus as a source may be generally underrated; on the other hand I have some doubt (of a subjective kind) whether Arrian was capable of systematically collating and dovetailing both narratives, and there are occasions when Ptolemy is not actually cited in which he is unquestionably the authority used, at least for military operations in which he played a large part himself. It may then seem *probable* that Ptolemy was more extensively used than Aristobulus.

In his preface Arrian adds that he has also recorded, but only as tales (*legomena*), statements he found in other writers, if he thought them memorable and not entirely untrustworthy; in fact he sometimes mentions such "tales," only to reject them as incredible, presumably because they were so prevalent that he felt bound to notice them, or because they illustrated his contention that the usual versions of Alexander's expedition were often worthless. It is conventional to refer to the accounts of Alexander which do not depend on Ptolemy, Aristobulus or Nearchus as "the vulgate." This is an expression I shall use for convenience. . . . I believe that he culled them from very late writers, those which were read in his own day, whereas our other authorities may preserve much earlier versions. . . .

Diodorus is generally held to have used only one source at a time, for instance in books 18 to 20 the excellent contemporary historian, Hieronymus of Cardia (ca. 360–260); evidence from these books which bears on Alexander is of first rate value. In book 17 his one source (if this theory is correct) was also used, perhaps at second hand, by Curtius, whose account often shows striking concurrences but preserves more of the common source than Diodorus' briefer story. Curtius, it is true, must also have drawn on another tradition, perhaps Ptolemy, for he is also sometimes at variance with Diodorus. As Clitarchus is named once by Diodorus (though not in book 17) and twice by Curtius, and as there are some (but very few) significant agreements between the fragments of his work and their accounts, he is generally identified as their common source, all the more readily as he was much read down to the first century B.C., though little respected. However, since the fragments of Clitarchus are meagre, this identification adds little to the picture we can form of their common source from the works of Diodorus and Curtius alone, and it is positively harmful if it induces the error of thinking that the evidence for Alexander in antiquity came to consist only of the "Clitarchean vulgate" and of Arrian's chosen authorities. In fact there was a multiplicity of versions of many events, and we should not disregard any of the historians of Alexander's own time or those who may later have distorted and embellished what they read.

Arrian's account is in general at once more detailed, clear and coherent than those given by Diodorus and Curtius, and it has less of the trivial and fabulous. . . . However, he himself was too much of an admirer of Alexander to detect that their histories were often apologetic, especially in tendentious omissions; nor did it occur to him that Ptolemy's version might have been affected by the feuds after Alexander's death in which he played a great part. Moreover, Arrian himself lacks some of the "documentary" material which other writers, notably Curtius, have preserved; it seems to me probable that he must have omitted much detail that his own main sources contained. We cannot, therefore, neglect other accounts of Alexander, even Diodorus and Curtius despite their general inferiority, and still less Plutarch and Strabo, especially when they themselves cite other contemporary authorities. Nor can it in my view be maintained that Arrian contributes much, if anything, of his own that is important to understanding Alexander. His merit was to have unearthed better accounts than were current in his day, and to have followed them without the embellishments of a Curtius, but just as his style is less brilliant than that of Curtius, so his own judgement is more naïve. He was a simple, honest soul, but no historian. . . .

During the Middle Ages many histories of Alexander were based on legendary traditions, some of which went back to Hellenistic times. This illustration, from a medieval history of Alexander, describes his birth accompanied by natural wonders, which indicate a divine favor. (Culver Pictures, Inc.)

The Macedonian Background: Macedonia, Philip II, and Alexander

Philip II and Macedonia

Arrian

Alexander's Account of His Father's Achievements

The selection below is excerpted from Arrian's account of a speech delivered by Alexander to his mutinous soldiers at Opis in 324. The passage enumerates Philip's and Alexander's services to the Macedonians

Reprinted by permission of the publishers and Loeb Classical Library from Arrian: *History of Alexander*, 7.9.2–5, vol. 9, translated by Peter A. Brunt, Cambridge, Mass.: Harvard University Press, 1976.

and describes Philip's great achievements, which enabled Alexander to embark on his campaign.

First of all, I shall begin my speech with Philip, my father, as is only fair. Philip took you over when you were helpless vagabonds, mostly clothed in skins, feeding a few animals on the mountains and engaged in their defence in unsuccessful fighting with Illyrians, Triballians and the neighbouring Thracians. He gave you cloaks to wear instead of skins, he brought you down from the mountains to the plains; he made you a match in battle for the barbarians on your borders, so that you no longer trusted for your safety to the strength of your positions so much as to your natural courage. He made you city dwellers and established the order that comes from good laws and customs. It was due to him that you became masters and not slaves and subjects of those very barbarians who used previously to plunder your possessions and carry off your persons. He annexed the greater part of Thrace to Macedonia and, by capturing the best placed positions by the sea, he opened up the country to trade; he enabled you to work the mines in safety; he made you the rulers of the Thessalians, who in the old days made you dead with terror; he humbled the Phocian people and gave you access into Greece that was broad and easy instead of being narrow and hard. The Athenians and Thebans were always lying in wait to attack Macedonia; Philip reduced them so low, at a time when we were actually sharing in his exertions, that instead of our paying tribute to the Athenians and taking orders from the Thebans it was we in our turn who gave them security. He entered the Peloponnese and there too he settled affairs, and his recognition as leader with full powers over the whole of the rest of Greece in the expedition against the Persians did not perhaps confer more glory on himself than on the commonwealth of the Macedonians. . . .

A. B. Bosworth

The Legacy of Philip

A. B. Bosworth is a professor of classics and ancient history at the University of Western Australia. Among his works is *From Arrian to Alexander* (Clarendon Press, 1988). In this selection, Bosworth describes how Philip transformed the Macedonian state and army and created the conditions that allowed Alexander to embark on his Asian campaign.

The period 336–323 B.C. is inevitably designated the age of Alexander. It marked a huge expansion of the imperial boundaries of Macedon, a virtually unparalleled outpouring of resources, material and human. . . . With equal justice the period might be termed the age of Philip. The Macedon that Alexander inherited was the creation of his father. The army he led was forged by Philip. The material resources of the Macedonian throne were acquired by Philip. The system of alliances which turned the Balkans into a virtual annex of Macedon was Philip's development, and the war against Persia was launched at the end of Philip's reign. In his first years, at least, Alexander was continuing a process begun by his father, and his reign cannot be understood without constant reference to his predecessor. What follows is in no sense a history of Philip, rather a contextual stage setting to introduce the accession of Alexander.

As is well known, Philip came to power in 359 B.C., when Macedon was threatened with dissolution, debilitated by a decade of dynastic feuding and crippled by military defeat at the hands of the Illyrians. During the next twenty-three years he made a world power out of that ruined inheritance, creating a political, military, and financial basis for empire. On the political front Macedon was

From *Conquest and Empire: The Reign of Alexander the Great* by A. B. Bosworth, Cambridge University Press, 1988, pp. 5–10, 12, 16–19. Copyright © 1988, Cambridge University Press. Reprinted by permission of the author and the publisher.

welded into a unity, focused on the person of the king. That came about partly by coercion. After his decisive early victory over the Illyrians (358) Philip was able to dominate the turbulent principalities of Upper Macedonia (Lyncestis, Orestis, Elimiotis and Tymphaea) which straddled the Pindus range between the upper Haliacmon and Epirus and had traditionally maintained their independence of the monarchy of Macedon proper, based on the lower plains. For the first time they became integral parts of the greater kingdom. Their nobility was absorbed into the court at Pella and achieved distinction under both Philip and Alexander. At the same time they offered a fertile recruiting ground for both infantry and cavalry; no less than three of the original six phalanx battalions of Alexander came from the upper principalities.

The political union was cemented by marriage. Unashamedly polygamous, Philip contracted a sequence of unions, particularly in the early years of his reign. . . . The most important was the formidable Olympias who came from the royal house of Molossia and was taken to Philip's bed by 357 at latest. This marriage linked together the two dynasties on either side of the Pindus and gave Philip direct influence on the Molossian throne. When he ultimately intervened in Epirus, the reigning king Arybbas was deposed in favour of his nephew, Alexander, the brother of Olympias. These marriages were the linchpins of the great nexus of guest-friends which was to support Philip's interests through the Balkans. At the same time the risk of dynastic conflict which they posed was obviated by the clear superiority that Olympias enjoyed over her fellow consorts.

As the king's network of alliances expanded, the influence of his nobility contracted. Philip increased the élite body of royal Companions (hetairoi), attracting immigrants from the wider Greek world. Men who would accept his patronage were given lavish donations of land and status at court. Of Alexander's close circle of boyhood friends three (Nearchus of Crete; Erigyius and Laomedon of Mytilene) were non-Macedonian. Other prominent figures, notably the chief secretary, Eumenes of Cardia, came from abroad. Their loyalty was to the king alone. However intimate and important their functions, they stood apart from the rest of the Macedonian hierarchy, never fully accepted and often resented. Even after Alexander's death Eumenes' foreign extraction was a liability when he commanded troops, and his own Macedonians were finally to turn against him with the bitter gibe "plague from the Chersonese."

Philip's lavishness to his new men was matched by benefactions to the old nobility. The new acquisitions of land in Chalcidice and Thrace were parcelled out to new and old alike. Polemocrates, father of the great marshal Coenus, obtained estates in the hinterland of Olynthus. His primary holdings were in Elimiotis, in Upper Macedonia, and he now had interests, directly conferred by the king, in the new territories. Philip was sharing the advantages of conquest while diversifying the power base of his nobility. He also, it seems, founded the institution of the Pages: the sons of prominent nobles received an education at court in the immediate entourage of the king, developing a personal attachment to him while necessarily serving as hostages for the good behaviour of their families. As a result the nobility was simultaneously coerced and rewarded, diluted and diversified. As the frontiers of the kingdom expanded, loyalty to the crown brought tangible rewards, and those rewards involved financial interests and military obligations outside the old baronial centres of power. In the climate of success and expansion there was less incentive to challenge the supremacy of the king at Pella, and even the influx of favoured Companions from beyond the borders was tolerable.

Philip reigned as an autocrat. The political institutions of Macedon were informal and rudimentary, and there were few practical constraints on a strong king. Like his son, Philip presumably consulted an inner council of intimates on major issues of state, but nothing suggests that the council was anything other than advisory. Again, it might be prudential to consult the opinions of the army on various occasions but there was nothing incumbent on the king to hold regular assemblies and he was in no sense bound by popular opinion. It is suggested that by tradition the army exercised capital jurisdiction, but that is a strictly limited area. Even there procedure was apparently fluid and informal, and there was certainly no body of Macedonian statute law. . . . For most effective purposes Philip *was* Macedon. He concluded treaties in his own name with sovereign states, sent his own ambassadors to the Amphictyonic Council, and (like his predecessors) struck coins in his own name. Perhaps the best illustration of the advantages of his position is the fate of the hapless Athenian embassy which travelled to Macedon in the summer of 346 to ratify the Peace of Philocrates. Ratification meant the physical presence of Philip, and the ambassadors were forced to wait impatiently at Pella while the king completed his campaigns in Thrace, increasing the territorial possessions which would be confirmed by the peace. . . .

This considerable freedom of action was underpinned by the huge financial resources of Macedon. The mineral reserves of the kingdom, previously centered in the territory east of the River Axios, were vastly expanded when Philip occupied the site of Crenides in 356 and exploited the rich veins of gold and silver in the neighbouring mines of Mt. Pangaeum. According to Diodorus (16.8.6) this area alone supplied revenues of more than 1,000 talents and Philip extended his mining operations to Chalcidice, exploiting the deposits in the mountainous terrain north of Olynthus. What is more, as the boundaries of the kingdom expanded, so did its fiscal basis: dues upon landed property and extraordinary levies (*eisphorae*). Philip's financial power was comparatively unmatched, except by the Great King [of Persia], and it gave him invaluable advantages. Diodorus mentions his capacity to keep a formidable mercenary force and to bribe collaborators in the Greek world. Though emotively expressed, the statement is true and important. Philip did attract a large and versatile body of mercenaries which he could use in the most remote theatres of operation and deploy independently of the Macedonian native levy. . . .

The diplomatic intrigue Diodorus speaks of is equally important. Philip attracted the most prominent figures of the Greek world to Pella, where he entertained lavishly and dispersed huge sums as gifts, in traditional Homeric hospitality. Bribery or guest-friendship, it depended on one's perspective. Philip could buy goodwill, encourage political cooperation or even finance dissidents to seize power in their home city. . . . Philip did not merely spend money, alleges the contemporary critic, Theopompus: he threw it away. His treasury was never flush with excess funds, and Alexander himself is alleged to have been severely embarrassed for ready money on the eve of his invasion of Asia. That is a measure of the expenditure. What is not in doubt is the magnitude of the royal revenues and the financial power of Macedon.

The greatest resource of Macedonia was probably its population. After his incorporation of Upper Macedonia Philip was master of a territory some 20,000 square kilometers in area, comprising some of the richest agricultural land in the Balkans. Its population was necessarily large and was certainly augmented by the internal peace that prevailed in his reign. . . .

Mere numbers are only part of the story. Macedon was populous before Philip, but its infantry was a primitive rabble. The mobilisation of the foot soldiers as a political as well as a military force may predate his reign, but it is highly probable that the introduction of the 12-cubit sarisa [a six-meter-long pike] as the fundamental offensive weapon was his innovation. From the beginning of the reign he imposed systematic training, to produce a cohesive and immensely strong formation that could surpass the depth and compactness of the Theban phalanx. This primary striking force was supplemented by light-armed auxiliaries, archers and, in due course, a siege train manned by the finest contemporary military engineers (retained by Philip's gold). The Macedonian cavalry was, as always, superb, and its discipline was sharpened by regular training which evolved the classic tactic of attack in wedge formation . . .

By the end of the 340s B.C. Macedon had become a superpower. Few realised it, certainly not the citizens of the Greek city states which might have been considered Philip's chief rivals. But in fact there was no real challenge. As early as 346 the Athenian orator Isocrates wrote an open letter to the Macedonian king, urging him to unite the four principal powers of Greece (Athens, Argos, Sparta and Thebes) and lead them in a crusade against Persia. These cities, he said in a memorable phrase, were reduced to a common level of disaster (Isocr. 5.40). The statement is overstressed for rhetorical purposes, but there is an element of truth in it. No single city state (or even coalition) was a match for Philip. . . .

In August 338 came the dénouement. Philip's army, a fraction of his total strength, faced a coalition of roughly equivalent numbers: the Theban and Athenian levies together with a few allied contingents, the most notable from Achaea. It was not an impressive array. The two principals had precious little support from the other Greek states, which were content to wait upon (and profit from) the result.

It was catastrophic. In the plain of Chaeronea the Macedonian phalanx proved its superiority over traditional hoplite forces. The

Athenians alone lost 1,000 dead and 2,000 prisoners, and the Boeotians suffered heavy casualties, including the entire Sacred Band. The end of the day saw Philip supreme in Greece. For Thebes it meant the end of her hegemony in Boeotia and the replacement of her moderate democracy by a strictly limited oligarchic junta, comprised mainly of returned exiles. Athens by contrast suffered only the loss of her remaining allies (but not her cleruchies [colonies], with the possible exception of the Chersonese) and was compensated by the acquisition of Oropus, territory which since 366 had been part of Boeotia. The price was formal alliance with Macedon. The same applied to the other states of southern Greece which, if they had not done so before, concluded treaties of alliance. The Spartans stood alone. They refused submission in any form, suffered invasion and lost border territories to their embittered neighbours. Elsewhere Macedonian garrisons occupied key citadels. They are attested at Thebes, Corinth, and Ambracia, and there may have been others. There was also a degree of political subversion, as Philip ensured that his partisans were established in government. In 337 a constitutive meeting of allies was convened at Corinth, and the political system Philip had created was confirmed by a common peace. Its pillars were the freedom and autonomy of all parties (under Macedonian hegemony) and the interdiction of political change and social revolution. It was administered by a *synedrion* [council] of delegates from all allied states and the executive officer was Philip himself. The propaganda was abolition of war and *stasis* [civil strife] under the benign presidency of Macedon; the reality all too often was the preservation of sycophantic and oppressive regimes by the threat of military action. Whatever ideological perspective one takes, the result of the common peace is the same. It entrenched a network of governments largely sympathetic to Philip and guaranteed them stability.

The forum of allies at Corinth also declared war on Persia. This was the climactic act of the reign and was carefully prepared. From the early years of the century the Persian empire had been ripe for attack. Plagued by succession disputes in the royal house and endemic revolts in the satrapies [Persian provinces], its whole fabric had been at times threatened with dissolution. In the late 360s practically the entire empire west of the Euphrates was alienated from the Great King at Susa. . . .

The Persian success depended on the Great King's ability to pay and keep mercenaries. That had long been evident, and the military weakness of the Persian empire was a commonplace by Philip's accession. Isocrates had repeatedly urged a crusade against Persia and the settlement of Greek refugees in the King's lands. . . . The satrapies of Asia Minor were undeniably a natural and lucrative target for aggression.

We cannot date the origins of Philip's ambitions against Persia. There is no literary evidence for them until the latter part of his reign. As late as his *Fourth Philippic* (341) Demosthenes can only argue on circumstantial evidence that Philip planned to attack the Persian king (Dem. 10.31–3). Philip, as always, had kept his ultimate intentions secret, deferring them (as was inevitable) until he had imposed a stable and permanent settlement on southern Greece. After Chaeronea the time for a declaration of hostilities was propitious. Shortly before the battle [the Persian king] Ochus was assassinated by his [minister], the sinister Bagoas, who then eliminated the immediate family of the deceased king, leaving his youngest son, Arses, to reign as his puppet. The dynastic convulsion provoked revolution in Egypt and Babylon, and the weakness of the empire was patent to all observers. Accordingly Philip had his allies declare war on Persia, with the avowed intention of avenging the sacrilege of Xerxes and liberating the Greek cities of Asia Minor. It was an explicit renewal of the aims of the Delian League*. . . . He would expand his realm by retaliating for past offenses against the Hellenes, and, far from promoting his private interests, he was acting for the entire Greek world. His allies endorsed the declaration of war, fixed the military contributions of each state and passed resolutions forbidding any Hellene to fight on the Persian side. The supreme commander of the combined forces was Philip, at once *hegemon* of the common peace and general in the war of revenge. In the spring of 336 campaigning began in earnest, when a Macedonian expeditionary force 10,000 strong crossed the Hellespont and began the work of liberation (and subjugation) on the coast of Asia Minor. Philip was never able to assume leadership. He was cut

---

*A league of Greek states, led by Athens, that aimed to punish the Persians for their invasion of Greece in 480–479.

down by assassination in the autumn of that same year, and command devolved upon his successor — with fatal results.

The Death of Philip

In both ancient and modern times, the capture of the killer of a prominent public figure has never stopped speculations about the nature of the crime and its author(s). The following selections examine the complex circumstances surrounding Philip's assassination and burial. The bulk of evidence on the affair comes from Diodorus and Plutarch, who describe the background of the murder and the slaying itself.

Diodorus

The Assassination of Philip

In this year [336], King Philip, installed as leader by the Greeks, opened the war with Persia by sending into Asia as an advance party Attalus and Parmenion, assigning to them a part of his forces and ordering them to liberate the Greek cities, while he himself, wanting to enter upon the war with the gods' approval, asked the Pythia [the priestess at the oracle of Delphi] whether he would conquer the king of the Persians. She gave him the following response: "Wreathed is the bull. All is done. There is also the one who will smite him."

Now Philip found this response ambiguous but accepted it in a sense favourable to himself, namely that the oracle foretold that the Persian would be slaughtered like a sacrificial victim. Actually,

Reprinted by permission of the publishers and the Loeb Classical Library from *Diodorus of Sicily*, 16.91–95, vol. 8, translated by C. B. Welles, Cambridge, Mass.: Harvard University Press, 1963.

however, it was not so, and it meant that Philip himself in the midst of a festival and holy sacrifices, like the bull, would be stabbed to death while decked with a garland. . . .

Straightway he set in motion plans for gorgeous sacrifices to the gods joined with the wedding of his daughter Cleopatra, whose mother was Olympias; he had given her in marriage to Alexander king of Epirus, Olympias's own brother. He wanted as many Greeks as possible to take part in the festivities in honour of the gods, and so planned brilliant musical contests and lavish banquets for his friends and guests. Out of all Greece he summoned his personal guest-friends and ordered the members of his court to bring along as many as they could of their acquaintances from abroad. He was determined to show himself to the Greeks as an amiable person and to respond to the honours conferred when he was appointed to the supreme command with appropriate entertainment.

So great numbers of people flocked together from all directions to the festival, and the games and the marriage were celebrated in Aegae in Macedonia. Not only did individual notables crown him with golden crowns but most of the important cities as well, and among them Athens. As this award was being announced by the herald, he ended with the declaration that if anyone plotted against King Philip and fled to Athens for refuge, he would be delivered up. The casual phrase seemed like an omen sent by Providence to let Philip know that a plot was coming. There were other like words also spoken, seemingly divinely inspired, which forecast the king's death.

At the state banquet, Philip ordered the actor Neoptolemus, matchless in the power of his voice and in his popularity, to present some well-received pieces, particularly such as bore on the Persian campaign. . . . Philip was enchanted with the message and was completely occupied with the thought of the overthrow of the Persian king, for he remembered the Pythian oracle which bore the same meaning as the words quoted by the tragic actor.

Finally the drinking was over and the start of the games set for the following day. While it was still dark, the multitude of spectators hastened into the theatre and at sunrise the parade formed. Along with lavish display of every sort, Philip included in the procession statues of the twelve gods wrought with great artistry and adorned with a dazzling show of wealth to strike awe in the beholder, and along with these was conducted a thirteenth statue, suitable for a god, that of Philip himself, so that the king exhibited himself enthroned among the twelve gods.

Every seat in the theatre was taken when Philip appeared wearing a white cloak, and by his express orders his bodyguard held away from him and followed only at a distance, since he wanted to show publicly that he was protected by the goodwill of all the Greeks, and had no need of a guard of spearmen. Such was the pinnacle of success that he had attained, but as the praises and congratulations of all rang in his ears, suddenly without warning the plot against the king was revealed as death struck. We shall set forth the reasons for this in order that our story may be clear.

There was a Macedonian Pausanias who came of a family from the district Orestis. He was a bodyguard of the king and was beloved by him because of his beauty. When he saw that the king was becoming enamoured of another Pausanias (a man of the same name as himself), he addressed him with abusive language, accusing him of being a hermaphrodite and prompt to accept the amorous advances of any who wished. Unable to endure such an insult, the other kept silent for the time, but, after confiding to Attalus, one of his friends, what he proposed to do, he brought about his own death voluntarily and in a spectacular fashion. For a few days after this, as Philip was engaged in battle with Pleurias, king of the Illyrians, Pausanias stepped in front of him and, receiving on his body all the blows directed at the king, so met his death.

The incident was widely discussed and Attalus, who was a member of the court circle and influential with the king, invited the first Pausanias to dinner and when he had plied him till drunk with unmixed wine, handed his unconscious body over to the mule-[drivers] to abuse in drunken licentiousness. So he presently recovered from his drunken stupor and, deeply resenting the outrage to his person, charged Attalus before the king with the outrage. Philip shared his anger at the barbarity of the act but did not wish to punish Attalus at that time because of their relationship, and because Attalus's services were needed urgently. He was the nephew of the Cleopatra whom the king had just married as a new wife and he had been selected as a general of the advanced force being sent into Asia, for he was a man valiant in battle. For these reasons, the king tried to mollify the righteous anger of Pausanias at his treatment, giving him substantial presents and advancing him in honour among the bodyguards.

Pausanias, nevertheless, nursed his wrath implacably, and yearned to avenge himself, not only on the one who had done him wrong, but also on the one who failed to avenge him. In this design he was encouraged especially by the sophist Hermocrates. He was his pupil, and when he asked in the course of his instruction how one might become most famous, the sophist replied that it would be by killing the one who had accomplished most, for just as long as he was remembered, so long his slayer would be remembered also. Pausanias connected this saying with his private resentment, and admitting no delay in his plans because of his grievance he determined to act under cover of the festival in the following manner. He posted horses at the gates of the city and came to the entrance of the theatre carrying a Celtic dagger under his cloak. When Philip directed his attending friends to precede him into the theatre, while the guards kept their distance, he saw that the king was left alone, rushed at him, pierced him through his ribs, and stretched him out dead; then ran for the gates and the horses which he had prepared for his flight. Immediately one group of the bodyguards hurried to the body of the king while the rest poured out in pursuit of the assassin; among these last were Leonnatus and Perdiccas and Attalus. Having a good start, Pausanias would have mounted his horse before they could catch him had he not caught his boot in a vine and fallen. As he was scrambling to his feet, Perdiccas and the rest came up with him and killed him with their javelins.

Such was the end of Philip, who had made himself the greatest of the kings in Europe in his time, and because of the extent of his kingdom had made himself a throned companion of the twelve gods. . . .

Plutarch

Conflicts in the Royal Family

While Philip was making an expedition against Byzantium, Alexander, although he was only sixteen years old, was left behind as regent of Macedonia and keeper of the royal seal. During this period he defeated the Maedi who had risen in revolt, captured their city, drove out its barbarous inhabitants, established a colony of Greeks assembled from various regions, and named it Alexandroupolis. He also took part in the battle against the combined armies of Greece at Chaeronea, and is said to have been the first to break the line of the Theban Sacred Band. Even in my own time an oak tree used to be pointed out near the river Cephisus which was known as Alexander's oak, because his tent had been pitched beside it at that time, and not far away is the mass grave of the Macedonians who fell in the battle. Because of these achievements Philip, as was natural, became extravagantly fond of his son, so much so that he took pleasure in hearing the Macedonians speak of Alexander as their king and Philip as their general.

But before long the domestic strife that resulted from Philip's various marriages and love affairs caused the quarrels which took place in the women's apartments to infect the whole kingdom, and led to bitter clashes and accusations between father and son. This breach was widened by Olympias, a woman of a jealous and vindictive temper, who incited Alexander to oppose his father. Their quarrel was brought to a head on the occasion of the wedding of Cleopatra, a girl with whom Philip had fallen in love and whom he had decided to marry, although she was far too young for him. Cleopatra's uncle Attalus, who had drunk too much at the banquet, called upon the Macedonians to pray to the gods that the union of Philip and Cleopatra might bring forth a legitimate heir to

From Plutarch, *Alexander*, 9–10 in *The Age of Alexander* by Plutarch, trans. by Ian Scott-Kilvert, Penguin Classics, 1973, pp. 260–263. Copyright © 1973, Ian Scott-Kilvert. Reproduced by permission of Penguin Books Ltd.

the throne. Alexander flew into a rage at these words, shouted at him, "Villain, do you take me for a bastard, then?" and hurled a drinking cup at his head. At this Philip lurched to his feet, and drew his sword against his son, but fortunately for them both he was so overcome with drink and with rage that he tripped and fell headlong. Alexander jeered at him and cried out, "Here is the man who was making ready to cross from Europe to Asia, and who cannot even cross from one table to another without losing his balance." After this drunken brawl Alexander took Olympias away and settled her in Epirus, while he himself went to live in Illyria.

Meanwhile Demaratus the Corinthian came to visit Philip. He was an old friend of the Macedonian royal family and so was privileged to speak freely. After the formal greetings and courtesies had been exchanged, Philip asked him whether the various city states of Greece were at harmony with one another. Demaratus retorted, "It is all very well for you to show so much concern for the affairs of Greece, Philip. How about the disharmony you have brought about in your own household?" This reply sobered Philip to such an extent that he sent for Alexander, and with Demaratus' help persuaded him to return.

In the following year Pixodarus, the satrap [governor] of Caria, tried to form a family union with Philip, hoping by this means to insinuate himself into a military alliance. His plan was to offer the hand of his eldest daughter to Philip's son Arrhidaeus, and he sent Aristocritus to Macedonia to try to negotiate the match. Alexander's mother and his friends sent him a distorted account of this manoeuvre, making out that Philip was planning to settle the kingdom upon Arrhidaeus by arranging a brilliant marriage and treating him as a person of great consequence. Alexander was disturbed by these stories and sent Thessalus, the tragic actor, to Caria to tell Pixodarus that he should pay no attention to Arrhidaeus, who was not only an illegitimate son of Philip's but was weak-minded as well: instead, he should offer his daughter's hand to Alexander.

Pixodarus was far more pleased with this suggestion than with his original proposal. When Philip discovered this, he went to Alexander's room, taking with him Philotas the son of Parmenio, one of the prince's companions. There he scolded his son and angrily reproached him for behaving so ignobly and so unworthily of his position as to wish to marry the daughter of a mere Carian, who was no more than the slave of a barbarian king. As for Thessalus, he wrote to the Corinthians ordering them to send him to Macedonia in chains, and at the same time he banished four of Alexander's friends, Harpalus, Nearchus, Erygius and Ptolemy. Later Alexander recalled all of these men and raised them to the highest honours.

Not long afterwards a Macedonian named Pausanias assassinated the king: he did this because he had been humiliated by Attalus and Cleopatra and could get no redress from Philip. It was Olympias who was chiefly blamed for the assassination, because she was believed to have encouraged the young man and incited him to take his revenge. It was said that when Pausanias met the young prince and complained to him of the injustice he had suffered, Alexander quoted the verse from Euripides' *Medea*, in which Medea is said to threaten. "The father, bride and bridegroom all at once."

However this may be, he took care to track down and punish those who were involved in the plot, and he showed his anger against Olympias for the horrible revenge which she took upon Cleopatra during his absence.

Stanley M. Burstein

The Tomb of Philip II and the Succession of Alexander the Great

Stanley M. Burstein is a professor of history at California State University, Los Angeles. He has written *Graeco-Africana: Studies in the History*

From S. M. Burstein, "The Tomb of Philip II and the Succession of Alexander the Great," *Echos du Monde Classique/Classical Views* 26 (1982): 141–163. Published by the University of Calgary Press. Reprinted by permission of the publisher and author.

of Greek Relations with Egypt and Nubia (Caratzas, 1993), and other works. In this selection, Burstein examines the various theories about Philip's death and tries to relate the literary evidence to the spectacular discovery of ancient tombs at Vergina (ancient Aegae) in the 1970s.

Clichés about history abound, but none is more common than the assertion that every generation rewrites its own history. Although, in actuality, it means only that historians' views of the past are conditioned by the available sources and the perspectives of their own time, the cynic may be forgiven if he sees in it proof that history is a pack of tricks the present plays on the past. For the ancient historian the cynical view is attractive, but the trick is one played on the present by the past. Everywhere he looks he finds himself to be the butt of time's jokes, of the loss of information essential to the understanding of important events and the survival of trivia. Nowhere is time's joke more bitter than with regard to the history of fourth century B.C. Macedon. . . .

In the twentieth century, fortunately, this situation has begun to change thanks to the progress of Macedonian archaeology, but until recently its discoveries have illuminated mainly either the prehistoric or the Hellenistic and Roman periods of Macedonian history, not the age of Philip and Alexander. It was, therefore, with understandable excitement that historians learned that in November of 1977 Professor Manolis Andronikos of the University of Thessaloniki had discovered at the village of Vergina an unlooted tomb of a Macedonian king and queen that could be securely dated to the second half of the fourth century B.C. The significance of Professor Andronikos' extraordinary find for the history of Greek art is as great as its importance for Macedonian history. Thus, not only has the old problem of the location of the Macedonian capital of Aegae finally been solved, but a flood of new light has been thrown on such important questions as the Hellenization of Macedon in the fourth century and the "Homeric" character of the Macedonian monarchy by the striking objects and decoration found in the tomb and the precise parallels between the burials of Greek heroes described in the *Iliad* and the royal burial ritual now documented at Vergina. It is about the tomb's political significance, however,

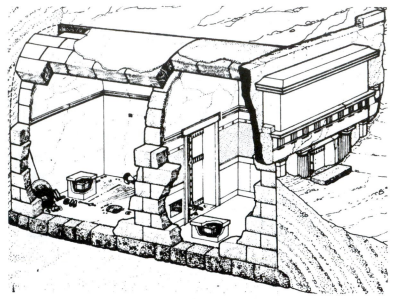

A diagram of Tomb II from Vergina, identified as that of Philip II. At right is the antechamber with a marble sarcophagus and a golden chest (larnax). The chest contained the bones of a young woman wrapped in cloth. The main chamber at left has a similar sarcophagus with a larger golden chest containing the bones of a male (Philip?). It included assorted weapons, silver vessels, and other artifacts.

that controversy has arisen, and rightly so, since by its very nature a royal burial is essentially a political act, a symbolic statement of the continuity between one reign and another, a ritual affirmation of the traditional acclamation of a new ruler, "the king is dead, long live the king." But which king?

The possibilities are limited. Between 350 and 300 B.C. only two adult kings died in Macedon, Philip II, the father of Alexander the Great, and Philip III Arrhidaeus, Alexander's mentally retarded half-brother and successor. Each is known to have received a royal burial from his successor, and, as the tomb contained no inscription identifying its occupants, both candidates have found supporters, who have rested their cases on this or that aspect of the finds. Thus, Professor Andronikos identified the king as Philip II and adduced in support of this theory several considerations. First were the now famous or, perhaps, infamous, five ivory heads, apparently once part of the decoration of a couch, which he identified with Philip's parents, Philip himself, his wife Olympias and Alexander and connected with the five statues of the Philippeum dedicated at Olympia by Alexander shortly after becoming king in 336. Additional support was found in the strangely mismatched set of greaves found in the antechamber of the tomb, the left of which was about 3 cm. shorter than the right, a fact that he explained by reference to the serious leg wound Philip received during his campaign against the [Triballians of the Danube valley] in 339, and, finally and most important, in the physical anthropologist's finding that the king was in his forties at the time of his death, which would fit Philip II who died at 46 but not Arrhidaeus who was not yet 40 at the time of his death in 317.

Unfortunately, none of these considerations is free of difficulty. In actuality, there are not five but twenty heads, and of Andronikos' identifications only those of Philip and Alexander can be said to be at all secure. The greaves are an even greater problem since they would fit a man whose lower left leg was shorter than his right leg, but Philip II's leg wounds were to the right thigh and shin, not the left shin. Far the greatest disappointment, however, is the skeletal analysis because its seeming precision is illusory since there is, in actuality, no way to distinguish accurately the skeleton of a man in his late thirties from that of a man in his mid-forties.

In this situation the historian has no choice but to fall back on circumstantial evidence and a number of pieces of such evidence do seem, in fact, to point toward Alexander's father as the king buried in the tomb. First and foremost is the scale of the monument itself. When first discovered, it was objected that the tomb was not splendid enough for so important a ruler as Philip II, but that was to ignore the monument complex as a whole, which ultimately included the tomb and its immediate neighbors, a hero shrine next to it and enclosing the whole group a vast artificial tumulus [mound] raised in three phases to a height of over 12 meters and a diameter of over 110 meters, making it among the largest of such monuments known from the Balkans. The construction of such a monument was truly a herculean labor, and it is difficult to believe that it would have been done for Philip III Arrhidaeus, a puppet for the whole of his brief reign from 323 to 317, whose burial by [the Macedonian ruler] Cassander masked the suppression of the dynasty of Philip and Alexander by a usurper and not the respect due an honored predecessor. The tomb itself also points in a similar direction since its unfinished main chamber and added antechamber — signs of haste easily understandable in the context of Philip II's untimely death and burial — accord poorly with the carefully staged interment of Philip III a year after his death. Then there is the matter of the hero shrine attached to the tomb, again explicable in the case of Philip II for whom cult is attested but less so for Philip III for whom none is indicated in the sources. Finally there is the number of bodies in the tomb itself. According to [the Greek historian] Diyllus of Athens, Cassander buried Philip III, his wife Eurydice and *with* them her mother Cynnane. Pressing the word *meta* ("with") is risky — particularly since it is possible that one of the looted tombs was that of Cynnane — but the phrasing does suggest a triple and not a double burial such as Andronikos found in the Vergina tomb. Taken together, these considerations create, I believe, a strong presumption that the tomb is indeed that of Philip II, the father of Alexander the Great. Why then the hesitation to accept this conclusion?

Partly, no doubt, a proper scholarly caution and partly also what one might call the "King Tut principle" (i.e., the feeling that only the tombs of historically insignificant rulers survive unlooted), but above all because of the question of the identity of the queen buried in the tomb's antechamber, for in that lies much of its historical interest. Philip II was polygamous — seven wives are attested — but only one is known to have died at the same time as he and hence to be a possible candidate for the queen sharing the tomb, Cleopatra, his last wife, whose marriage so embittered relations between Philip and both Olympias and Alexander. The tentative finding that the female skeleton is of a woman in her mid-twenties is surprisingly high but certainly possible for Cleopatra; it is, it should be noted, too high for Arrhidaeus' wife Eurydice who was in her late teens at the time of her death in 317. Resistance to this conclusion, however, has been strong, and desperate measures have been taken to avoid it by supporters of the identification of the tomb as that of Philip II, even to the extent of inventing a Scythian warrior-wife, a veritable Amazon, for Philip on the basis of the weapons found in the antechamber. This desperation is understandable since the alternative implies that Alexander buried Cleopatra with royal honors despite his passionate love of his mother and Olympias' bitter hatred of Philip's last wife. In the words of Professor Lindsay Adams: "It would not only have been out of place for Alexander to give her a state funeral and burial along with Philip, it would also serve as a painful reminder of Olympias' role in their deaths. . . . The wreath acknowledged Cleopatra to be a queen, officially, which would add insult to injury as far as Olympias was concerned. Given Alexander's well known devotion to his mother, this is not only doubtful, it is almost unthinkable." Or is it? New evidence forces us to confront the unthinkable and see if it is not, after all, thinkable, and, indeed, a consideration of the circumstances surrounding Alexander's succession suggests that he may well have found himself forced to give Cleopatra a state funeral.

The wedding of his daughter Cleopatra in the early summer of 336 to Alexander, king of Epirus, should have been a happy event for Philip II, then 46, ruler of Macedon for twenty-three years and at the peak of his power. . . .

Master of the Balkans, Philip was on the verge of his greatest undertaking, the war against Persia. Already an army commanded by his best general Parmenio and the uncle of his wife Cleopatra, Attalus, was in the field and had won notable successes among the Greek cities of western Asia Minor. After the wedding, Philip himself intended to join the campaign and lead it — no one knows how far, probably not even Philip knew his ultimate goal — but it was not to be. As he entered the theatre at Aegae after the wedding, his guards withdrawn to demonstrate his popularity to the representatives of the Greek cities who had been invited to witness the spectacle, he was struck down by Pausanias of Orestis, one of his own bodyguards.

Pausanias' personal motives have never been in doubt. Aristotle, writing shortly after the event in the *Politics*, classified the assassination of Philip II as an example of an attack on a ruler out of a desire for revenge for an unrequited insult, noting that it was because Philip "allowed Pausanias to be insulted by Attalus and his friends." Diodorus preserves the whole sordid story of a homosexual rivalry for Philip's affection, of the tragic death of a promising young warrior caused by Pausanias' frustrated slurs against his manhood, the brutal and degrading humiliation inflicted on Pausanias by the dead warrior's patron Attalus, the uncle of Philip's wife Cleopatra, and Philip's attempt to preserve peace at court by fobbing off Pausanias' demand for revenge with an appointment as a bodyguard. Previously, believing these events to have taken place almost a decade earlier, scholars wondered at Pausanias' delay in seeking revenge and his choice of Philip as victim. J. Rufus Fears, however, has shown that Pausanias' grievance was fresh, perhaps only a few months old, so that it is possible, as Fears suggested, that Attalus' sudden rise to glory as promoter of Philip's marriage and co-commander of the Asian expedition unbalanced him and drove him to seek his moment of glory and revenge in this theatrical manner. Certainly, the story (Diod. 16.94.1) that his teacher, a sophist named Hermocrates, once told Pausanias that fame could be obtained "by killing him who had achieved the most" suggests that a similar explanation was current in antiquity.

Given the fact that Pausanias was killed by Philip's bodyguards while trying to escape and our own experience of the aftermath of President Kennedy's assassination, however, it is understandable that people suspected something more sinister, that Pausanias had been a tool, used and discarded by the members of a conspiracy, and with reason suspicion fell on those who benefited the most from Philip's death, Alexander and, especially, his mother Olympias. A selection of the rumors is preserved in the sources. In conversation Alexander is said to have quoted to Pausanias the line from Euripides' *Medea*, "The father, bride and bridegroom all at once" (Plut. 10.6); Olympias, it was alleged, urged Pausanias to revenge, held the horses for his escape, honored his crucified body, and gave him a princely burial next to Philip (Justin 9.7). No matter that she probably was not even in Macedonia at the time of the assassination, suspicion clung to her and her son and understandably so in view of her recent estrangement from Philip and the well-known tension between him and Alexander.

Alexander was born in 356, the first child of Philip and his Epirote wife Olympias, a marriage that sealed an alliance between Epirus and Macedon that lasted throughout Philip's reign. The sources for Alexander's childhood and youth are meagre in the extreme, hardly more than a few anecdotes in Plutarch's *Life* of Alexander, but, such as they are, they make two things clear, first, that Alexander's closest emotional attachment was to his mother Olympias and not Philip and, second, that nevertheless relations between him and his father down to 337 were close and marked by mutual trust and respect.

Despite his growing estrangement from Olympias, Alexander was his heir, and Philip and his queen cooperated in preparing him for that role. Both seem to have agreed on his tutors during his boyhood and probably also on the selection in 343 of Aristotle, a long-time student and colleague of Plato with hereditary ties to the Macedonian court and useful political connections in Asia Minor, to give the thirteen-year-old Alexander and his companions a proper Greek education. . . . Responsibilities followed in due time. In 340 Alexander governed Macedon as regent in his father's absence and suppressed a Thracian rebellion during his tenure of office (Plut. 9.1). The next year he accompanied Philip on his Scythian campaign, in 338 he commanded one wing of the Macedonian army at the decisive battle of Chaeronea that established Philip's supremacy over all Greece (Plut. 9.2; Diod. 16.86), and in 337 he conducted his first independent campaign against the Illyrians (Curt. 8.1.25). Within a few months, however, all was changed. Alexander's hopes for the throne were seemingly gone and he and his mother were both in exile, Olympias in Epirus and he among his father's bitterest enemies, the Illyrians.

The cause of this sudden reversal of Alexander's fortunes is not in doubt. In 337 Philip married for the seventh time and, significantly, a Macedonian woman, Cleopatra, niece of the Attalus who humiliated Philip's assassin Pausanias. Olympias had endured Philip's previous marriages, but this one was different. Arrian (3.6.5), probably quoting Ptolemy, provides the explanation when he notes that "Alexander became suspect to Philip when he married Eurydice and disgraced Olympias, Alexander's mother." As has recently been pointed out, the nature of Olympias' disgrace is indicated by the reference to Cleopatra under the name Eurydice. Eurydice had become one of the dynastic names during Philip's reign and his bestowal of it on Cleopatra indicates that she was not to be yet another consort but his new queen, displacing Olympias from the position of honor and influence she had held for almost two decades. Philip may well have thought that he could thus eliminate Olympias without threatening his relations with Alexander; certainly his son's presence at his wedding indicates that no action had been taken to prejudice his position as Philip's heir. Be that as it may, Attalus clearly had grander hopes and the storm broke at the wedding banquet when Attalus' toast to a future legitimate heir to the throne of Macedon revealed the nature of those hopes. A drunken brawl ensued between Philip and his enraged son that ended with the flight of the latter and his mother into exile (Plut. 9.6–11).

To be sure, the rift between Philip and his son was patched over quickly. A mutual friend, Demaratus of Corinth, reconciled father and son. Alexander's position at court even improved a bit when Cleopatra gave birth to a daughter, Europa, but only a bit. Philip's motives for marrying Cleopatra must remain matters for speculation; perhaps he was simply infatuated with her as Plutarch (9.6) claims, but one thing is clear, the marriage meant entering into an alliance with a political faction whose great influence is readily apparent in its members' offices — Attalus and his father-in-law Parmenio were co-commanders of the Asian expedition — and whose hostility to Alexander and his mother is clear from Attalus' toast at the wedding banquet. Just how insecure Alexander's position at court actually was is revealed by an incident that happened after his return from exile.

Pixodarus, the semi-independent satrap [governor] of Caria in southwestern Asia Minor, wrote Philip asking for a son as husband for his daughter. The alliance would be valuable for the war against Persia so Philip agreed and offered him Alexander's retarded half-brother Arrhidaeus. His suspicions roused by the warnings of his mother and his friends, Alexander secretly sent a personal envoy, the tragic actor Thessalus, to advise Pixodarus of Arrhidaeus' mental condition and to suggest that he request Alexander instead. As a result the marriage negotiations collapsed, and Philip, on learning of his son's meddling, confronted him, rebuked him for his presumption and his willingness to stoop to so menial a marriage and then ordered the exile of Alexander's closest friends, thus leaving him even more isolated at court. True, Alexander was still the heir apparent, but merely a thought of his cousin Amyntas, proclaimed king in 359 with Philip as regent, deposed shortly thereafter and ejected from the succession entirely following the birth of Alexander, would suffice to convince him of the insecurity of his position should Philip live, as well he might, for another decade or two and have a son by his influentially connected Macedonian wife. Philip's assassination, thus, could not have been more opportune for Alexander and Olympias, and it is not surprising if people, reflecting on that fact, suspected their involvement in it.

Quick action by Antipater, Philip's senior advisor, and Alexander's principal ally at court, in having Alexander acclaimed by the troops at Aegae assured his succession; and the equally quick discovery, trial and execution of Pausanias' alleged employers in the persons of two princes of the royal house of Lyncestis in upper Macedonia, a house whose restlessness under Argead rule was well known, satisfied at least temporarily the need to discover a conspiracy, but then what? The consensus of modern scholarship is well summed up by E. Badian, who wrote that "the opposing faction (led by one Attalus), which only a little earlier had carried all before it, was taken entirely by surprise . . . and wiped out even to infants in arms, and Alexander's rule was made secure." If one adds the execution of Alexander's cousin and chief rival to the throne, Amyntas, as some scholars do, the picture of a sudden and ruthless massacre of all Alexander's opponents, real and imaginary, as the first act of the regime is complete, but is it true?

True, all were dead by the time Alexander invaded Asia in 334, but not as a result of a sudden pre-emptive strike by him. With the loyalty of the Asian army under Parmenio and Attalus open to question and Greece restive under Macedonian domination, such precipitate action, which might well drive his enemies to desperate resistance, would be folly and Alexander was neither foolish nor rash. Rather, after burying Philip and executing the "conspirators" Alexander quickly made appearances in Thessaly and central and southern Greece where he was confirmed as *tagos* [leader] in Thessaly and, after cowing Athens and Thebes, as head of the Corinthian league and commander of the war against Persia. Against Amyntas and Attalus no overt action was taken for some time, perhaps not for several months, until they could be isolated from their supporters and their deaths justified on the grounds of their own compromising actions, that of Amyntas apparently on the basis that he allowed himself to become involved in a plot to dethrone Alexander, a plot whose reality has been made more likely by inscriptions dating to this period from Boeotia to him as king, and that of Attalus on the grounds of a treasonable correspondence he had entered into with Demosthenes, the Athenian patriot.

If Alexander was willing to be patient until the proper moment to strike arrived, the same was not true of his headstrong mother Olympias. Alexander had taken no action against Cleopatra. After all, with Philip dead and her only child a daughter, she posed no danger to him and might be useful as a hostage for the good behavior of her family. To Olympias, however, Cleopatra was the hated symbol of her disgrace, and she took advantage of Alexander's absence in Greece to murder her and her infant daughter Europa by, according to the 2nd century A.D. guide-book writer Pausanias (8.7.7), roasting them over a brazier or, less melodramatically, by forcing Cleopatra to hang herself after killing her daughter in her mother's arms (Justin 9.7.12). According to Plutarch (*Alex.* 4) Alexander was furious with his mother when he learned what she had done and well he might be since the murders amounted to a declaration of war on the members of Attalus' faction and seriously compromised the cautious policy Alexander had adopted in dealing with them. If one asks what Alexander could do to counter the damage wrought by Olympias, the answer surely is what is suggested by Plutarch's reference to his anger and the proposed identification of the queen in the Vergina tomb as Cleopatra, namely, to try to put the best face possible on the situation by dissociating himself from Olympias' act and giving Cleopatra a burial appropriate to her status as Philip's widow and queen.

This paper began with the question, was it thinkable that Alexander buried Cleopatra with the honors of queen together with

Philip II? Pending the full publication of the tomb, and perhaps not even then, no answer to that question can be definitive, but if the analysis of the political situation confronting Alexander in 336 at the time of Olympias' murder of Cleopatra is correct, then the answer is probably yes. . . .

The tomb of Philip II, should it so prove to be, would illuminate a different and less glorious time, the first uncertain weeks of his [Alexander's] reign when his very survival as king was open to question, when, as Plutarch (*Moral.* 327C) says, all Macedon was looking to his cousin Amyntas as a possible king, and a less well known aspect of Alexander's character emerged, his ability to master his passions and play the game of court politics with a skill equal to that of his older and more experienced rivals. The tomb also suggests the need for a reconsideration of the view generally held by ancient historians of the strong if not dominant influence exerted on him by Olympias. Antipater does not understand, he is reported to have said, that one tear of hers was enough to wipe out ten thousand letters of complaint about her interference in Macedonian affairs, and references to letters of political advice as well as maternal admonishment to her son survive in the sources. Psycho-historians have even suggested that an unsatisfactorily resolved Oedipus complex is the key to understanding Alexander. Yet perhaps more attention should be devoted to another of Alexander's reported remarks about his mother, namely, that she was wise to leave Macedon because Macedonians would never endure being ruled by a woman, for there is reason to believe that it reflects more accurately his real views. At least that is what is suggested by the fact that he did not support her attempts to usurp power in Macedonia from his regent Antipater with the result that finally in 331 she left Macedonia in frustration and returned to Epirus whence, in the absence of her brother, she ejected her daughter Cleopatra and ruled until her return to Macedonia as guardian of Alexander's young son Alexander IV in 317. If, as I suggested above, Alexander did in fact bury Cleopatra, the queen who had replaced Olympias and whom his mother so hated, with full royal honors, then his refusal to tolerate Olympias' attempts to interfere in Macedonian politics, despite his love for her, must be considered a fixed part of his policy from the very beginning of his reign.

A bronze statuette from Herculaneum of Alexander on his horse
Bucephalas, now in the National Museum, Naples. It may be modeled
after Lysippus' group of statues that commemorated the Battle of
Granicus. (Art Resource)

III Alexander and the Greeks

Demosthenes

On the Treaty with Alexander

After a prolonged struggle with the Greek states, especially Athens, Philip defeated a Greek coalition at Chaeronea in 338 and established Macedonian hegemony in Greece. He formalized his relationship with the Greeks in the League of Corinth, a military and political alliance under his leadership. The following selection from a speech, falsely attributed to the Athenian orator Demosthenes, attacks Alexander for violating his treaty with Athens. Scholars generally assume that similar clauses to the passages cited here appeared in agreements between the Macedonian king (Philip and later Alexander) and other Greek states.

"On the Treaty with Alexander." Reprinted by permission of the publishers and the Loeb Classical Library from Demosthenes: *Orations*, 17, vol. 1, trans, by J. H. Vince, Cambridge, Mass.: Harvard University Press, 1989.

Our hearty assent, men of Athens, is due to those who insist that we should abide by our oaths and covenants, provided that they do so from conviction; . . . But from the very terms of the compact and from the oaths which ratified the general peace, you may at once see who are its transgressors; and that those transgressions are serious, I will prove to you concisely. . . .

Therefore when Alexander, contrary to the oaths and the compacts as set forth in the general peace, restored those tyrants, the sons of Philiades, to Messene, had he any regard for justice? Did he not rather give play to his own tyrannical disposition, showing little regard for you and the joint agreement? . . . For it is further stipulated in the compact that anyone who acts as Alexander has acted shall be the enemy of all the other parties to the compact, and his country shall be hostile territory, and all the parties shall unite in a campaign against him. So if we carry out the agreement, we shall treat the restorer of the tyrants as an enemy. . . .

Again, the compact at the very beginning enjoins that the Greeks shall be free and independent. Is it not, then, the height of absurdity that the clause about freedom should stand first in the compact, and that one who has enslaved others should be supposed not to have acted contrary to the joint agreement? . . .

I come to another claim sanctioned by the compact. For the actual words are, "If any of the parties shall overthrow the constitution established in the several states at the date when they took the oaths to observe the peace, they shall be treated as enemies by all the parties to the peace." But just reflect, men of Athens, that the Achaeans in the Peloponnese enjoyed democratic government, and one of their democracies, that of Pellene, has now been overthrown by the Macedonian king, who has expelled the majority of the citizens, given their property to their slaves, and set up Chaeron, the wrestler, as their tyrant. . . .

Now for a still greater absurdity. For it is provided in the compact that it shall be the business of the delegates at the Congress and those responsible for public safety to see that in the states that are parties to the peace there shall be no executions and banishments contrary to the laws established in those states, no confiscation of property, no partition of lands, no cancelling of debts, and no emancipation of slaves for purposes of revolution. . . .

I will point out a further breach of the compact. For it is laid down that it shall not be lawful for exiles to set out, bearing arms, from the states which are parties to the peace, with hostile intent against any of the states included in the peace; but if they do, then that city from which they set out shall be excluded from the terms of the treaty. Now the Macedonian king has been so unscrupulous about bearing arms that he has never yet laid them down, but even now goes about bearing arms, as far as is in his power, and more so indeed now than ever, inasmuch as he has reinstated the professional trainer at Sicyon by an edict, and other exiles elsewhere. . . .

But to prove to you still more clearly that no Greeks will accuse you of transgressing any of the terms of the joint agreement, but will even be grateful to you for exposing the real transgressors, I will just touch upon a few of the many points that might be mentioned. For the compact, of course, provides that all the parties to the peace may sail the seas, and that none may hinder them or force a ship of any of them to come to harbour, and that anyone who violates this shall be treated as an enemy by all the parties to the peace. Now, men of Athens, you have most distinctly seen this done by the Macedonians; for they have grown so arrogant that they forced all our ships coming from the Black Sea to put in at Tenedos, and under one pretence or another refused to release them until you passed a decree to man and launch a hundred war-galleys instantly, and you put Menestheus in command. . . .

Arrian

The Destruction of Thebes

In 335 the city of Thebes rebelled against the Macedonians in a political and military challenge to Alexander and the settlements that Philip

"The Destruction Of Thebes." Reprinted by permission of the publishers and the Loeb Classical Library from Arrian: *History of Alexander,* 1.7–10, vol. 1, translated by Peter A. Brunt, Cambridge, Mass.: Harvard University Press, 1976.

imposed on Greece. The destruction of Thebes was a departure from Philip's generally conciliatory policy in the mainland and influenced Alexander's relationship with Greek city-states.

Meanwhile some of the exiles from Thebes slipped into Thebes by night on the invitation of persons in the city with revolutionary designs, and seized and killed Amyntas and Timolaus, members of the force occupying the Cadmea [the citadel], who had no suspicion of hostile movement outside. Then appearing in the assembly they incited the Thebans to rebel against Alexander, on the pretence of freedom and of liberty of speech — time-honoured and fine sounding words: now at last had come the time to shake off Macedon's heavy yoke. They won readier trust from the populace by affirming that Alexander had died in Illyria: in fact this was common talk, and many put it about; he had been long away and no word had come from him, so that, in ignorance of the facts, they conjectured (as often happens in such cases) what they most desired.

Alexander hearing of what occurred at Thebes was fully convinced that it had to be taken seriously; for he had long had suspicions of Athens, and was much concerned about the Theban coup, in case the Lacedaemonians (long ago rebels at heart) as well as some other Peloponnesians and the Aetolians, who were unreliable, should join in the revolutionary movement of the Thebans. He marched, therefore, past Eordaea and Elimiotis, and the heights of Stymphaea and Paravaea, and on the seventh day reached Pelinna in Thessaly. Thence in five days he entered Boeotia, so that the Thebans did not learn that he was within the Gates until he arrived, with all his force, at Onchestus. At that time the authors of the revolt were saying that a force of Antipater had come from Macedon, but confidently affirmed that Alexander himself was dead, getting annoyed at anyone who reported Alexander's own proximity at the head of his men; it was, said they, a different Alexander, the son of Aeropus.*

---

*Alexander, son of Aeropus, was from the dynastic family that ruled Lyncestis in Upper Macedonia. He was arrested later in Asia and executed for conspiring against the king.

Alexander left Onchestus and next day reached Thebes, near the enclosure of Iolaus, where he encamped, giving the Thebans a period of grace, in case they should repent of their bad decisions and send an embassy to him. They were so far from making any concession that might lead to an agreement that their cavalry and many of their light troops sallied out against the camp, discharged volleys at the outposts, and actually killed a few Macedonians. Alexander sent out some of his light troops and archers to hold up their sally; they easily checked the Thebans, who by now were approaching the camp. Next day Alexander moved his whole force and came round to the gates leading to Eleutherae and Attica, yet even then he did not actually assault the walls, but pitched camp not far from the Cadmea, so that support would be close at hand for its Macedonian garrison. The Thebans were investing the Cadmea with a double stockade, so that no one from without could help those shut up inside, nor could they sally out and harm the Thebans when engaged with their enemies without. But Alexander still hoped to win Theban friendship rather than to incur any danger and waited, encamped near the citadel. At this point those Thebans who best saw the city's advantage were anxious to go out to Alexander and obtain pardon for the Theban people for their revolt; but the exiles and those who had called them in, not expecting to receive kind treatment from Alexander, especially some of them who were Boeotarchs, used every method of urging their countrymen to war. Yet even so Alexander did not attack.

Ptolemy son of Lagus, however, says that Perdiccas, who was officer in charge of the camp guard with his own battalion and lay not far from the enemy palisade, did not await Alexander's signal for battle, but himself first attacked the palisade and tearing it apart broke in upon the Theban advance guard.* Amyntas son of Andromenes followed, as he was brigaded with Perdiccas, and led on his own battalion when he saw Perdiccas had advanced within the palisade. Seeing this, Alexander brought up the rest of the army, so that they might not be stranded and at the mercy of the Thebans. . . . Then Perdiccas, trying to force his way into the second palisade, was wounded and

---

*According to Diod. 17.12, Perdiccas, in fact, followed Alexander's orders.

fell on the spot; he was borne off to the camp in a serious condition; only with difficulty was he healed of his wound. . . .

As the Macedonians pressed on them from all sides, and Alexander appeared, now here, now there, the Theban cavalry, pushing their way through the city, streamed out upon the plain; with the infantry [trying to save themselves as best they could]. And then, in hot blood, it was not so much the Macedonians as Phocians and Plataeans and the other Boeotians who slaughtered the Thebans without restraint, even when they no longer offered resistance, some in their houses, which they broke into, some showing fight; others actually suppliant at the shrines; — they spared neither woman nor child.

This Greek disaster, because of the size of the captured city, the sharpness of the action, and not least the general unexpectedness of the event, both to victors and victims, horrified the other Greeks as much as those who had a hand in it. . . .

With Thebes, . . . the hastiness and lack of consideration in the revolt, her sudden capture, with so little trouble to the victors, the great massacre, a natural act to kindred people working off old feuds, the complete enslavement of the city, then foremost in Greece for power and military prestige, were quite naturally set down to divine wrath: Thebes, men said, had thus paid the price, at length, for betraying the Greek cause in the Persian wars, for seizing Plataea in time of truce, for completely enslaving the Plataeans, for her responsibility for the un-Greek massacre of men who had surrendered to Sparta, and for the desolation of the Plataean countryside, on which the Greeks, ranged shoulder to shoulder against Persia, had repelled the common danger of Greece, and last, for voting for the destruction of Athens when a motion was put before the allies of Sparta that the Athenians should be sold into slavery. People said that the coming disaster cast its shadow before, in many divine warnings neglected then, but the memory of them later made people realize that there had long been prognostications, now confirmed by the event.

The allies who took part in the action, to whom Alexander actually entrusted the settlement of Thebes, decided to garrison the Cadmea, but to raze the city to the ground, and to apportion its land among the allies, in so far as it had not been consecrated, and to enslave the women and children and any Theban survivors, save for priests and priestesses, and any guest-friends of Philip or Alexander, or [guest-friends] of Macedonians. They say that Alexander saved the poet Pindar's house and any of his descendants out of reverence for Pindar. Besides this, the allies determined to rebuild and fortify Orchomenus and Plataea.

When the fate of Thebes was notified to the other Greeks, the Arcadians who had left home to help Thebes condemned to death those who had persuaded them to take this step, while the Eleans restored their own exiles, as they were persons ready to serve Alexander. The Aetolians sent embassies, tribe by tribe, and begged forgiveness for revolting on the news brought from Thebes. The Athenians, who were celebrating their great mysteries when some of the Thebans arrived hot foot from the action, abandoned the mysteries in consternation and began to get in their belongings from the country into the city. The people met in an assembly, and on the motion of [the orator] Demades chose ten ambassadors from the whole body of citizens, men known to be most acceptable to Alexander, and sent them to him bearing the city's rather belated congratulations on his safe return from the Illyrians and Triballians and on his punishment of the Theban revolt. Alexander replied in a friendly way to the embassy, except that he wrote a letter to the city demanding the surrender of [the Athenian leaders] Demosthenes and Lycurgus, as well as Hyperides, Polyceutas, Chares, Charidemus, Ephialtes, Diotimus and Moerocles, whom he held responsible for the city's disaster at Chaeronea and for the wrongs later committed, at Philip's death, against himself and Philip. He also showed that they were just as guilty of the Theban rebellion as the Theban revolutionaries themselves. The Athenians did not give up the men, but sent a second embassy to Alexander, begging him to relent to those whose surrender he had demanded. Alexander did so, whether from reverence for Athens, or because he was anxious to hurry on his Asian expedition and did not wish to leave any ill-feeling behind in Greece. Charidemus alone, however, of those men whose surrender he had demanded but not obtained, he ordered to be exiled; and he took refuge in Asia with King Darius. . . .

Diodorus

The Exiles' Decree

In 324 Alexander proclaimed that Greek exiles should be allowed to return to their native lands. This decree not only violated the king's promise not to interfere in Greek internal affairs but also created great difficulties, political and economic, for the home governments. The following is a report by Diodorus on the decree.

A short time before his death, Alexander decided to restore all the exiles in the Greek cities, partly for the sake of gaining fame, and partly wishing to secure many devoted personal followers in each city to counter the revolutionary movements and seditions of the Greeks. Therefore, the Olympic games being at hand, he sent Nicanor of Stageira to Greece, giving him a decree about the restoration, which he ordered him to have proclaimed by the victorious herald to the crowds at the festival. Nicanor carried out his instructions, and the herald received and read the following message: "King Alexander to the exiles from the Greek cities. We have not been the cause of your exile, but, save for those of you who are under a curse, we shall be the cause of your return to your own native cities. We have written to Antipater about this to the end that if any cities are not willing to restore you, he may constrain them." When the herald had announced this, the crowd showed its approval with loud applause; for those at the festival welcomed the favour of the king with cries of joy, and repaid his good deed with praises. All the exiles had come together at the festival, being more than twenty thousand in number.

Now people in general welcomed the restoration of the exiles as a good thing, but the Aetolians and the Athenians took offence at the action and were angry. The reason for this was that the Aetolians had

Reprinted by permission of the publishers and the Loeb Classical Library from *Diodorus of Sicily*, 18.8, vol. 9, translated by R. M. Geer, Cambridge, Mass.: Harvard University Press, 1969.

exiled the Oeniadae from their native city and expected the punishment appropriate to their wrongdoing; for the king himself had threatened that no sons of the Oeniadae, but he himself, would punish them. Likewise the Athenians, who had distributed Samos in allotments to their citizens, were by no means willing to abandon that island. Being no match, however, for the forces of the king, they remained quiet for the time being, waiting for a favourable opportunity, which Fortune quickly gave them. . . .

A. J. Heisserer

Alexander and the Greeks of Asia Minor and the Mainland

A. J. Heisserer was a professor of ancient history and classics at the University of Oklahoma. Among his works is *Alexander the Great and the Greeks: The Epigraphic Evidence* (U. of Oklahoma, 1980), from which the following discussion is taken. He, and A. B. Bosworth in the next selection, examine Alexander's relationship with Greek communities on the Greek mainland and in Asia Minor during his reign.

The Greeks of the Eastern Aegean

I believe that the evidence reveals that it was Philip's policy to attach the Greek states in the eastern Aegean to the League of Corinth during the preparatory campaign of 336. The crucial testimony appears on the complicated Eresos stelae [inscribed stone blocks], which show that Eresos and Antissa on the island of Lesbos

From *Alexander the Great and The Greeks: The Epigraphic Evidence.* by A. J. Heisserer. Copyright © 1980 by the University of Oklahoma Press. Reprinted with permission.

were incorporated within Macedonian hegemony by being enrolled in the League for the first time at that date. Analogy with other epigraphical and literary passages confirms that at least Mytilene, Chios, and Ephesos (the latter on the mainland) were also joined to the League at that time. Since these places were members, it follows that many other cities (the evidence for which has been lost) were enrolled both among the island and on the mainland.

Philip's strategy of "freeing" the Greek cities and aligning them within his new organization had several advantages. In the interesting document describing institutions of the League we discover that, once a state was admitted, its laws were to be rewritten in order to assure that city's future membership and subordination to Macedonian hegemony: there were to be no banishments and no executions "contrary to the laws" established in those states, no confiscation of property, no partitioning of land, no cancelling of debts, and no emancipation of slaves for evolutionary reasons. These enactments, apparently made during admission or shortly thereafter, substantially modified each state's constitution, and it was furthermore forbidden to overthrow those constitutions set up "when they [the participants] took the oaths concerning the [common] peace." This situation insured the continued existence of the pro-Macedonian "democracies" and explains why in general the *hegemon** would oppose any change in the governments of the allied cities. . . . Those in each town who opposed admission seem to have been banished before the constitution was altered, or at least could be banished later by a measure that would be declared not "contrary to the laws." For this reason it was stipulated in the constitution that it was not permissible for exiles to set out armed "from the states which share in the peace with hostile intent against any of the states participating in the [common] peace; but if they do, that city shall be excluded from the treaty." Clearly the *hegemon* was concerned over the possibility of exiled opponents attempting a coup d'état to recover their former positions, and since it was likely that those exiled would seek refuge in neighbor-

---

Hegemon (leader) and *strategos autokrator* (commander in chief) were the official titles of the leader of the Corinthian League.

ing cities, we can deduce something about the character of Philip's program in Asia Minor. His plan of "liberation" of the Greek cities necessarily committed Parmenion to a policy of political revolution wherein the existing regimes (often pro-Persian tyrants or oligarchs) were to be toppled and new governments friendly to Macedonia were to write new (League) constitutions and exile the pro-Persians. The most certain way for Philip (or Alexander) to extend Macedonian hegemony into a given area was to attach its cities to the League, as the anonymous author of oration 17 in the Demosthenic corpus realized. But because of the expected activities of the exiles, the *hegemon*, having taken one city for the League, discovered that it was necessary to take the next city and after that still another in order to insure the continued loyalty of his first conquests. To maintain Macedonian influence in any single major city of Ionia or Aeolis [in northwest Asia Minor], it was necessary to control as many of them as possible. Indeed, this must have been one of the motivations behind enrolling an allied force for the campaigns; a purely Macedonian army will have given the impression of an invasion instead of an "emancipation," whereas a League force, even if its contingents were compelled to serve in the manner of hostages, offered the appearance of a united panhellenic host opposing the Persian enemy and "freeing" its Greek subjects.

This interpretation makes sense of the many references in the sources to Alexander's reviving various governments during his campaign of 334. He ordered his general Alcimachus to destroy the oligarchies of Ionia and Aeolis, to set up democracies, and "to restore to each of the cities its own laws," while his determination to bring back the (pro-Macedonian) exiles who had been expelled by [the Persian general] Memnon is attested both in Arrian and [by inscriptions]. The conqueror recognized his own partisans and knew that they would declare their respective towns loyal once again to the Corinthian League.

That Alexander pursued such a policy is corroborated by the kind of activity undertaken by Darius. In 333, when his admirals successfully ventured into the Aegean, they offered terms to (at least) Mytilene and Tenedos on the basis of "the peace of Antalcidas" and demanded that these cities pull down the stelae that recorded the terms binding them to Alexander. The "peace of

Antalcidas" was the so-called King's Peace of 387, according to which the cities of Greece (but not Asia Minor) were to be free from tribute and garrisons. To Chios, which received a Macedonian garrison with tribute in the form of a *syntaxis* [contribution tax] of twenty ships, these terms will have been appealing, and we can imagine the same for Mytilene, Tenedos, and any number of other places. Before the time of Philip and Alexander many of the Aegean cities had been members of the Second Athenian Confederacy, a status that did not violate the King's Peace. But that was not true of the Corinthian League, one of whose major purposes was making war on the Great King. Darius, for his part, wished to have the cities declare their recognition of the principles of the King's Peace, which had authorized the Persian overlord to be the arbitrator of Greek affairs. Darius's policy in itself confirms that he wanted the cities *not* to recognize another League, and the only one in question was that founded by Philip. The cities of many Aegean islands, therefore, were joined to the League certainly by 334, but as the Eresos stelae reveal, the whole policy was initiated by Philip in 336 and then continued by Alexander afterward. That Philip went so far as to include Ephesos (on the mainland and technically a part of the Great King's land) testifies to how aggressive his program was.

Such were the conditions of "liberation" and "sharing in the common peace" of the Macedonians (the latter being the euphemism for membership in the Corinthian League). The insidiousness of the propaganda is reflected substantially in both the literary and epigraphical sources for Alexander's reign. . . . [The] Macedonian hegemony meant a new form of the old imperialistic spirit and not any true "freedom and autonomy" for the member states.

Alexander and the League of Corinth

In general Alexander's reign witnesses two common themes with respect to his relations with the Greek city-states. At first the king acted in accordance with treaty obligations made in the name of, or under the aegis of, the League. He made an attempt to associate himself with the Greeks on a "legal" basis, one prescribed by his role as *hegemon* and *strategos autokrator*, and this basis was intended to elicit a positive response for the panhellenic character that he and his father wished the campaign to have. The treaty he concluded with Athens reveals his willingness to bind himself by a written agreement, even though it must be admitted that his overriding powers as *hegemon* and *strategos autokrator* gave the Athenians and other Greeks little choice in the matter. . . . The inscribed stones all attest to his readiness to intervene in the local affairs of the city-states, even those as small as Eresos, but in the early part of his reign those interventions were based on a politico-legal relationship: Alexander was keenly aware of his position as head of the League and apparently wanted to assure the Greeks he was acting in accordance with the authority vested in him. Consequently his restoration of the exiles at Mytilene could be termed "legal" and would have prompted resentment against him only upon the part of the pro-Persian Greeks of the islands and Asia Minor. A "constitutional" basis for his interventions was available in the League documents, and Alexander seems to have referred to these regularly.

A second common theme, and also a corollary to the first, is that, as Alexander's reign wore on, the League meant less and less, and in this situation he came to rely increasingly upon extralegal procedures with the Greek states. The critical change came in 330 when the king, on his way to complete victory over the Persians, dismissed the last (infantry) contingents of the Corinthian League and released the city-states from their *syntaxeis*. This was a monumental step, for although still officially *hegemon* and *strategos autokrator*, no longer was he able to perform effectively the roles associated with these positions. The stele that records Alexander's treaty of alliance with Athens was probably still standing, but its clauses became otiose for both parties. Alexander had no further need of Athens, or of any other Greek ally, to supply foodstuffs or to pay for the *hypaspistai* [foot soldiers]. Furthermore, since the treaty of alliance was connected with the treaty of common peace, the atrophy of the one could not but affect negatively the condition of the other. Once Alexander ceased to exercise his office of panhellenic *strategos autokrator*, his position as *hegemon* became anomalous. In theory the League of Corinth was still in existence, for no act is known by which it was dismantled, but its *dogmata* [decrees] are not heard of again, and for all practical purposes it had ceased to function entirely. Its absence would not have been missed by the Greeks but left them with no other alternative than to send envoys individually to the king far away in the east. The difficulty was that king and cities could no longer readily approach each other (even if they so wished) through the channels that had been operating previously. Communication with the city-states was slowly converted into a unilateral relationship. . . . At the end of his life Alexander appears simply to have been issuing orders (*diagrammata*) to the Greeks to carry out his will; if they objected, it was another edict that determined the course of action and not any *dogma* of the *synedrion* [council], a state of affairs remarkably well revealed in the famous Tegea decree. The only other alternative for the Greeks was to oppose Alexander directly, and this occurred when Athens led various Greek states in the Lamian War (324–22). To be sure there had been mistrust in 336 between king and cities, but by the end of his reign, although he might satisfy the hopes of the Samians, the conqueror had alienated many city-states earlier bound to him by oath. . . .

A. B. Bosworth

Alexander and the Greeks: Power and Diplomacy

The Exiles' Decree and Its Effects

At the Olympic Games of 324 B.C. (which probably culminated at the full moon of 4 August) Alexander pronounced the restoration of exiles throughout the Greek world. His letter, delivered by

From *Conquest and Empire: The Reign of Alexander the Great* by A. B. Bosworth, Cambridge University Press, 1988, pp. 220–228. Copyright © 1988, Cambridge University Press. Reprinted by permission of the author and the publisher.

Nicanor of Stagira, was read out by the victorious herald to a vast and expectant audience comprising more than 20,000 exiles who had gathered for the occasion (Diod. 18.8.3–5). It was a grand gesture and had wide repercussions, almost causing open war with Athens, whose interests on Samos were threatened, and inflicting grave disruption upon thousands of communities, who were forced to receive back and compensate families long estranged, some of them second- and third-generation expatriates. In addition it breached one of the fundamental tenets of the Corinthian League, which prohibited the return of exiles, at least when backed by force (Dem. 17.16). More seriously, Alexander was acting in blatant violation of Greek autonomy in issuing a general command which struck at the economic and political stability of every city, great and small. The sources give no hint of debate in the Corinthian *synedrion* [council] or of any sort of diplomatic consultation. Instead they speak of a unilateral declaration by Alexander, delivered by letter. As quoted by Diodorus (who here excerpts the contemporary Hieronymus of Cardia), it was a brief communiqué disclaiming responsibility for the exiles, guaranteeing return to all but those guilty of sacrilege, and revealing that Antipater had instructions to coerce any city which was uncooperative. That is the language of autocracy. Alexander was conferring a general benefaction and nothing was to impede it, least of all the laws of the individual city-states. Philip at least had not issued general edicts; he had intervened politically, by direct and indirect methods, and ensured that most regimes were responsive to his wishes. By 324 Alexander had transcended such procedures. Now the Greeks of the mainland were treated as his subjects, the recipients of direct commands. He was prepared to listen to representations, to modify his general edict to accommodate the problems of particular cities, but there was to be no questioning his powers to organise the Greek world as he thought fit. His monarchy was now universal, and there were to be no areas of exemption and privilege.

The Decree was probably formulated over a period of months. It was promulgated at Olympia but conceived in Mesopotamia. Both Curtius and Diodorus associate it with the dismissal of the veterans from Opis in the summer of 324; . . . The decree for the restoration of the exiles, the sole subject of the Olympic announcement, was only one of the orders conveyed by Nicanor. He had more specific instructions concerning two problem areas. The Aetolians had their occupancy of the Acarnanian city of Oeniadae threatened, and the Athenian cleruchies on Samos were to be withdrawn, so that the native Samian populace, in exile since 365, could be restored to its homeland. These rulings were not promulgated at Olympia, but they had been foreshadowed in earlier pronouncements by Alexander and negotiations were already afoot. Significantly it was Demosthenes who led the official Athenian delegation to Olympia, and he used the occasion to open discussions with Nicanor, who was clearly both messenger and ambassador. As well as the specific rulings concerning Oeniadae and Samos there were mysterious instructions which dealt with the federal assemblies of the Achaean and Arcadian Leagues. The text of [the Athenian orator] Hypereides (the only source for this) is sadly fragmentary, and it remains very dubious what Alexander intended to do with these communities. But it is more than a possibility that he planned to abolish the federal assemblies altogether, so destroying their legislative machinery. Nicanor brought more than a single letter; he was commissioned with a whole package of regulations designed to reorganise the political structure of Greece.

These regulations were hardly conceived overnight. Alexander had probably been mulling over the affairs of Greece ever since his return from the east. His motives, as always, are difficult to disentangle. Diodorus (18.8.2) gives two reasons for the Exiles' Decree — Alexander's desire for glory and his wish to have partisans in every city as a counter against revolution and defection. This information comes from [the Greek historian] Hieronymus [of Cardia] and it is intrinsically credible. The popularity of the move was obvious enough. There were exiles in plenty at the royal court who agitated constantly for their restoration. If they were not themselves prominent courtiers, there were often powerful friends who could give support. There is epigraphical evidence for the efforts of Gorgus of Iasus in support of the dispossessed Samians; he constantly made representations for them at court, and, when the king announced their restoration, he offered him a crown in recognition and sent concrete assistance to the Samian refugees in Iasus. Exiles at court were not the only petitioners. There was a constant influx of embassies from communities in exile, soliciting Alexander's help. . . .

Alexander was well aware of the misfortunes of exiles and avid for the glory of a general restoration. The passion to display magnanimity was always a driving force with him, and his letter to Olympia underscores it; he is not responsible for the exiles' condition but he will assume responsibility for their restoration. It was his royal benefaction, and a benefaction not to be refused. Behind the diplomacy of Nicanor was the coercive power of the armies of Antipater, and Alexander's letter made it clear that it would be used.

The reverse of the coin was the political advantage accruing from the return of the exiles. Diodorus stresses Alexander's wish to have his own partisans to counteract revolution in the cities. . . . Families which had spent generations in exile would return to reclaim a portion of their own and, almost by definition, they would be hostile to the existing regimes. At Tegea for instance the exiles of several generations returned together. Some had been away long enough for their previous wives and daughters to marry or remarry and produce offspring who were later exiled in their turn. Those restored in 324 would have included the survivors and descendants of the families exiled during the democratic revolution of the 360s, when the Arcadian League was founded. There were exiles of equally long standing elsewhere, notably the Samians, who had been refugees since 365. Such long-term expatriates would necessarily be out of touch with their home cities and the only real guarantor of their interests was the man who had restored them. Their gratitude and loyalty were therefore dependable. But there were also more recent exiles, many of whom opposed Macedon before the establishment of the Corinthian League and had been expelled during the constitutional rearrangements of 338–337. Alexander was to some degree subverting the policies of his father, and it is not difficult to see why he did so. The governments supported by Philip, particularly those in the Peloponnese, had not been reliable in the recent past. The states which gave material assistance to Agis* included the Achaean League, the Arcadian League except Megalopolis, and Elis. . . .

---

*Agis III, king of Sparta, led an unsuccessful movement against Macedon in 333 while Alexander was in Asia.

The Exiles' Decree accordingly struck at the guarantees of political stability which were the foundation of the Corinthian League. Tens of thousands of exiles would return *en masse,* and the home governments would have their hands too full with domestic problems to plan or support any military uprising. In that context the subsidiary instructions relating to the Achaean and Arcadian Leagues make excellent sense. Both had been involved in the war of 331–330, and the Arcadians had sent an army to monitor events at Thebes in 335. It might have seemed prudent to set limits on the common assemblies and prevent collective votes which might commit a whole federation against Macedon. Philip had operated in much the same way against the Aetolians when he divided the *koinon* [confederacy] into its constituent tribes. Now his son was apparently planning to fragment and weaken the two federal states in the Peloponnese which had offered most opposition during his reign. The Decree, then, was Alexander's considered response to the problem of Greek resistance. It was deliberately disruptive, aiming to increase the tensions in Greek city-states while at the same time augmenting Alexander's own partisans in each community.

The amnesty though general was not unrestricted. Alexander's letter to Olympia specifically excluded those guilty of sacrilege, and Diodorus (17.109.2) extends the exclusion to murderers. Now it is very unlikely that individuals exiled as a result of Alexander's own actions or policies were restored. The letter disclaims responsibility for the exiles' fate, and that is not hypocrisy. Alexander did not consider the people he had exiled as covered by the Decree; he was restoring those persons expelled before his accession and by actions other than his own. The largest group of his victims, the Thebans, had no city to return to. Their territory was divided into [plots of land], farmed by other Boeotians (Diod. 18.11.3–4), and there was no suggestion of changing the situation before Cassander [who ruled Macedon after Antipater] invaded Boeotia in 316 (cf. Diod. 19.53. 2). Other exiles could easily be excluded. . . .

Not surprisingly the news of the Decree triggered off a flurry of diplomatic activity. Early in 323 Alexander received a number of embassies which protested against the return of the cities' exiles

(Diod. 17.113.3), and for the rest of his life there was doubtless a continuous stream of representations, as the general terms of the Decree were modified to the conditions of the individual cities. Modifications there certainly were. At Tegea the regulations finally inscribed on stone followed a royal rescript making corrections to meet the city's specific objections. Those objections largely concerned property, and from them we can to some degree trace the amount of disruption caused by the Decree (even though the number of the restored exiles and their financial status is completely unknown). Exiles were to regain part of their property (paternal property or maternal, in the case of women with no surviving male blood relatives), and they were guaranteed a house at the controlled price of two *minae* per room. Disputes were to be heard in the first instance outside the city, probably in Mantineia; Tegean courts only operated if suits were not filed within sixty days of return. The stipulation of outside jurisdiction was probably Alexander's and it was prudent. Tegean courts were not likely to look with favour on residents being dispossessed of property acquired maybe generations ago. The return of the exiles inevitably meant hardship and loss, particularly in the propertied classes, and it must have been bitterly resented. There was no general refusal, for no city and no regime wished to face reprisals from the world conqueror.

The Athenians were the supreme diplomats, and they managed to retain control of Samos until the end of the reign. But it was a close-run thing and they came to the brink of outright war. The crisis came when Harpalus [Alexander's treasurer who had fled Asia] reached Athens in the midsummer of 324. Athens' objections to the loss of Samos were already well known to Alexander, and the arrival of a notorious defector off the coast of Sunium naturally appeared prearranged and a prelude to war (Curt. 10.2.1–2). It was when the news reached Ecbatana that Gorgus of Iasus made his famous offer of 10,000 panoplies and catapults for the siege of Athens. Alexander was seriously planning a campaign and war was imminent. Fortunately there were strong forces at work in Athens to prevent open conflict. The key issue was the retention of the Samian cleruchies and it was not to be prejudiced by Harpalus, however great a debt the city owed him. Demosthenes, initially at least, urged the *demos* [people] not to involve the city in a major war for an unjust and unnecessary cause, an argument reminiscent of the peroration of the *De pace* [On Peace], delivered over twenty years before (Dem. 5.24–25). Within a matter of weeks from his admission to Athens, Harpalus was under guard on the Acropolis awaiting extradition, and in due course he slipped from custody. The Athenians were spared the humiliation of surrendering their suppliant and fellow-citizen, and the *casus belli* was removed. Harpalus had gone; only his money remained. For the moment Athens was reprieved, but preparations for war continued secretly. Leosthenes, the mercenary commander at Taenarum, was retained with his men for the service of Athens after secret negotiations with the *boule* [council] and he held his forces in readiness for action (Diod. 18.9.2; 17.111.3). At the same time he acted as intermediary between Athens and Aetolia, laying the diplomatic groundwork for the formal alliance which was concluded immediately after Alexander's death was known. These negotiations were strictly unofficial, but they were provocative and Antipater cannot have been unaware of them (cf. Diod. 18.9.2). Fortunately Antipater himself was insecure. He was shortly to be replaced as regent by Craterus and was to lead an army of fresh recruits to Babylon. The last thing he desired was a major conflagration in Greece to distract his attention and drain his reserves of manpower. He therefore tolerated the seditious negotiations in the south and even made overtures on his own behalf to the Aetolians (Plut. 49.14–15).

The Athenians had domestic worries caused by the Decree. Exiles from the city expected their immediate restoration, and by the time of the trial of Demosthenes they had gathered as a group in Megara. They were regarded as a threat to the constitution. Communications with them were prohibited and subject to prosecution. Demosthenes himself began (and later dropped) impeachment proceedings against his enemy Callimedon on the grounds that he was intriguing with the exiles to subvert the democracy; and given Callimedon's later record of collaboration with Macedon the charge may not have been unfounded. There was also trouble at Samos, where the exiled Samians apparently made an abortive attempt to return. This episode, only recently revealed by Samian decrees of the restoration, was dramatic. A group of exiles had gathered at Anaea, on the slopes of Mt. Mycale facing the island. At some time they crossed the strait into Samos and actually engaged in conflict with the Athenian cleruchs. The attempt was a failure. The insurgents were captured by the Athenian general delegated to Samos and were shipped to Athens where the *demos* condemned them to death. While in prison awaiting execution they were ransomed by a sympathiser, Antileon of Chalcis, who transported them to safety in his home city and was later honoured for his action by the restored Samians. These events are difficult to date, but clearly they did not occur after the battle of Crannon (322) when Athens was at the mercy of Antipater. . . . It remained to be seen which way Alexander would finally decide, whether he would recognise the Athenian claims in some measure or view their resistance as a deliberate affront to his authority. What was not now in doubt was that the Athenians would fight to preserve their hold on Samos.

The other state directly threatened by the Decree was the Aetolian League. The Aetolians were far more openly at loggerheads with Alexander than were the Athenians. They had clearly revoked Philip's settlement and reconstituted their federal polity. They had also occupied the Acarnanian town of Oeniadae and expelled its inhabitants, an action which made them liable to the collective sanctions of the Corinthian League to which the Acarnanians were signatories. They would ultimately face reprisals and Alexander had already promised punishment in the most explicit terms. For the moment they were preserved by their remoteness and the fact that the major actors in the drama had more pressing concerns. But there was necessarily a reckoning to be faced, and the Aetolians were the automatic allies of any state which resisted Macedon. They were still too insignificant to be the focus of a general rising and could only hope that others, above all the Athenians, would make the first move.

There is no evidence for the reaction elsewhere. Presumably the majority behaved like Tegea, first protesting and pleading special circumstances and then allowing their exiles to return under fixed conditions. But there must have been widespread discontent, and resentment of the Exiles' Decree was probably a major cause of the defections from Macedon in the early months of the Lamian War. The Thessalians in particular reversed thirty years of loyalty to the Argead house when they changed sides *en masse* during the autumn of 323 (Diod. 18.11.1–3). They had recently been faced with the return of families exiled during the long years of conflict between the Thessalian League and the tyrants of Pherae. The beneficiaries of that conflict had been Philip's partisans, the nobles who dominated the great cities of Larisa and Pharsalus — men like Daochus, Cineas and Thrasydaeus, whom Demosthenes (18.295) stigmatised as traitors; and significantly it was Pharsalus, the city most favoured at the end of Philip's reign, whose cavalry was the élite of the Thessalians with Alexander, that formed the centre of Thessalian resistance during the Lamian War. In Pharsalus at least the restoration of the exiles of Philip's reign will have made many (certainly the most important) citizens feel defrauded and it is not surprising that they reacted violently.

Alexander was not given time for his policies to work. He died only ten months after the Decree was promulgated at Olympia, too short a time for the exiles to be returned, re-established and entrenched as his loyal supporters. The destabilisation he planned never eventuated. It is clear, however, that the Exiles' Decree amounted to a repudiation of the policies and partisans of Philip. The settlement imposed after Chaeronea had been no safeguard against armed resistance to Macedon, and the regimes sanctioned by Philip had been of equivocal loyalty. Alexander accordingly reversed his policy and struck against the whole fabric of the Corinthian League, whose keystone was the maintenance of existing governments and the enforcement of sentences of exile. His new supporters were to be the old dispossessed, and there was now not even lip service to the concept of autonomy. Alexander simply imposed his will by fiat. He might subsequently be swayed by diplomacy but the final decision was his alone. It was absolute rule by royal command, the polar opposite of the façade of consensus which Philip had attempted to create. At all events, when Alexander died, the regents at Babylon considered it prudent to send a circular letter to the cities announcing the restoration of "the peace and the constitutions which Philip had established" (Diod. 18.56. 2). It was a proclamation for propaganda purposes, to gain popularity, and was a reaction against the despotism of Alexander's last months. By comparison even the militarily enforced peace and the political inertia of the Corinthian League [were] a welcome change.

Staircase at Persepolis: relief portraying the bringing of offerings to King Darius the Great. (The Oriental Institute)

IV Alexander's Aims

Diodorus

Alexander Lands in Asia Minor

Part of the mystique of leadership comes from the uncertainty of followers about their leader's plans. The question "what next?" must have weighed on the mind not only of Alexander's contemporaries but of the king himself. Alexander's ambitions and plans have long inspired both observers and scholars to try to open windows into his personality. The following statements are from our sources regarding Alexander's objectives at different stages of his campaign.

In the selection below, Diodorus describes the king's first symbolic act upon landing in the Troad in northwestern Asia Minor in 334.

Reprinted by permission of the publishers and the Loeb Classical Library from *Diodorus of Sicily*, 17.17, vol. 8, translated by C. B. Welles, Cambridge, Mass.: Harvard University Press, 1963.

Alexander advanced with his army to the Hellespont and transported it from Europe to Asia. He personally sailed with sixty fighting ships to the Troad, where he flung his spear from the ship and fixed it in the ground, and then leapt ashore himself the first of the Macedonians, signifying that he received Asia from the gods as a spear-won prize. . . .

Arrian

Alexander and Darius Exchange Letters

In 333 Alexander defeated the Persian king Darius in the Battle of Issus and captured his family (see Part V). Soon he received a letter from Darius, who had fled to Mesopotamia. The letter offered terms of peace. Alexander's victory was not decisive, but his reply, as reported by Arrian in the selection below, justifies his Asian campaign and leaves no doubt about his ambitions.

While Alexander was still at Marathus, envoys reached him from Darius, bringing a letter from him; they were themselves to plead by word of mouth for the release to Darius of his mother, wife and children. The letter argued as follows: Philip had been in peace and alliance with Artaxerxes [Ochus, king of Persia, 358–338], and when Arses son of Artaxerxes became king, Philip first did wrong to King Arses, although he had sustained no injury from the Persians. From the time Darius had been King of Persia, Alexander had sent no envoy to him to confirm the ancient friendship and

Reprinted by permission of the publishers and the Loeb Classical Library from Arrian: *History of Alexander*, 2.14, vol. 1, translated by Peter A. Brunt, Cambridge, Mass.: Harvard University Press, 1976.

alliance, but had crossed with an army into Asia and had done great harm to the Persians. That was why Darius had come down to defend his country and to rescue his ancestral dominion. The battle had been decided as some god had willed; but as a king he begged a king to restore his captive mother, wife and children; and he was ready to make friendship and an alliance with Alexander, and for these arrangements he thought it fitting that Alexander should send to him along with Meniscus and Arsimes (the envoys who had come from Persia) persons appointed to exchange pledges.

Alexander wrote a reply and sent Thersippus along with Darius' envoys with instructions to deliver the letter, but not to discuss anything with Darius. This is how Alexander's letter runs: "Your ancestors invaded Macedonia and the rest of Greece and did us great harm, though we had done them no prior injury; I have been appointed *hegemon* of the Greeks, and invaded Asia in the desire to take vengeance on Persia for *your* aggressions. For you assisted Perinthus [in Thrace, south of Byzantium] which wronged my father, and Ochus sent a force into Thrace, which was under our rule. My father was murdered by conspirators, whom you Persians organized, as you yourselves boasted in your letters to all the world; you assassinated Arses with the help of [the minister] Bagoas, and seized the throne unjustly and in actual contravention of Persian law, doing wrong to Persians; you sent unfriendly letters to the Greeks about me, urging them to make war on me. You despatched sums of money to the Lacedaemonians and certain other Greeks, which no other city accepted but the Lacedaemonians. Your envoys destroyed my friends and sought to destroy the peace I had established in Greece. Although I marched against you, it was you that started the quarrel. As I have conquered in battle first your generals and satraps [Persian provincial governors], and now yourself and your own force, and am in possession of the country by the gift of heaven, I hold myself responsible for all of your troops who did not die in the field but took refuge with me; they are with me of their own free will, and voluntarily serve in my army. You must then regard me as Lord of all Asia and come to me. If you fear that by coming you may receive some harm at my hands, send some of your friends to receive pledges. Ask for your mother, wife and children and what you will, when you have come, and you will receive them. You shall have whatever you persuade me to give. And in future when you send to me, make your addresses to the king of Asia, and do not correspond as an equal, but tell me, as lord of all your possessions, what you need; otherwise I shall make plans to deal with you as a wrongdoer. But if you claim the kingship, stand your ground and fight for it and do not flee, as I shall pursue you wherever you are. . . .

Diodorus

Alexander's Last Plans

Shortly after Alexander's death, his regent Perdiccas presented the king's last plans to an assembly of Macedonians; the plans were rejected. Although some historians question the authenticity of these memoranda, many scholars consider them an authentic reflection of the king's aims and state of mind in the year of his death. Below, Diodorus gives an account of the presentation of the plans.

For when Perdiccas found in the memoranda of the king orders for the completion of the pyre of Hephaestion [Alexander's closest friend, who died in 324], which required a great deal of money, and also for the other designs of Alexander, which were many and great and called for an unprecedented outlay, he decided that it was inexpedient to carry them out. But that he might not appear to be arbitrarily detracting anything from the glory of Alexander, he laid these matters before the common assembly of the Macedonians for consideration.

The following were the largest and most remarkable items of the memoranda. It was proposed to build a thousand warships,

Reprinted by permission of the publishers and the Loeb Classical Library from Diodorus of Sicily: *Diodorus of Sicily,* 18.4, vol. 9, translated by C. B. Welles, Cambridge, Mass.: Harvard University Press, 1969.

larger than triremes [warships using a three-level oar system], in Phoenicia, Syria, Cilicia, and Cyprus for the campaign against the Carthaginians and the others who live along the coast of Libya and Iberia and the adjoining coastal region as far as Sicily; to make a road along the coast of Libya as far as the Pillars of Heracles [Gibralter] and, as needed by so great an expedition, to construct ports and shipyards at suitable places; to erect six most costly temples, each at an expense of fifteen hundred talents; and, finally, to establish cities and to transplant populations from Asia to Europe and in the opposite direction from Europe to Asia, in order to bring the largest continents to common unity and to friendly kinship by means of intermarriages and family ties. The temples mentioned above were to be built at Delos, Delphi, and Dodona, and in Macedonia a temple to Zeus at Dium, to Artemis Tauropolus at Amphipolis, and to Athena at Cyrnus. Likewise at Ilium in honour of this goddess there was to be built a temple that could never be surpassed by any other. A tomb for his father Philip was to be constructed to match the greatest of the pyramids of Egypt, buildings which some persons count among the seven greatest works of man. When these memoranda had been read, the Macedonians, although they applauded the name of Alexander, nevertheless saw that the projects were extravagant and impracticable and decided to carry out none of those that have been mentioned. . . .

Peter A. Brunt

The Aims of Alexander

In this selection, Brunt considers the realistic as well as mystical features of Alexander's goals and personality from the beginning of the campaign until his death.

"The Aims of Alexander" by Peter A. Brunt from *Greece And Rome* 12 (1965), pp. 205–209, 211–215. Reprinted by permission of Oxford University Press and the author.

Sir William Tarn wrote that "the primary reason why Alexander invaded Persia was, no doubt, that he never thought of *not* doing it; it was his inheritance." The invasion had been planned and begun by Philip. It was, in name, a Panhellenic enterprise, to exact retribution for the devastation wrought by Xerxes in Greece and to liberate the Greeks of Asia Minor. These aims Alexander faithfully fulfilled. From the spoils of the [Battle of] Granicus he dedicated three hundred Persian panoplies to Athens' tutelary goddess; he sent back to Athens the statues of [the tyrant-slayers] Harmodius and Aristogiton which Xerxes had carried off to Susa; and he excused the burning of Persepolis as a reprisal for the sack of Athens. The Panhellenic war was then over, and Alexander sent the Greek contingents home (Arr. 3.19.5). In general he freed the Greek cities of Asia from the control of satraps [governors]; they were to pay no taxes, to receive no garrisons and to live under their own laws. By expelling tyrants or oligarchs and setting up democratic governments, he not only removed the partisans of Persia from power but did homage to the growing tendency in Greece to equate freedom with democracy. The gratitude of the liberated cities was long-enduring; it was here that his cult survived into Roman times. In reality of course they were as much subject to his will as less privileged subjects. And to Greek cities that opposed him he was less accommodating. . . . Sentiment and principle gave way to his own interests, as they always did.

Polybius says that Philip launched the crusade against Persia to win goodwill in the Greek world. If he entertained such a hope, it was plainly delusory. The persistent propaganda of Isocrates for a national war against Persia had fallen on deaf ears. Since 412 all the leading Greek cities had vied with each other in seeking Persian subsidies or diplomatic support. None had any reason to fear Persian aggression; like the Romans after Augustus' death, the Persian kings were content with [the borders of the empire]; bent on restoring control over Asia and Egypt, they had been very willing to promote internal discords among the Greek cities under the name of "the freedom and autonomy of every city, great or small." The sense of natural antagonism between Greeks and barbarians can easily be exaggerated, and in any event to Greeks of the fourth century, even to Isocrates, Macedonians too were barbarians (though the ruling dynasty had a recognized claim to be regarded as Greek), and it was they, not Persia, whose power menaced Greek freedom. Demosthenes and king Agis took Persian gold, and the Thebans in 335 called on their fellow Greeks to fight for liberty in concert with the great king. They were right; in his last year Alexander showed that he meant to be master in Greece. Between 336 and 322 most Greek cities were in arms at one time or another against the Macedonian power. Alexander himself suffered no illusions; he knew that he could not in 334 rely on a Greek fleet to dispute the mastery of the seas with the Persians, and the Greek contingents in his army played only a subordinate role in the fighting, apart from the Thessalians who owed Philip special gratitude for restoring peace and order in their country. The Panhellenic crusade was a fiction for everyone but modern scholars who suppose that Isocrates' pamphlets were widely admired for anything but their languid eloquence. . . .

We cannot say how far Philip intended to go. Perhaps he could not have said himself. In 332 Darius offered to cede all his territory west of the Euphrates. Parmenio declared that he would close with the offer, if he were Alexander. "So would I," replied Alexander, "if I were Parmenio." It is often supposed that Philip would have agreed with his old general rather than with his son. There is no warrant for this belief. Philip was an opportunist and his ambitions expanded with his successes. . . .

Even Isocrates had envisaged a war with a different purpose. Retribution for long distant wrongs hardly interested him; he even showed surprisingly little concern for the "enslaved" Greeks in Asia. In the *Panegyricus* he had urged that it was folly for the Greeks to contend with each other over a few barren acres, when the wealth of the Persian empire was theirs for the taking. In 346 he had recommended Philip to win fame by conquering lands in Asia for the surplus population of Greece. Philip had sufficient power and wealth already; his reward was to be glory, and the material fruits of his victories were to enure to the Greeks. At Pella this can only have evoked ridicule. For attacking Persia Philip had a Macedonian as well as a Panhellenic pretext, that by aiding Perinthus in 340 the Persians had broken a treaty concluded with him, and he surely intended to annex Persian territory himself. Certainly this was Alexander's purpose from the first. As soon as he had won the battle of the Granicus, he appointed satraps and imposed tribute on the king's Asiatic subjects. . . .

There is then no difficulty in supposing that when Alexander cast a spear on the Asian shore, he meant to symbolize his intention of conquering Asia, that is to say, the whole Persian empire; to Isocrates "Asia" is a synonym for the king's dominion. The story indeed comes from Diodorus and the source is poor. But it was Aristobulus, a well-informed authority, who told how early in 333 Alexander untied the Gordian knot and offered sacrifice in thanksgiving to the gods for manifesting by this sign that he was destined to rule over Asia. All the evidence suggests that Alexander was a deeply religious man, sedulous in performing the ceremonies sanctioned by custom, and that he came to believe that he was upheld in his victorious career by the favour of the gods. After Gordium then he can have been in little doubt that he was destined to rule over Asia. He proclaimed this aim before Issus, in his negotiations with Darius in 332, and again before Gaugamela. That victory seemed decisive, and he was then apparently acknowledged as king of Asia by the army. A change soon came over his attitude to Darius. In 332 he had castigated him as a usurper; after his death, he paid him respect as the legitimate ruler, and seems to have represented himself in some peculiar way as the heir of the Achaemenids, whose tombs he was zealous to restore. This was natural enough; he had seen the loyalty and courage of the Iranian nobility in defending their king, and he wished to bind them to himself by similar sentiments.

It is not likely indeed that Alexander was guided at any time in his life by purely rational calculations. Devoted to the reading of Homer, he conceived himself as a second Achilles, born "to always excel and be above others." The spirit of heroic adventure mingled with an insatiate curiosity. The oft-recurring phrase that he was seized with a longing to do or see things that no one or only a few had done or seen before seems to come down from Ptolemy and Nearchus, who were among his most intimate companions. His almost uninterrupted successes engendered in him the conviction that he was permitted to achieve what was denied to ordinary mortals. More than once we are told that the more impracticable a project appeared, the more he was determined to undertake it; though at other times, it is true, he was ready to adopt the prudent courses that caution recommended, this unparalleled audacity served him well by making enemies surrender at the mere terror of his name.

In the Indian campaigns a new motif comes to the fore in the emulation of Heracles and Dionysus. The Macedonians, misinterpreting what they heard of local legends, thought that they had found traces that Heracles and Dionysus had preceded Alexander on his march. This idea was very congenial to Alexander. At the rock of Aornus he even found himself able to do what Heracles had failed to do. When he heard of Dionysus' presence at Nysa, and of his foundation of the city, he *wanted* the story to be true and conceived the hope that he might also outstrip the god. Many such stories come from inferior sources and may be disbelieved; but the particular incidents mentioned (and indeed others) were recorded by the best authorities and must be credited. Tarn indeed ridicules the whole tradition on the ground that it makes Alexander into an imitative character. This is a very curious view. To excel the achievements of beings who were thought to have attained to godhead by their terrestrial beneficence was an ambition that could be entertained only by a man conscious of his own transcendent powers, and to Greeks might well have been the basis of a charge of *hybris* [insolent transgression]. Again, it was Nearchus who told that Alexander sought to outdo Cyrus and [the legendary Babylonian queen] Semiramis by traversing the desert of Baluchistan; and this must be believed against the official apologia for an enterprise probably hardly less disastrous than Napoleon's Russian campaign. Here *hybris* was indeed attended by *ate* [infatuation] and *nemesis* [divine wrath]. . .

Long ago Empedocles, one of the most religious of Greek thinkers, had written: "I go among you as an immortal god, no mortal now, honoured among all as is right, crowned with fillets and flowery garlands." Why should we not suppose that Alexander too was imbued with a sense of divine inspiration, power and beneficence, sown in his mind by the teaching of Ammon and other oracular responses and confirmed by his superhuman achievements which made him feel himself to be the equal of Dionysus, entitled to the adoration of mankind? He knew of course that he would die, or rather quit this life; but that had been the fate of Heracles and Dionysus. At any rate the belief in his divinity was accepted even by his proud Macedonian officers; for after his death his former secretary, Eumenes, induced them to set up a golden throne in the camp, before which they all did daily sacrifices and obeised themselves to Alexander as a god, taking counsel from his divine will and ever-living spirit. Like Caesar, and unlike any other deified king, Alexander commanded genuine veneration.

To a god upon earth the allegiance of all mankind was rightly due. In India Alexander expected universal submission and treated resistance as revolt, even when he had passed beyond the confines of the empire the Achaemenids had once ruled. Some held that he aimed at reaching the mouth of the Ganges and the encircling Ocean stream. Even on [the geographer] Eratosthenes' later reconstruction of the eastern hemisphere he was not seemingly so far distant from this objective when he had reached [the river Hyphasis in India]. Here mutiny turned him back; but he had not forsworn conquests, and took his army homewards by a devious route that involved more fighting and brought him to the Ocean at the Indus delta. Certainly he did not (as Tarn holds) abandon any of his Indian acquisitions; the principalities of Porus and Taxilas were still regarded as parts of the empire after his death, and their status was not different in principle from the kingdoms of Cyprus and Phoenicia. After his return to Mesopotamia he was still bent on more wars; he promised his veterans at Opis to give them rewards enough to incite the new Macedonian drafts to be ready to share the same dangers and exertions. His immediate projects comprised the exploration of the Caspian, surely as a prelude to the deferred campaign against the Scyths, and the conquest, not the mere circumnavigation, of Arabia; Aristobulus said that he intended to take possession of the country and found colonies there as part of a design to be "lord of all." We are told that he left behind him memoranda for a gigantic plan of conquest in the west that would have taken him along the southern shore of the Mediterranean to the Ocean at Gibraltar (where Heracles once again had preceded him) and then along the northern shore back to Macedon. . . .

The authenticity of Alexander's reputed memoranda has been questioned, but in my view on quite insufficient grounds. The plan attributed to him is in keeping with all that we know of his character. It would have marked a new stage in the attempt to reduce the whole inhabited world, bounded by the Ocean, a world which in the west as in the east appeared much smaller than we know it to be.

A prudent ruler, governed by rational calculations, would

clearly not have embarked on such an enterprise. Large tracts of the old Persian Empire were still not pacified.... Greece was smouldering with discontent; even the loyalty of Macedon and its vice-regent, Antipater, who did not comply with Alexander's summons to his court in 324, could not be counted on. To secure the gains he had already made, Alexander needed decades of patient organizing work. It was not enough to remove or punish (as he did) officials whom he suspected of infidelity or oppression. But there is no sign that he had any taste for the humdrum routine of administration.

Not that he lacked statesmanlike views. He sought to turn nomads into settled, peaceful cultivators of the soil, to foster economic development, and to create cities as centres of civilization. In some, but not all, of his foundations there were Greek and Macedonian settlers; as, even in these, natives were brought within the walls and the Greeks and Macedonians were no doubt expected to solace themselves with native wives, mixed communities were likely to be formed, in which the culture would surely be Hellenic, as in the older ethnically mixed cities of Ionia, and from which Hellenic ideas would radiate to barbarians, as in fourth-century Caria and Lycia. Alexander himself was devoted to Greek culture, and I suspect that he never thought of his realm as being other than fundamentally Hellenic; it is said that he had Greek taught to Darius' family and to the children his soldiers had had by native women. Not that he despised barbarians. We are told that he rejected Aristotle's advice to treat barbarians as enemies and to behave to them as a master might towards slaves; experience showed him, as indeed it showed Aristotle, that the distinction between natural masters and slaves was not to be equated with that between Greeks and barbarians. Phoenicians, Iranians, Indians, all rendered him valuable services; he needed Orientals to fill the ranks of his army and to administer subjects with whose languages and customs they were familiar. He recognized local laws, left natives to manage local affairs, and even appointed Iranians to satrapies and admitted them to his entourage. To reconcile them to his rule, he progressively adopted Persian dress and court ceremonial. All this aroused opposition among old-fashioned Macedonians. Alexander was prepared to crush it without mercy, but he wished also to effect a genuine union of hearts. . . .

He always assumed that his invincible will would surmount every obstacle, of sentiment no less than of armed resistance. His colonies illustrate this: established in sites carefully chosen for strategic or commercial value, they were designed to become great cities and by their names to perpetuate his own; for the feelings of conscribed settlers who "yearned for the Greek way of life and had been cast away in the extremities of the kingdom" he cared nothing. Admirable as these aims were, one may yet feel that he did not possess *"le tact des choses possibles."* But who can say what his iron resolution might not have achieved, if fate had not denied him the long life needed to bring his purposes to fruition?

His early death would have mattered less if he had had an able successor to carry on his work. The rise of Macedon to power had long been retarded by disputes over the succession and by the turbulence of the nobility. Philip had attached the great nobles more closely to the court, but the danger of dynastic quarrels remained, and it was not unreasonable for Demosthenes and other Greeks to hope, after 346 and even after 338, that Macedonian power would disintegrate. Alexander's old advisers, Antipater and Parmenio, had pressed him not to invade Persia before he had married and begotten an heir. He rejected the advice, and at his death he still had no child. Roxane was indeed pregnant, and her unborn son was recognized as the future king. But like all minors who ascended the Macedonian throne, Alexander IV was not suffered to survive for long. The chief Macedonian generals were bent on securing their own power, if necessary at the expense of the unity of the empire. . . .

According to Plutarch Alexander had sought to be "a governor from God and a reconciler of the world; using force of arms against those whom he failed to bring together by reason, he united peoples of the most varied origin and ordered . . . all men to look on the *oikoumene* [inhabited world] as their fatherland, the army as their citadel and guardian, good men as kin, and wicked as foreigners; he taught them that the proof of Hellenism lay in virtue and of barbarism in wickedness." This objective could be achieved only by blood and iron, and by the will of a despot who was prepared to override the sentiments of his subjects; and though the world was to be united in government and culture, there is no concept here of the brotherhood of all men as sons of a common Father, but at best only of those who possessed *arete* [excellence]. Neither Alexander nor anyone else realized the objective, and it may be doubted if in his own mind it was so clearly defined as in Plutarch's ideal description. But his work tended in this direction and helped to inspire not only perhaps Stoic philosophers but the Romans, who were also to transcend national differences and to conceive that Italy had been marked out to unite scattered empires, to humanize customs, to give mankind a common speech, and to become *"una cunctarum gentium in toto orbe patria"* [the single homeland to all races in the whole world].

A mosaic found in the House of the Faun at Pompei (now in the National Museum, Naples), depicting what was most likely a scene from the Battle of Issus, when Darius (in the chariot) turned and fled the battlefield. Alexander is portrayed riding on a horse wielding a spear. The mosaic was probably made after a contemporary painting by Philoxenus. (Art Resource)

Alexander in Battle

Nicholas G. L. Hammond

The Armed Forces of the King

When Alexander reached the eastern Mediterranean in the autumn of 333, he faced for the first time the king of Persia, backed by the imperial army. The ancients appreciated not grand strategies but tactical acumen and personal example in a general. In the Battle of Issus, Alexander established his military fame and confirmed contemporary expectations of him, but not without difficulties. Alexander of course, owed his success chiefly to his army. In the selection below, Nicholas G. L. Hammond examines the king's army as a military, political, and social institution. Hammond was a professor of ancient history and Greek at Clare College, Cambridge, and the University of Bristol. His works include *Sources for Alexander the Great: An Analysis of Plutarch's Life and*

From N. G. L. Hammond, *Alexander the Great: King, Commander, and Statesman* (London: Chatto & Windus, 1981), pp. 24–34.

Arrian's Anabasis Alexandrou (Cambridge University Press, 1993), among others.

The Macedones

The relationship between the army and the king in Macedonia was particularly close, in that they were the two parts which made up the Macedonian state: the men under arms being the "Macedones," and the king the head and the superscription of the state. The army chose its commander only when it elected a man to be king, and it was a real choice even if the candidates were restricted to members of the Temenid house by a convention which lasted for more than three centuries. On making the election the soldiers clashed their spears against their shields to indicate their defence of their chosen king, and once elected the king exercised command for the rest of his life without let or hindrance or question, except on the rare occasion when a king was deposed by the army with or without foreign intervention (Amyntas, the father of Philip, for instance, was deposed but subsequently reinstated). Thus Philip and Alexander held the supreme and total command of their armed forces with an absolute constitutional right from the moment each was elected king. Moreover, the king's powers of command were limited only by the condition that charges of treason had to be tried and decided by the army. In all else his orders were to be obeyed. He alone enlisted a man, making him thereby a "Macedon"; he made all appointments and promotions; and he provided pay and bounties, set the conditions of service and granted exemptions, leave, and discharge. . . .

In the Macedonian army the highest prestige was enjoyed by the cavalry. The king and his entourage were horsemen, hunting on horseback and fighting as cavalrymen, and the king honoured his best cavalrymen with the title "Companion" *(hetairos)*. . . . To those who, like Alexander, were steeped in the poems of Homer, the ties which bound the king and his Companions were as strong in the religious and the social sense as those which had bound Achilles and his Companions. Already in the period before Alexander II (369–368 B.C.) we know that the king selected from the ranks of his Companions the "Friends" (*philoi*) who were his closest associates and the "Commanders" (*hegemones*) to whom he delegated his own power of command. Entry to the charmed circle of the Companionship depended entirely on the king's favour, and he was concerned to choose men of integrity and ability. But the conditions of horsemanship in war were such that candidature was not open to all men.

[The Greek historian] Thucydides described the Macedonian cavalry in action against vastly superior numbers of Thracian cavalry and infantry in 429 B.C. as being "brave horsemen and cuirassiers [soldiers armed with breastplates]," who "dashed in among the Thracian host wherever they pleased and no one withstood their onset." The men wore the cuirass (a bronze breastplate or coat of mail), their mounts were stronger than the horses of their neighbours, and they fought not as skirmishers but as shock-troops at close quarters. Their horsemanship was superb; for the stirrup being as yet unknown, they had to grip the horse with their thighs and wield a weapon in battle, sometimes with both hands. To acquire this skill it was necessary to start in childhood; already by the age of fourteen the royal pages were so far advanced in horsemanship that they hunted and fought on horseback with the king. . . .

In the period before Philip the cavalry of Lower Macedonia and Upper Macedonia were separate entities; indeed they sometimes took different sides and even fought against one another. But Philip fused them into one body. His squadrons were named after a centre or centres of recruitment, near which the estates of the Companions were located; for instance, one after Bottiaea, a district in Lower Macedonia, and another after Amphipolis, a city in the coastal basin of the Strymon. One or more squadrons were called the *asthippoi* (a contraction of *astoi hippoi*), "townsmen-cavalry," and were recruited from the towns of Upper Macedonia; some of these served in Alexander's Balkan campaign, being referred to as "the cavalry from Upper Macedonia." Thus there was a territorial basis for the Companion cavalry squadrons. When able Greeks or other non-Macedonians were made Companions by Philip and Alexander, thus becoming "Macedones," they were allocated to the squadron of their place of residence. The total number of the Companion cavalry at the accession of Alexander is uncertain. In Asia Minor Alexander had about 1,800 in eight squadrons of some 225 each. We are told that he left 1,500 cavalry with Antipater in Macedonia; if these included both heavy and light cavalry, as is probable, and the proportion between them was as for the Asiatic campaign, there were about 1,000 Companion cavalry at home, so that the overall total was about 2,800 Companion cavalry in some fourteen squadrons of 200 each.

Thucydides described the Macedonian infantry in 423 B.C. as a mob. . . . Attempts to improve the sorry state of the infantry were made by two kings, Archelaus (ca. 413–399 B.C.) who trained and equipped infantrymen on the lines of contemporary Greek armies, and Alexander II (369–368 B.C.), who probably first introduced the title of Infantry Companionship, calling the best infantrymen "Foot-Companions." The latter was an important step; for it placed the best infantrymen on a level with the best cavalrymen, admitted them also to the closest association with the king, and led to a selected number serving as the king's bodyguard. We see these new infantry in action twice, in 359 B.C. as part of an army utterly defeated by the Illyrians with a heavy loss, and in 358 B.C. as the spearhead of victory under Philip's personal leadership against the Illyrians. The transformation was due to the personality and the methods of Philip. . . . [who] "improved the military formations, equipped his men appropriately with weapons of war, and held frequent exercises under arms and competitions in physical fitness." He was thus beginning to train an army of infantry on professional lines and equip them at his expense.

Names of army units and personnel were used in both a general sense and a restricted one, and their literal meaning is sometimes uncertain. What follows is the author's opinion in a controversial subject. In 359 B.C. (as in most of the preceding decade), the king's authority hardly extended beyond Lower Macedonia. Then Philip drew his "Foot-Companions" (*pezhetairoi*, being a contraction of *pezoi hetairoi*) from Lower Macedonia, and by the end of his reign he had at least six brigades of them. As far as our sources tell us, these brigades of *pezhetairoi* were named after their commanding officer only, e.g., "the brigade of Meleager." Late in the 350s, when Upper Macedonia had been assimilated and new towns were being planted, Philip began to raise and train infantrymen on the same lines from the people of the towns. These were called

"Townsmen-Companions" (*asthetairoi*, being a contraction of *astoi hetairoi*). When Alexander went to Asia, he took six brigades, three of *pezhetairoi* and three of *asthetairoi*; and the implication of the equal number is that the total of brigades of each kind was about the same. As a brigade consisted of some 1,500 men and as 12,000 infantry were left behind in Macedonia, the total number of brigades probably was fourteen. The brigades of *asthetairoi* were named, in one source, after both the commanding officer and the canton of Upper Macedonia from which they came; for example, "the brigade of Coenus from Elimeotis" and "the brigade of Polyperchon from Tymphaea."

Within the forces which we have mentioned the king developed certain élites. Seven of the Companion Friends served as personal Bodyguards (*somatophylakes*) to Alexander; and it seems that the assassin of Philip, Pausanias, being both a Bodyguard and a Friend, was one of such a special group during Philip's reign. There was next a special group of *pezhetairoi* who acted as Philip's guard when he was walking on a ceremonial occasion or in action if he was fighting on foot; for example in the battle against the Illyrians in 358 B.C. They were chosen for their courage and physique. Of the Companion cavalry one squadron (*ile*) was the "Royal Squadron" or "King's Own Squadron"; it fought beside the king, and so was sometimes called the Guard (*agema*).

Another group of infantry recruited by Philip was called the Hypaspists ("shield-bearers"). The name was taken from the king's squire who carried his shield into battle (Peucestas did this for Alexander), and it was extended first to the Royal Guard (*agema*) and then to two other brigades. The Hypaspists numbered 3,000, and they all went with Alexander to Asia. They were Companions and Macedones and in a particular sense the King's Own infantry. Their sons were trained for the army, and these sons served in 321 B.C., being named "the descendants of the Hypaspists" or just the "Hypaspists"; for the original corps' name was changed to the "Silver-Shields" (*argyraspides*) just before the invasion of India.

It is probable that the king gave special rewards to the King's Own men: the seven Bodyguards, the royal squadron of Companion cavalry, Philip's guard of *pezhetairoi*, and the royal guard of Hypaspists. These rewards were in land-grants or in cash. In addition, the king paid for the maintenance and training of the royal pages, many of whom were relations of the Companions; he seems to have done the same for the sons of the Hypaspists.

Non-Macedones of the Kingdom, Balkan Troops, Greek Allies, and Greek Mercenaries

Some cavalry units which served in Asia with Alexander were not Macedones: Thracians, Scouts (*prodromoi*), and Paeonians — five squadrons in all. That the Scouts, who constituted three of the five squadrons, were recruited from within the kingdom is very probable because they were given no ethnic label in our sources; they came perhaps from the mixed peoples of southeast Macedonia. The Paeonians came presumably from Paeonia which had been incorporated into the kingdom by Philip. If we are right about the Scouts and the Paeonians, it seems likely that the Thracians were also from within the kingdom. The squadrons numbered some 200 men each, and other squadrons of these light-armed cavalry were left behind in Macedonia.

The archers at first had no ethnic label. Although there were Macedones among them, the bulk may have come from east Macedonia and the Balkan empire. Greeks, and especially Thessalians, as well as a few Macedones, developed the siege-train to a high level of efficiency under Philip; and there were probably Greeks as well as Macedonians among the surveyors (*bematistai*), who recorded distances and planned communications. The ancillary services were manned by persons from the kingdom who were not Macedones. . . .

To sum up, the forces which came from within the kingdom were of two kinds. The heavy cavalry, called the Companions of the king, and the heavy infantry who fought in the battle-line or phalanx, called the Foot-Companions, the Townsmen-Companions and the Hypaspists — all were Macedones. Together with a few specialists in other arms it was these troops which represented the people under arms who elected the king in an armed assembly. This was apparent most clearly in the assembly and purification of the army which followed after the death of Alexander. Second to them in privilege and not possessing the status of Macedones were the light cavalry, the ancillary services, and the personnel of the fleet. They had no say in the election of the king or the hearing of a case of treason. For example, Callisthenes, a Greek from Olynthus, who served Alexander as the court historian, was not qualified to attend the hearing which resulted in his being put to death. The Macedones in Alexander's expedition to Asia were thus an army within the army and a state within the kingdom. . . .

The Balkan empire was rich in ferocious, if ill-disciplined troops, and there is no reason to suppose that Philip disarmed them. He was able to use some of them against such perpetual enemies as the Scythians and other raiders, and Alexander took to Asia 5,000 infantry who were described as Illyrians, Triballians, and Odrysians, the last being the leading tribe of central Thrace. They were not infantry of the phalanx-line but light-armed skirmishers, useful in mountain warfare and on subsidiary duties. A particularly fine unit of which Alexander made continuous use was supplied by the Agrianes, a tribe at the head of the Strymon valley (near Sofia), whose royal house was on excellent terms with that of Macedonia. Some of the archers who served with Alexander may have been recruited in the empire.

Among the Greek allies the Thessalians provided squadrons of heavy cavalry which rivalled the Macedonians in excellence. Led by a noble house of Heraclid descent, the Aleuadae, they had cooperated with Philip throughout his reign and fought on his side at Chaeronea, taking part in the charge led by Alexander. And for the war against Persia they sent 1,800 horsemen, equal in number and quality to Alexander's own Companion cavalry, who were to play a decisive part. The other Greek allies supplied 600 cavalry, 7,000 infantry, and 160 triremes with a complement of some 32,000 men for the war against Persia. Thus the Greek commitment of almost 40,000 men in all surpassed in number the troops sent from Macedonia and the Balkan empire. The expeditionary force at the start was a well-balanced partnership between the two states, Macedonia and "the Greeks."

A market which was open to all bidders was provided by Greek mercenary soldiers, available in many tens of thousands throughout the Greek world. Philip had made much use of these professional soldiers for training his own Macedonians and for campaigns in the Balkans, and Alexander employed 4,000 Greek mercenaries at the start in Asia. These were mainly infantrymen, probably with different kinds of expertise. It is interesting that he preferred to hire them rather than to take more infantry from his Balkan empire.

Equipment, Movement, and Supply

The Companion cavalryman fought wearing a metal helmet, metal cuirass (sometimes with shoulder-pieces extending to the upper arm), flowing cloak, short tunic, short metal or leather kiltlet covering the abdomen and private parts, and sandal-type shoes. His chief weapon was a lance of cornel-wood, light and tough, with counter-balancing butt and tip of metal, which he wielded with one arm. In a massed charge the lance gained its momentum from man and horse alike and was broken or dropped on impact, lest the rider was himself unseated. The Macedonians were the first to use the lance successfully. Next he fought with a rather long, slightly curving sword, of which the blade was designed for slashing. He did not normally carry a shield in battle; but a groom might be at hand to provide one at need. Thus equipped the cavalrymen rode in a close wedge-shaped formation, apex to the enemy, so that they could readily incline to right or left and charge into any gap (a formation used on occasion by Epaminondas of Thebes, but regularly first by Philip). It required much training, for every man had to keep his eyes on the one leader, "as happens in the flight of cranes." Their function was to shatter the enemy cavalry by the shock of their onset, and they proved under Philip superior to the fine horsemen of Illyria, Thrace, and Scythia. They could not charge an infantry-line; but as soon as an infantry-line lost its cohesion, they could push their way in, using the lance and the horse's weight, and they were deadly in attacking the open flank or the rear of an infantry force, and in pursuing a broken enemy, as Philip showed in his victory over the Illyrians in 358 B.C. The mounts were usually geldings, controlled by a spiked bit and spurs. They were bred from sturdy stock and expertly trained, but were often killed or wounded in battle, and maimed in long pursuits, since they were not shod. The relatively light armour of these cavalrymen, as compared with that of some Persian cavalrymen or the medieval knight, was in part due to the fact that Macedonian horses were less heavily built and smaller, perhaps around fourteen hands.

Light-armed cavalrymen, drawn probably from the eastern part of the Macedonian kingdom, served in Philip's time, as they appear early in Alexander's activities. Of these the Paeonians and the Thracians were armed with missiles as well as side-arms; and the Paeonians at least had no breastplate but used a shield. The Scouts or Lancers (*sarissophoroi*) carried a long *sarissa*, similar to that of the Companion infantryman which we shall shortly describe. As Alexander was sometimes portrayed wielding such a *sarissa*, it is possible that the Companion cavalrymen were trained to fight on occasion with the *sarissa*.

For centuries the Thessalian nobles had bred the finest horses and been the best cavalrymen in Greece. Equipped in the Greek manner, they carried two short spears, hurling one as a javelin and using the other as spear or javelin to suit the occasion and they were armed with a curving sword for slashing. They wore protective armour like the Companion cavalrymen, but sometimes had bronze guards on the forehead, chest, and flanks of their chargers. Thessalians were said to have invented the diamond formation.

The Companion infantrymen, both *pezhetairoi* and *asthetairoi*, were equipped with a metal helmet, metal greaves, a metal circular shield some two feet wide which was suspended from neck or shoulder, a long pike (*sarissa*) of light cornel-wood to be wielded with both hands, and a dagger as a second weapon. Pikes varied in length, probably from 15 to 18 feet; they were held in the middle by a metal band; and the foot-long blade at the tip was counterbalanced by a spiked butt of metal. During much of Philip's reign only the officers seem to have worn a metal cuirass, but in his later years, as prosperity developed, the wearing of it or of a metal frontlet (a "semi-cuirass") probably became general. This was so under Alexander. This equipment was designed primarily for fighting in the long close-packed line, known as the phalanx, against an enemy line of a similar kind. Normally each man in the front rank occupied a metre of space.

Behind him there were at least seven men. His front was protected not only by the blade of his own fifteen-foot pike but also by the blades of three or four pikes from behind him, these being progressively longer. When they faced an enemy of a different kind, other formations were adopted, such as a wedge or column. On the march into action the infantrymen were quick to change their pace and direction, and they had to maintain their dressing on different kinds of terrain. Strict discipline and precise drill were essential, and the best training of all was provided by experience in battle. For this reason Alexander chose not young but seasoned infantrymen for the brigades which went to Asia.

The Hypaspists were equally infantry of the line in that they formed part of the phalanx in every set battle. Then they too used the pike, which was the characteristic weapon of the Macedonian phalanx, and had the same equipment as the Companion infantrymen except that the cuirass was worn only by their officers. To be without a cuirass made for greater mobility on forced marches and night operations. Thus the Hypaspists were used sometimes with light-armed units for special tasks. They saw more action and had a greater reputation for toughness and endurance than any other soldiers.

That the men of the phalanx, *when in that formation*, fought with the pike is clear from the battles at Chaeronea and Pelium, where the king was leading his best infantrymen (whether called *pezhetairoi* or *hypaspistai* at the time) and also from the battle at Gaugamela, for the serried points were mentioned in the descriptions. It was this weapon which gave the Macedonians the advantage over Balkan infantry and Greek hoplites; and it did so also in the set battles in Asia against both cavalry and infantry. Ideally they fought on flat ground, but also on difficult ground, for instance on the steep banks of the Granicus and Pinarus rivers. That they were able to fight with other weapons under other conditions is obvious; for instance when mounted in the final stage of the pursuit of Darius, or in leading an assault on a breached wall at Tyre, or in mountain warfare. The shaft of the *sarissa* seems to have been made of two pieces joined together; these were probably dismantled on the march, and one length alone was of a normal spear's length and may on occasion have been used as such.

The infantry known as *hoplites* were the Greek equivalent of the Companion infantry. They were more heavily armed, having helmet, breastplate and greaves, a large bronze shield with two grips which was attached to the left arm at elbow and hand, a spear, six to eight feet long, and a sword. They too were trained to fight in a close-packed phalanx, eight men deep, but one which was less flexible and needed flatter terrain. Because their weapons and their methods did not marry with those of the Companion infantrymen, they were not used as troops of the line in Alexander's major battles.

The remarkable feature of the European army which Alexander inherited from his father and led into Asia was its composite nature and the specialised expertise of each part. Alexander had at his disposal almost every known variety of cavalry and infantry, heavy or light, regular or irregular, as well as experts in siegecraft, artillery, roadmaking, bridge-building, surveying and so on. Each unit was the best of its kind, properly equipped and highly trained. The fleet too, though relatively small, was supplied by the leading naval states in Greece, Athens among them, and the reputation of Greek triremes and Greek seamen was still the highest in the Mediterranean.

"Philip used to train 'the Macedones' for dangerous service by taking them on frequent route marches of some thirty-seven miles, fully armed with helmet, shield, greaves, pike and, as well as their arms, rations and all the gear they needed for daily life." This type of training, familiar today in commando or parachute courses, was of general application, and it produced the physical fitness and capacity for endurance which were found in the best guerrilla troops of the Balkan resistance movements of World War II. On such marches over rough country there was no question of keeping step in a column of fours or waiting for a soup kitchen. The troops spread out and each man made his best speed; each man too was his own mule, carrying a load which might include a month's stock of flour, and he prepared his own food in his metal dixie (the Macedonian name being *kotthybos*).

Whereas a Greek hoplite had a slave boy to carry his shield and gear, Philip allowed only one bearer (carrying grinders and ropes) to ten soldiers on the march. Troopers and horses were trained on similar lines so that they were capable of maintaining long pursuits over rough country. Philip allowed only one groom to a cavalryman.

The movement of goods and especially of heavy materials for the building of siege-towers and bridges was best undertaken by a fleet, whenever possible, as in Philip's campaign of 340–339 B.C. and in the early phase of Alexander's expedition to Asia. On land, when advanced troops had repelled an enemy, the baggage-train followed at its own slow pace, wheeled carriers and wagons being drawn by horses or by requisitioned oxen, and men also putting their shoulders to the task. But sometimes, as in Alexander's Balkan campaign, the baggage-train had to keep up with a fast-moving army; and this was achieved by careful planning, frequent relays of draught-animals, and knowledge of the country.

Communications and supply were related matters. We have already mentioned road-making in Macedonia and the Balkans, and Alexander put his Thracian troops to the task of making a road in mountainous Lycia, for example. Even where there were Persian roads or newly made roads surfaced with rubble or flagstones, haulage was slow; and messages carried by riders or cross-country runners took months even in summer to pass from Macedonia to India. Philip and Alexander had to find local solutions as far as possible to the problems of supply. The army often split and moved in separate groups, so that they could live mainly on foodstuffs officially requisitioned or privately purchased from the villagers; and where local supplies were short, the army had to make double speed to get into a better feeding-ground for men and horses, as between Susa and Persepolis. Hardships were relieved by feasting and drinking at times of rest and relaxation. Even so, long-term plans had to be made and executed when shipwrights and their equipment were brought from Phoenicia to the Indus valley, or an army was marched across the Hindu Kush. That these problems of communication and supply, which Wavell regarded as the supreme test of generalship, were solved by Alexander is one of the clearest signs of his genius. . . .

Arrian

The Battle of Issus

In the selections below, Arrian recounts the Battle of Issus, and N. G. L. Hammond analyzes Alexander's generalship and the army's performance in this battle, based on visits to the scene and ancient descriptions of the fighting.

Alexander was still at Mallus when a report came that Darius with his full force was encamped at Sochi, a place in Assyrian territory,

Reprinted by permission of the publishers and the Loeb Classical Library from Arrian: *History of Alexander*, 2.6–11, vol. 1, translated by Peter A. Brunt, Cambridge, Mass.: Harvard University Press, 1976.

about two marching days from the Assyrian Gates. Alexander therefore assembled the Companions and told them the news of Darius and his army, on which they urged him to advance without more ado. He then thanked them and dismissed the council and marched next day to attack Darius and the Persians. On the second day he passed the Gates and camped near a city called Myriandrus, and in the night a severe storm came on with rain, and a violent gale, which kept Alexander in his camp.

Darius meanwhile was marking time with his army. He had selected a plain in the Assyrian land open all round, convenient for the great number of his army and suitable for the manoeuvres of his cavalry. Amyntas son of Antiochus, the deserter from Alexander, advised him not to leave this place; there was, he said, elbow-room favourable for the numbers and equipment of the Persians. So Darius stayed where he was. But as Alexander spent a long time in Tarsus on account of his illness,* and a good deal at Soli, where he sacrificed and held the parade, and was delayed by his raid on the Cilician hillmen, all this made Darius waver in his decision. He himself was readily induced to adopt any opinion it was most agreeable to hold; and ingratiating courtiers, such as do and will haunt each successive king to his detriment, encouraged him to conclude that Alexander was no longer willing to advance further, but was hesitating on hearing of Darius' own approach. On all sides they egged him on, telling him that he would trample the Macedonian force underfoot with his cavalry. Amyntas, however, persisted that Alexander would come wherever he found Darius to be, and urged him to remain where he was. But the worse counsels prevailed, as they were more agreeable to hear at the time; moreover, some divine power led Darius into the very position where his cavalry did not much help him, nor the number of his men and javelins and arrows, where he could make no display even of the splendour of his army, but delivered the victory easily to Alexander and his force. In fact it was destined that the Persians should forfeit the sovereignty of Asia to Macedonians, just as Medes had lost it to Persians, and Assyrians even earlier to Medes.

Darius then crossed the mountains by the so-called Amanian

*Alexander fell ill in Cilicia after he had taken a swim in the cold waters of the Cydrius River.

Gates, advanced towards Issus and slipped in behind Alexander. On seizing Issus, he savagely tortured and killed all the invalid Macedonians left behind there whom he captured. Next day he advanced to the river Pinarus. Alexander heard that Darius was in his rear but did not credit the report; he embarked some of the Companions in a thirty-oared ship and sent them back to Issus, to see if it was true. They discovered the more easily that the Persians were camped there, since the sea takes the form of a bay there, and reported to Alexander that Darius was at hand.

Alexander summoned the generals, squadron leaders and officers of the allies and urged them to be confident in view of the dangers they had successfully surmounted in the past; already conquerors they were to fight men they had conquered, and God was a better strategist on their own side, putting it into Darius' mind to bring his force out of the open country and hem it into the narrow pass, an area just the size for the deployment of their phalanx; in the battle the Persians would have no benefit from their numbers, while their physique and morale were no match for their own. "We Macedonians," he continued, "are to fight Medes and Persians, nations long steeped in luxury, while we have now long been inured to danger by the exertions of campaigning. Above all it will be a fight of free men against slaves. And so far as Greek will meet Greek, they will not be fighting for like causes; those with Darius will be risking their lives for pay, and poor pay too; the Greeks on our side will fight as volunteers in the cause of Greece. . . . In addition you have Alexander commanding against Darius." Besides rehearsing these advantages they had in the contest, he pointed out the greatness of the rewards for which they were incurring danger. It was not Darius' satraps [Persian provincial governors] whom they were now to overcome, nor the cavalry that lined the Granicus, nor the twenty thousand foreign mercenaries, but the flower of Medes and Persians and all their subject nations living in Asia; the Great King was there himself; nothing remained after this final struggle but to rule the whole of Asia and set an end to their long exertions. . . . He also told them of anything else which at such a time, before dangers, a brave general would naturally tell brave men by way of encouragement. They crowded round and clasped their king's hand, and with cries of encouragement urged him to lead them on at once.

For the moment, however, Alexander told his troops to take their meal, but he sent a few horsemen and archers on [towards the

Gates] to reconnoitre the road that lay behind them; then at nightfall he himself marched with his whole force to seize the Gates again. When about midnight he was in possession of the passes once more, he rested his army for the remainder of the night there on the crags, after carefully setting outposts. Just upon dawn he descended from the Gates along the road; as long as the defile enclosed on every side remained narrow, he led the army in column, but when it grew broader, he deployed his column continuously into a phalanx, bringing up battalion after battalion of hoplites [heavy infantry], on the right up to the ridge, and on the left up to the sea. His cavalry so far had been ranged behind the infantry, but when they moved forward into open ground, he at once drew up his army in battle order; on the right wing towards the mountain ridge he placed first of the infantry the *agema* [royal guard] and hypaspists [elite infantry] under Nicanor son of Parmenio, next to them Coenus' battalion, and then that of Perdiccas. From right to left these regiments stretched to the centre of the hoplites. On the left, Amyntas' battalion came first, then Ptolemaeus', and next Meleager's. Craterus had been put in command of the infantry on the left and Parmenio of the entire left wing, with orders not to edge away from the sea, for fear the barbarians should surround them, since with their great numbers they were likely to overlap them on all sides.

When the approach of Alexander in battle order was reported to Darius, he sent about 30,000 of his cavalry across the river Pinarus with 20,000 light infantry, so that he might deploy the rest at his leisure. He placed the Greek mercenaries, about 30,000, foremost of his hoplites facing the Macedonian phalanx; next, on either side, 60,000 of the so-called Cardaces, who were also hoplites; this was the number which the ground where they stood allowed to be posted in one line. He also stationed about 20,000 men on the ridge on his left over against Alexander's right; some of these actually got to the rear of Alexander's force, since the mountain ridge where they were posted was deeply indented in one part and formed something like a bay as in the sea; then bending outwards again it brought those posted on the foothills to the rear of Alexander's right wing. The general mass of his light and heavy troops, arranged by their nations in such depth that they were useless, was behind the Greek mercenaries and the barbarian force drawn up in phalanx formation. Darius' whole force was said to amount to some 600,000 fighting men.

Alexander, however, finding the ground opening outwards a little as he went forward, brought into line his cavalry, the so-called Companions, the Thessalians . . . whom he posted with himself on the right wing while the Peloponnesians and other allies were sent to Parmenio on the left.

His phalanx once in due order, Darius recalled by signal the cavalry he had placed in front of the river to cover the deployment of the army and posted most of them opposite Parmenio on the right wing by the sea, because it was rather better ground for cavalry, though some were sent to the left wing near the hills. But as they appeared useless there for want of space, he ordered most of them too to ride round to their right wing. Darius himself held the centre of his whole host, the customary position for Persian kings; [the historian] Xenophon son of Gryllus has recorded the purpose of the arrangement.

At this Alexander, observing that nearly all the Persian cavalry had been transferred to his left, resting on the sea, while he had only the Peloponnesians and the other allied horse on this side, despatched the Thessalian cavalry at full speed to the left, with orders not to ride in front of the line, so that their change of position might not be sighted by the enemy, but to pass unobserved behind the phalanx. He posted the *prodromoi* [scouts] under Protomachus' command in front of the cavalry on the right, with the Paeonians led by Ariston, and in front of his foot the archers commanded by Antiochus. The Agrianians under Attalus, with some of the cavalry and archers, he threw back at an angle with the heights in his rear, so that on his right wing his line forked into two parts, one facing Darius and the main body of Persians across the river, the other towards the force posted in the Macedonian rear in the heights. On the left wing of the infantry the Cretan archers and the Thracians under Sitalces had been posted in front, with the cavalry of the left wing further in advance. The foreign mercenaries were drawn up in support of the whole line. But as his phalanx did not seem very solid on his right, and the Persians seemed likely to overlap them considerably there, he ordered two squadrons of the Companions from the centre, that from Anthemus, commanded by Peroedes son of Menestheus, and that called the Leugaean, under Pantordanus son of Cleander, to transfer unobserved to the right wing. He brought over the archers and some of the Agrianians and Greek mercenaries to the front of his right and so extended his phalanx to out-flank the Persian wing. For since the troops posted on the heights had not descended, but on a sally made by the Agrianians and a few archers at Alexander's order, had been easily dislodged from the foothills and had fled to the summit, Alexander decided that he could use those who had been posted to hold them in check to fill up his phalanx. To watch the hill-troops he reckoned it enough to tell off three hundred horsemen.

His forces thus marshalled, Alexander led them on for some time with halts, so that their advance seemed quite a leisurely affair. Once the barbarians had taken up their first positions, Darius made no further advance; he remained on the river bank, which was in many places precipitous, in some parts building up a stockade, where it appeared more accessible. This made it plain to Alexander and his staff that Darius was in spirit a beaten man. When the two armies were close, Alexander rode all along his front and bade them be good men and true, calling aloud with all proper distinctions the names not only of generals but even of commanders of squadrons and companies, as well as any of the mercenaries who were conspicuous for rank or for any brave action. An answering cry went up from all sides to delay no longer, but to charge the enemy. He continued to lead on in line, at marching pace at first, though he now had Darius' force in view, to avoid any part of the phalanx fluctuating in a more rapid advance and so breaking apart. Once within missile range, Alexander himself and his entourage were the first, stationed on the right, to charge in the river, in order to strike panic into the Persians by the rapidity of the attack, and by coming more quickly to close quarters to reduce losses from the Persian archers. Everything happened as Alexander guessed. The moment the battle was joined hand-to-hand, the Persian left gave way; and here Alexander and his followers won a brilliant success. But Darius' Greek mercenaries attacked the Macedonian phalanx, where a gap appeared as it broke formation on the right; while Alexander plunged impetuously into the river, came to close quarters with the Persians posted here, and was pushing them back, the Macedonian centre did not set to with equal impetus, and finding the river banks precipitous in many places, were unable to maintain their front in unbroken line; and the Greeks attacked where they saw that the phalanx had been particularly torn apart. There the action was severe, the Greeks tried to push off the Macedonians into the river and to restore victory to their own side who were already in flight, while the Macedonians sought to rival the success of Alexander, which was already apparent, and to preserve the reputation of the phalanx, whose sheer invincibility had hitherto been on everyone's lips. There was also some emulation between antagonists of the Greek and Macedonian races. Here it was that Ptolemaeus son of Seleucus fell, after showing himself a brave man, and about a hundred and twenty Macedonians of note.

At this point the battalions on the right wing, seeing that the Persians opposed to them were already routed, bent round towards Darius' foreign mercenaries, where their own centre was hard pressed, drove them from the river, and then overlapping the now broken part of the Persian army, attacked in the flank and in a trice were cutting down the mercenaries. The Persian cavalry posted opposite to the Thessalians did not keep their ground behind the river, once the engagement had actually begun, but crossed manfully and charged the Thessalian squadrons, and here there was a desperate cavalry fight; the Persians did not give way till they realized that Darius had fled and till their mercenaries were cut off, mowed down by the phalanx. But then the rout was patent and universal. The Persian horses suffered much in the retreat, with their riders heavily armoured, while the riders too, hurrying by narrow paths in a crowded horde in terror and disorder, suffered as heavy losses from being ridden over by one another as from the pursuit of their enemies. The Thessalians fell on them with vigour, and there was as much slaughter in the cavalry-flight as in the infantry.

As for Darius, the moment his left wing was panic-stricken by Alexander and he saw it thus cut off from the rest of his army, he fled just as he was in his chariot, in the van of the fugitives. So long as he found level ground in his flight, he was safe in his chariot; but when he came to gullies and other difficult patches, he left his chariot there, threw away his shield and mantle, left even his bow in the chariot, and fled on horseback; only night, speedily falling, saved him from becoming Alexander's captive, since Alexander pursued with all his might as long as daylight held, but when it was growing dark and he could not see his way, turned back towards the camp, though he took Darius' chariot, and with it his shield, mantle and bow. The fact is that his pursuit had become slower because he had wheeled back when the phalanx first broke formation and had not himself turned to pursue till he had seen the mercenaries and the Persian cavalry driven back from the river.

The Persians killed included Arsames, Rheomithres and Atizyes who had been among the cavalry commanders on the Granicus, and also Savaces the satrap of Egypt and Bubaces among the Persian nobles; as for the rank and file, some 100,000 fell, including over 10,000 cavalry, so that Ptolemy son of Lagos, who was then with Alexander, says that the pursuers of Darius meeting a deep gully in the pursuit crossed it over bodies of the dead. Darius' camp was stormed at once, and captured with his mother, wife, who was also his sister, and his infant son; two daughters were taken too, with a few noble Persian ladies in their suite. The other Persians had in fact despatched their women-folk and baggage to Damascus; Darius too had sent there the greater part of his money and everything else a great king takes with him even on campaign for his extravagant way of living; so they found no more than three thousand Talents* in the camp. However, the money at Damascus too was captured soon after by Parmenio, who was specially detailed for the purpose. So ended this battle, fought in the archonship at Athens of Nicocrates and in the month Maimacterion [November–December 333]. . . .

Nicholas G. L. Hammond

The King and His Army at Issus

At Issus Alexander consulted his staff. The question was whether to await Darius on the borders of Cilicia or to advance into Syria. The staff favoured advance. . . . Marching from Issus he reached

---

*One hundred drachmas made a mina, and sixty minas a talent. In 329 a skilled laborer in Athens received 2 to 2⅓ drachmas per day.

From N. G. L. Hammond, *Alexander the Great: King, Commander, and Statesman* (London, Chatto & Windus, 1981), pp. 94–110.

Myriandrus in two days, as Cyrus had done in 401 B.C., and drove the Persian troops back towards the Belen Pass. That night there was a severe storm with much wind and rain, and next day Alexander rested his men and horses at Myriandrus.

Meanwhile, unknown to Alexander, Darius had decided to advance from Sochi into Cilicia. He chose the northern route, because he knew that Parmenio held the Jonah Pass. In preparation for the advance he had sent his baggage-train and treasure to Damascus; for he drew his supplies mainly from the south and probably intended to follow up the defeat of Alexander by a move in that direction. At the time of his decision Darius believed that Alexander's forces were spread out from Cilica Tracheia or Tarsus to the Jonah Pass and that his own army, descending from the Hasanbeyli Pass and some lesser passes to Castabalum, would cut the enemy forces in two. In fact Darius reached Castabalum without opposition, captured Issus and mutilated or killed the sick. There he learnt to his surprise and delight that Alexander was not at Tarsus but had left Issus two days before en route for Myriandrus. He was sitting on Alexander's tail with a larger army, and he knew that Alexander would have to turn back and fight his way through or starve. So he advanced next day to the best defensive position, the line of the river Pinarus, and encamped there. On that day Alexander was resting his army at Myriandrus.

The news that Darius was not in front of him but behind him reached Alexander at Myriandrus during the ensuing night or early next day. He was at first incredulous. He sent some of his Companions in a thirty-oared boat to ascertain the truth. They not only found where Darius was but they rowed right into the mouth of the Pinarus and noted the disposition of his forces. Their action was the more courageous, because the Persians must have commandeered and manned any shipping along the coast. When they reported back, Alexander consulted his staff. He then ordered his men to take their afternoon meal and started back as night was falling. The army reached the Jonah Pass at midnight; detachment after detachment marched through the narrows and slept among the crags. Both Alexander and Darius knew that a decisive battle was about to be fought on or near the Pinarus river.

It is this battle which scholars have named the Battle of Issus. It was not fought there, but there has been considerable argument as to which of the rivers north of the Jonah Pass was the Pinarus. One important source of information is Callisthenes, the court historian, who stood high in the confidence of the king. He was probably present at the battle and could have obtained information on the spot. As Tarn observes, Callisthenes must have read his account to Alexander; and he must have had comments from him and other participants. Matters of fact then are as certain to be correct as anything can be, and it is these matters of fact which enable us to establish the scene of the battle beyond any reasonable doubt.

We owe our knowledge of Callisthenes to Polybius, who read and criticised his predecessor's work and so transmitted to us some of Callisthenes' statements. One is that when Alexander, having already passed "the narrows" (i.e., Jonah's Pass) going south, learnt of the presence of Darius in Cilicia (i.e., at the Pinarus river), they were 100 stades (18.5 kilometres) apart (Polybius 12.19.4). Alexander heard this news at Myriandrus. Since the distance from Iskenderun to the Payas river is 20 kilometres by the modern motor-road, the Pinarus river should be identified with the Payas. Most scholars prefer to identify it with the Deli Cayi, 10 kilometres farther north. Its distance from Iskenderun, 30 kilometres, is incompatible with the distance given by Callisthenes. . . .

If we ask how Callisthenes came to know these distances, the answer is from Alexanders' surveyors, the *bematistae*. Alexander had been a student of war from boyhood and as a commander he had to assess distances in relation to battle formations with an accurate eye. If then, the distance between coast and mountainside at the Payas river, as given by Callisthenes, is not the same as it is today, the logical deduction is not that Alexander or Callisthenes got it wrong, but that the terrain has changed since 333 B.C. . . .

Darius was in camp at the Pinarus river for more than thirty-six hours before Alexander's army appeared. His choice of the Pinarus position was therefore deliberate. It may seem to us that he could have put his superior numbers to better effect by positioning himself on either of the rivers father north, the Uzerli Cayi or the Deli Cayi, because the distances there between coast and mountainside were almost twice as much as at the Payas river, and his cavalry forces in particular would have had more space to manoeuvre. But the banks of these rivers lacked the runs of precipitous places which we have seen at the Payas river. We must conclude then that Darius preferred to man these precipitous places even at the cost of being unable to put his superior numbers to the best effect. How did he intend to use these places? Evidently as means of defence for the infantry which he placed on the north bank; which is clear from the fact that he had stockades built on such accessible places as occurred between the precipitous ones. The plan then was to hold the centre by the defensive action of Darius' best infantry, fighting against the only force which could attack them frontally, the Macedonian phalanx. Curtius was then correct in saying that Darius believed the chief strength of the Macedonian army to be its phalanx (3.10.11, *phalangem Macedonici exercitus robur*). The very erection of the stockades meant that Darius did not intend his best infantry to take the offensive. Callisthenes made a similar point (Polybius 12.17.6).

The best infantry, being heavy-armed, were the Greek mercenaries (30,000 according to Callisthenes); next came their Persian imitators, the Cardaces (60,000 according to Arrian). When the whole force was encamped, before the Macedonian army appeared, Darius had his cavalry on the right near the sea, then the Greek mercenaries along the river, and then the Cardaces. When the enemy first began to approach, Darius sent across the river towards them a cavalry force of 30,000 and a light-armed infantry force to the number of 20,000. One effect of this was to screen Darius' rearrangement of the infantry, which is mentioned by Callisthenes but not by Arrian. Darius summoned the Greek mercenaries to the centre where he stationed himself (Polybius 12.18.9); presumably he moved part of the Cardaces to the position vacated by the Greeks, i.e., to the right wing of the infantry line, next to the cavalry. Thus he put himself and his finest infantry in the most defensible place. There was also with him the 3,000-man Royal Cavalry Guard. The revised positions, as indicated by Callisthenes (Polybius 12.18.9), are shown in Figure 1.

In advance of his left wing Darius placed troops on the foothills which curved round in the shape of a sickle. They were in position before the Macedonian army reached the point of the sickle. When the enemy came closer, Darius recalled his cavalry by signal and stationed the majority on the right of the phalanx and a part only on its left. But even of this part he withdrew most and

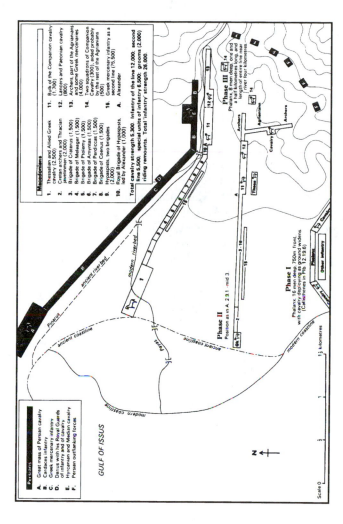

FIGURE 1. The Phases of the Battle of Issus [from N. G. L. Hammond, *Alexander the Great: King, Commander and Statesman* (London, Chatto & Windus, 1981) p. 101.]

113

reallocated them to his right wing, the reason being that they were cramped for suitable space on the left wing (Arr. 2.8.10–11). We learn from Curtius (3.9.5) that the cavalry who stayed there were Hyrcanians, Medes, and a heterogeneous squadron. They fitted between two groups of Cardaces (Arr. 2.8.6.).

The Persian order of battle, in its final form, is shown on Figure 1, apart from archers, slingers, and other skirmishers (Curt. 3.9.1–5). Darius clearly intended to deliver an attack with the cavalry massed on his right by the sea, and at the same time to deliver a left hook with the forces on the sickle-shaped high ground taking the enemy in the flank and partly in the rear. Meanwhile his phalanx had to hold firm and keep the Macedonian phalanx at bay. Success against both wings or even one wing would enable the successful troops to take the Macedonians in the rear.

Let us turn now to Alexander. On the day before the battle he learned from the Companions who rowed into the bay of Payas that the order of the encamped troops from coast to mountainside was cavalry, Greek mercenaries, and "peltasts," who were Cardaces or others. Just before dawn, when he was mustering his army near Jonah's Pass, he sent horsemen off to reconnoitre. The column of march formed at dawn. It was led by the phalangites, 12,000 strong. When the strip between the sea and the mountainside became a kilometre or so, the column deployed into a front of 375 men and a depth of 32 men. When the strip widened to two kilometres, the front changed to 750 men and the depth to 16 men (Callisthenes in Polybius 12.19.6). At about the time of the changeover, the horsemen returned to report what they had seen at dawn, namely that the Persian army was standing to arms in the order of encampment as reported on the previous day, and that some troops were moving on the higher ground of the mountainside south of the Pinarus river. As the march continued, Alexander riding ahead saw the 30,000 Persian cavalry and the 20,000 light-armed coming towards him. But they were soon recalled by Darius and withdrew north of the river.

When the Macedonian phalanx, sixteen men deep, passed the tip of the sickle-shaped high ground, it began to enter the flat area of the dead ground and its extension to the coast. Here the front of the phalanx was extended to 1,500 men and the depth reduced to eight men, the normal depth for engaging an army of hoplites [heavy infantry]; and he was able also to deploy his cavalry. Alexander himself rode immediately on the right of the phalanx. He had under his command there the Companion cavalry, the Thessalians, the Lancers and the Paeonians [cavalries]. He posted the Greek cavalry and the allied cavalry on the left of the phalanx and put them under the command of Parmenio. A force of Cretan archers and Thracian infantry was brought forward to form a link between Parmenio's cavalry and the left of the phalanx. The remainder of the infantry marched as a second phalanx behind the Macedonian brigades (Arr. 2.9.3).

From this point, perhaps two kilometres from the river Payas, Alexander made his army advance very slowly, with frequent halts. There were two reasons for this. He wanted to see the final dispositions of Darius before his own men left the dead ground, in which they were out of sight of Darius and his staff. He also had time to deal with the threat to his right flank and — as he advanced — to his right rear, for he deployed a force of Agrianians [infantry], archers, and cavalrymen at a right angle to the line of his advance and ordered them to attack the enemy on the sickle-shaped higher ground (Arr. 2.9.2 and 4). This they did successfully.

When the right-hand half of the line was about to reach the ridge where they would see and be seen by the enemy on the Payas river, Alexander made his last dispositions. He knew now the final dispositions of Darius, because he or his aides riding to the top of the ridge could watch the enemy movements. He moved the Thessalian cavalry from the right wing to the left wing, but he made them ride *behind* the phalanx, i.e., in the dead ground, so that Darius and his staff did not see the change of disposition. In the second place he filled the gap created through the withdrawal of the Thessalian cavalry by bringing forward the archers, some of the Agrianians, and some Greek mercenaries (the last from the second phalanx) and making them into an extension of the line on the right wing. He also detached two squadrons of Companion cavalry and sent them to a position on the right which they were to reach unobserved by moving *behind* other troops (Arr. 2.9.3–4). He did this, says Arrian, because his right wing up to that point was not strong and was in danger of being much outflanked by the longer Persian line. He posted 300 cavalrymen, evidently those of the two squadrons of Companion cavalry, to his right rear to deal with any threat from the enemy on the sickle-shaped piece of high ground.

The front men of the Macedonian army came slowly over the top of the ridge and across the level ground near the coast in the final order of battle, which is shown in Figure 1. They were in perfect line, cavalrymen and infantrymen, as on a parade ground. They halted at the order of Alexander. He rode along the front of the line, some four kilometres in length. While he harangued the troops, the enemy made no attempt to attack. When his 31,000 or so men roared their approval, he returned to his position on the right of the phalanx, and the slow advance was resumed "step by step" (Arr. 2.10.3). As the line came within range of the Persian archers on the far bank of the river, some eighty metres away, the Royal Infantry Guard, led by Alexander on foot, charged "at the double" into and through the river to hurl themselves upon a battalion of Cardaces [infantry], the Hyrcanian and Median cavalry being on the Cardaces' left. . . .

We must pause to emphasise the point that the charge was on foot and not on horseback. The expression "dromo" which I have translated "at the double" is generally used of an infantry charge, though not exclusively. More decisive is the nature of the ground. Cavalry at the charge would have broken the horses' legs in the boulder-strewn riverbed described above. But Alexander, his entourage, and the Royal Brigade of Hypaspists [elite infantry] (Arr. 2.8.3) could pick their way at the run through the riverbed and emerge in line on the far side. It was, indeed, an axiom of ancient warfare that cavalry never delivered a frontal charge on an infantry line. Scholars have assumed this to be an exception, because the Cardaces were Persians, albeit trained as hoplites (Arr. 2.8.6); but there is no need to postulate such an invidious exception.

As in the case of the other battles, the attention of the narrator and so of the reader is focussed upon the doings of Alexander and any unit he is leading. We hear less of what happened in other parts of the battlefield. Of course, once the two lines were locked in conflict, no one had an overall knowledge of what was happening, far less any overall control. Alexander had anticipated this by decentralising the command in advance: he had given to Parmenio command of the entire left half of the line with orders not to lose contact with the coast (i.e., not to be outflanked), and within that command he had given command of the left half of the phalanx to

Craterus, himself commander of the leftmost brigade of phalangites (Arr. 2.8.4). Alexander retained command of the entire right half of the line, both infantry and cavalry. He led the Royal Infantry Guard in the initial charge, and later, as we shall see, a group of Companion cavalry. As he was himself to be a combatant, he must have given his orders to unit commanders in the right half of the line before he had led the charge. We may assume that what ensued in this part of the line came about through the execution of these orders.

Alexander and his Royal Infantry Guard succeeded brilliantly. They punched a hole through the line of Cardaces, and as they did so the Hypaspists, Coenus' battalion, and Perdiccas' battalion were coming into action against the Cardaces (up to almost the middle of the Persian line), and on Alexander's right the Companion Cavalry crossed the wide river bed in their own time and attacked the Hyrcanian and Median cavalry. Further to the right, lancers, Paeonians, Agrianian infantry, and archers swept into action, outflanking and overwhelming their opponents. After some fighting the whole of the Persian left wing gave way and fled. The task of Alexander's right wing was now to swing left and attack the Persian centre on the flank and in the rear; and he himself, now mounted, went first with his own Companions and the leading squadron of cavalry, forcing his way through the disrupted battalions of Cardaces towards Darius and his Royal Cavalry Guard, conspicuous among the sea of infantrymen.

Meanwhile the left half of the Macedonian line was in considerable difficulty. Whereas Alexander had taken the initiative on his right, the cavalry of the Persian right had crossed the river and attacked the Greek and Thessalian cavalry under Parmenio. Although the Persian cavalry far outnumbered their opponents in this part of the field, the actual front was so narrow that it is doubtful whether there was much disparity at first between the numbers effectively engaged. Squadrons of heavy Persian cavalry, in which man and horse were both protected by corselets of metal discs, overbore one Thessalian squadron by the weight of its charge; but other Thessalian squadrons, being quicker in movement, and using the wider space behind their infantry for regrouping, outmanoeuvred and slaughtered the Persians.

As the limitless Persian reserves came through the gap, the cavalry battle became very fierce. The connecting link of infantry seems to have held its own, but the four battalions of the left half of the Macedonian phalanx had to deal not only with some beetling cliffs on both sides of the river and some stockades on the far side but also with the opposing Greek mercenaries, whose fighting quality was high (their superior numbers was not a factor, since the limited space made the numbers equal in the first eight files). It was not possible for the Macedonians to maintain the phalanx line either in getting down into the riverbed or in forcing their way up the accessible parts of the opposite bank and through the stockades. Whenever a group of Macedonians established a bridgehead on the north bank, the Greeks charged them and tried to hurl them back into the river.

Both sides fought with a bitterness in which racial animosity played its part. One battalion commander, Ptolemy son of Seleucus, and 120 phalangites lost their lives in this struggle. There was also some dislocation on the right half of the phalanx line, where a sudden shift to the right had been made necessary by the impetuous charge of Alexander (Arr. 2.10.4–7).

While the fate of the left half of the line was hanging in the balance, Alexander was drawing near to the Persian Royal Guard. Alexander and his Companions evidently passed behind the Greek mercenaries in order to make a drive on Darius, and it was the victorious infantry Guardsmen, the Hypaspists, and the phalangites of Coenus and Perdiccas who were coming in on the flank and in the rear and mowing down the Greek mercenaries. In this way the phalangites of the left part of the line received relief, and the Greek mercenaries were in danger of being surrounded (Arr. 2.11.3 fin.). However, Alexander and the Companion Cavalry had pressed on towards the extreme left wing, where the Persian cavalry were at last being driven back. Aware now of the complete defeat which Darius had suffered and of Darius' own flight, the swarms of Persian cavalrymen set off at the gallop for any routes of escape through the Amanus range.

The pursuit, led by Alexander, the Companions, and the Thessalians, lasted as long as there was light. The distance covered, 200 stades (37 km) (Diod. 17.37.2), is that from the Payas river to Toprakkale, beyond which the enemy turned east into the hills.

Alexander did not submit his tired horses to pursuit in the hills as darkness was falling. This is another indication that the Payas is to be identified with the Pinarus; for if the Deli Cayi is proposed, he had to carry the pursuit into the hills for some ten kilometres. The pursuit was directed not against the Greek mercenaries (who escaped in large organised units) but against the Persian Empire's élite, the cavalrymen of the central and eastern satrapies, and Darius himself. The losses in men and mounts on the Persian side were very great, some narrow defiles being filled with their corpses; but Darius rode through the night and collected survivors next day, including 4,000 Greek mercenaries, before crossing the Euphrates to safety. Alexander lost 150 cavalrymen and 302 infantrymen; he was one of the 4,500 wounded. The proportion of killed to wounded is a testimony to the effectiveness of protective armour.

To criticise Darius is not difficult. The position which he chose for the inevitable battle had grave defects. It was too narrow for the full deployment even of his best troops, let alone the mob of light-armed who became engaged only in the horrors of the flight. For example, if the 30,000 Greek mercenaries had been used in the same depth as the 12,000 Macedonian phalangites, they would have had a front of 3.75 kilometres, whereas in fact they were concentrated beside the king with a front of probably less than half a kilometre. The great numbers of fine Persian cavalry had the same experience on the Persian right wing. . . . Darius' personal example, in choosing a safe place behind his centre instead of leading the left wing, may have been the sort of factor which caused the light-armed infantry on the higher ground to show so little spirit. . . .

In the preliminary phase Darius seems to have made changes of disposition rather through indecision or miscalculation than for tactical reasons. It was the view of Callisthenes that Darius meant at first to fight on his left wing where he would face Alexander if Alexander followed the usual practice of Greek commanders, but that later he decided otherwise and moved to the centre where he held a backward position (Polybius 12.22.2; Curt. 3.9.4). If he thought he and his staff could direct the course of the battle better from there, once action started, he was mistaken. Again, his motive for moving the Greek mercenaries from the right wing, where they had the best chance of breaking and outflanking the left wing of the Macedonian phalanx, seemed tactically unwise. Perhaps the transfer of them to the centre gave him a greater sense of security. The moving of cavalry units from one wing to another seems to have been due to changes of mind or miscalculation, and the final result was to weaken the left wing which had to face the superb Companion Cavalry.

Alexander might well have been disconcerted when he realised that his sick and wounded had been captured, his lines of supply cut, and his return barred by an army of superior numbers in a strong defensive position. However, when he called a meeting of his commanders, he said they had grounds for confidence. Then he ordered his army to take their main meal — the last they were to have for some twenty-four hours. When night fell, he led the army back to Jonah's Pass. There, after a few hours of sleep, they began a slow confident march down towards the enemy. The deployment in three stages from a marching column to a moving line of battle was a superb piece of drill, executed by more than 30,000 men, and was itself a demonstration of the cohesion and integration of the various arms and races in Alexander's army. Thus the men realised their interdependence and their interdependability on the eve of action.

Whereas Darius failed to use so many of his men, Alexander used his men with a precise economy. The threat to his right wing and right rear was contained finally by 300 cavalrymen. The phalanx, about one and a half kilometres in length, was of the standard depth, eight men, although the enemy infantry was in much greater depth. The right number of Companion Cavalry to break through the opposing Persian cavalry was so assessed that two squadrons could be detached to ensure the outflanking of the Persian left wing. The distribution of his 5,000 or so cavalry between the two wings when they faced some 30,000 Persian cavalry was so capably calculated that he ensured success on his right and held the enemy on his left. It is not possible to fault his final order of battle, either in theory or in practice, and that is a very remarkable thing when we realise that Alexander developed it stage by stage during a slow but continuous march, in such a way that it fitted the final dispositions of the enemy. He made the last moves, and he made them so that they were not seen by Darius and his staff.

The decentralisation of command was another thing which distinguished Alexander from Darius. The authority entrusted in advance to Parmenio enabled him to hold together the hard-pressed left wing, and that entrusted to Craterus enabled him to coordinate the four battalions which were under severe pressure, whereas the Persian left wing seems to have disintegrated rapidly. But this was only possible because Alexander's planning mind gave him a clear idea of the way in which the whole action would develop. "It turned out as Alexander supposed" (Arr. 2.10.4).

"Alexander carried out the duties of a soldier no less than those of a commander" (Curt. 3.11.7). Even in the more remote relationships of modern warfare the known courage in action of a Field Marshal — Birdwood, Montgomery, Harding for instance — is an inspiration to officers and men, a challenge to emulation. Alexander had the fearlessness of the born fighter. In the deadly struggle of the Macedonian infantry against the Greek mercenaries on the precipitous banks "it was the conspicuous success of Alexander in action which made the Macedonians determined not to fall behind him and not to dim the glorious record of the phalanx, famed as invincible up to that day." (Arr. 2.10.6).

Both as a commander and as a fighter, whether on foot or on horse, Alexander knew his officers and men with a personal intimacy which it is impossible to conceive as ever existing between the Great King of Persia and his subjects. . . .

All the [other accounts of the battle] were written at a later date, when the myth of Alexander's invincibility was already established. They conceal the fact that only a freak of chance prevented Darius from cutting Alexander's forces in two, and that only the folly of Darius gave Alexander the opportunity to fight under favourable conditions and recover from being outmanoeuvred. The victory was commemorated later by the foundation of Alexandria ad Issum, named in relation to the Gulf of Issus. . . .

A detail from the so-called Alexander sarcophagus made for his ally
Abdalonymus, king of Sidon, now in the Istanbul Museum. It depicts
Alexander on horseback in combat between Macedonians and Persians.
(Hirmer Fotoarchiv)

VI Alexander and the Macedonian Generals

Plutarch

Philotas and His Enemies

The Roman historian Ronald Syme suggests that behind every con-stitutional facade an oligarchy lurks. The charges of conspiracy brought against the prominent Macedonian Philotas (in Drangiana in 330) affords a close-up view of how the king and the Macedonian upper class managed their mutual relationships and how the compo-sition (and perhaps even the character) of the elite was transformed by this crisis.

Below is Plutarch's account of the conspiracy against Alexander that culminated in the execution of both Philotas and his father Parmenio. Plutarch, in typical fashion, dwells on the characters of

From Plutarch, *Alexander*, 47–49, in *The Age of Alexander* by Plutarch, trans. by Ian Scott-Kilvert, Penguin Classics, 1973, pp. 303–306. Copyright © 1973, Ian Scott-Kilvert. Reproduced by permission of Penguin Books Ltd.

the people involved in the affair but also points to the role played by Philotas's enemies.

From this point [some time after Darius's death] he [Alexander] began to adapt his own style of living more closely to that of the country and tried to reconcile Asiatic and Macedonian customs: he believed that if the two traditions could be blended and assimilated in this way his authority would be more securely established when he was far away, since it would rest on goodwill rather than on force. For this reason he selected thirty thousand boys and gave orders that they should be taught to speak the Greek language and to use Macedonian weapons, and he appointed a large number of instructors to train them. . . .

Alexander noticed that among his closest friends it was Hephaestion who approved of these plans and joined him in changing his habits, while Craterus clung to Macedonian customs, and he therefore made use of the first in his dealings with the barbarians and of the second with the Greeks and Macedonians. In general he showed most affection for Hephaestion and most respect for Craterus, for he had formed the opinion and often said that Hephaestion was a friend of Alexander's, while Craterus was a friend of the king's. For this reason a feeling of hostility grew and festered between the two and they often came into open conflict. Once on the expedition to India they actually drew their swords and came to blows, and as their friends appeared and began to join in the quarrel, Alexander rode up and publicly reprimanded Hephaestion: he told him that he must be a fool and a madman if he did not understand that without Alexander's favour he was nothing. Then later in private he sharply rebuked Craterus. Finally he called both men together and made them be friends again. He swore by Zeus Ammon and the rest of the gods that these were the two men he loved best in the world, but that if he ever heard them quarrelling again, he would kill them both, or at least the one who began the quarrel. After this, it is said, neither of them ever did or said anything to offend the other even in jest.

Among the Macedonians at this time few men enjoyed a more prominent position than Philotas, the son of Parmenio: he had a high reputation for courage and for his ability to endure hardship and after Alexander he had no equal for generosity and devotion to his friends. At any rate we are told that when one of his intimate friends asked him for money and his steward replied that he had none to give, he asked the man, "What do you mean — have I no plate or furniture to sell?" However, Philotas also displayed an arrogance, an ostentation of wealth, and a degree of luxury in his personal habits and his way of living which could only cause offence in his position as a private subject. At this time in particular his efforts to imitate a lofty and majestic presence carried no conviction, appeared clumsy and uncouth, and succeeded only in provoking envy and mistrust to such a degree that even Parmenio once remarked to him, "My son, do not make so much of yourself." And indeed Philotas had fallen under suspicion a long while before this. When Darius had been defeated in Cilicia and his treasure captured at Damascus, one of the many prisoners who were brought into Alexander's camp was discovered to be a beautiful Greek girl who had been born in Pydna and was named Antigone. She was handed over to Philotas and he — like many a young man who, when he has drunk well, is apt to talk freely to his mistress in the boastful fashion of a soldier — often confided to her that all the greatest achievements in the campaign had been the work of his father and himself. Then he would speak of Alexander as a mere boy who owed his title of ruler to their efforts. Antigone repeated these remarks to one of her friends, and he naturally enough passed them on until they reached the ears of Craterus, who took the girl and brought her privately to Alexander. When the king heard her story, he ordered her to continue visiting Philotas, but to come and report everything that she learned from him.

Philotas had no suspicion of the trap that was being set for him and in his conversations with Antigone he uttered many indiscretions and often spoke slightingly of the king, sometimes through anger and sometimes through boastfulness. Even so Alexander, although he now had overwhelming evidence against Philotas, endured these insults in silence and restrained himself either because he had confidence in Parmenio's loyalty, or perhaps because he feared the power and prestige of father and son. But meanwhile a Macedonian from Chalaestra named Dimnos organized a conspiracy against Alexander, and invited a young man named Nicomachus whose lover he was to take part in the plot. Nicomachus refused to be involved, but told his brother Cebalinus of the attempt. Cebalinus then went to Philotas and demanded that he should take them both to Alexander, as they had something of the greatest urgency to tell him. Philotas, however, for some unknown reason, did not arrange the interview, making out that the king was engaged on more important business, and he did this not once but twice. By this time the brothers had become suspicious of Philotas, and so they turned to somebody else who brought them into the king's presence. First of all they revealed Dimnos' plot and then they made a number of insinuations against Philotas, because he had twice disregarded their requests to see the king.

This news enraged Alexander, and when he learned that Dimnos had resisted arrest, and had been killed by the men who had been sent to fetch him, he became still more disturbed, as he concluded that he had lost the chance to uncover the plot. He felt bitter resentment against Philotas and became all the more ready to listen to those who had long hated his friend. These enemies now said openly that it was folly on the king's part to suppose that a man such as Dimnos who came from the obscure town of Chalaestra would ever have undertaken such a daring enterprise on his own account: it was obvious that he was a mere agent, a tool in the hands of somebody of much greater power, and that Alexander must look for the source of the conspiracy among those who had most interest in keeping it concealed. Once the king had begun to listen to these insinuations and suspicions, Philotas' enemies brought innumerable accusations against him. He was arrested, interrogated, and tortured in the presence of the king's Companions, while Alexander himself listened to the examination from behind a curtain. We are told that when he heard Philotas uttering broken and pitiful cries and pleas for mercy to Hephaestion he exclaimed, "Ah, Philotas, if you are so weak and unmanly as this, how could you involve yourself in such a dangerous business?" Philotas was executed, and immediately afterwards Alexander sent messengers to Media and had Parmenio put to death as well. This was a man who had rendered many great services to Philip and who, of all Alexander's older friends, had urged him most strongly to undertake the invasion of Asia: of his three sons he had seen two die in battle and now he was put to death with the third. . . .

Quintus Curtius Rufus

The Philotas Affair

Curtius is our most informative source for the conspiracy, and his account of the plot forms the basis for many modern interpretations of the affair.

Alexander could better cope with warfare than peace and leisure. As soon as he was free of these worries that beset him, he yielded to dissipation, and the man whom the arms of Persia had failed to crush fell before its vices. There were parties early in the day; drinking and mad revelry throughout the night; games; women by the score. It was a general decline into the ways of the foreigner. By affecting these, as though they were superior to those of his own country, Alexander so offended the sensibilities and eyes of his people that most of his friends began to regard him as an enemy. For the Macedonians clung tenaciously to their own practices and were used to satisfying their natural requirements with a diet that was sparing and easily accessible; and these he had now driven into the depraved customs of foreigners and conquered nations. This explains the increase in the plots against his life, the mutiny of his men and the more-public displays of resentment and mutual recrimination among them; it explains why Alexander subsequently oscillated between anger and suspicion which arose from groundless fears, and it explains other similar problems which will be recounted later. . . .

Alexander was not merely undefeated by foreign assailants but secure from attack, when after eight days back in camp he became the object of an internal conspiracy. Dymnus, a man of slight influence or favour with the king, had a passionate infatuation for a catamite called Nicomachus; he was totally devoted to the boy,

From *The History of Alexander*, 6.2.1–4, 7–11, by Quintus Curtius Rufus, trans. by John Yardley, Penguin Books, 1984, pp. 119–120, 131–145. Translation copyright © 1984, John Yardley. Reproduced by permission of Penguin Books Ltd.

whose favours he alone enjoyed. Practically beside himself, as one could see from his face, Dymnus went with the young man into a temple, with no one else present, saying to him first that what he had to tell him were secrets that were not to be divulged. Nicomachus was now on tenterhooks, and Dymnus begged him in the name of their mutual affection and the pledges each had made of their feelings to swear on oath to remain silent about his disclosures. Nicomachus did not think that Dymnus would tell him anything he would be obliged to divulge even if it meant perjury on his part, so he took the oath by the gods of the place. Then Dymnus revealed that a plot had been hatched against the king which was to be executed in two days' time, and that he was involved in the plan along with some courageous and distinguished men.

On hearing this, the youth resolutely denied that he had sworn to be party to treason and asserted that he could not be constrained by any religious consideration to cover up a crime. . . . In fact, Nicomachus possessed the steadfast resolve appropriate to a clean-living man; he had not wavered from his earlier decision but pretended that out of love for Dymnus he could deny him nothing. He now proceeded to inquire about the identity of the accomplices in this important enterprise, saying that the quality of the people involved in so significant an undertaking made all the difference. Crazed as much by love as by guilt, Dymnus offered him both thanks and congratulations on unhesitatingly joining a brave group of young men, comprising the bodyguard Demetrius, Peucolaus and Nicanor. To these Dymnus added the names of Aphobetus, Iolaus, Dioxenus, Archepolis and Amyntas.

Following this conversation Nicomachus relayed what he had heard to his brother, whose name was Cebalinus. They decided Nicomachus should remain in the tent in case, by entering the royal quarters, he made the conspirators aware that they had been betrayed, for he was not an intimate of the king's. Cebalinus himself stood before the entrance to the royal tent, not being permitted to proceed further, and waited for someone of the first order of Alexander's friends who would take him in to the king. As it happened, only Parmenio's son Philotas had remained in the royal quarters after the others had been dismissed; why he did so is not known. To him Cebalinus, noticeably in great agitation, disclosed in confused speech what he had learned from his brother, and in-

sisted that it be reported to the king without delay. Philotas commended him and straightway went in to Alexander but, after engaging him in lengthy conversation on other matters, he reported
none of the information he had received from Cebalinus. Towards
evening the young man caught Philotas at the entrance to the royal
tent as he was on his way out, and asked if he had carried out his
request. Philotas claimed Alexander had had no time to talk to him
and then went on his way. The next day Cebalinus was there when
Philotas came to the royal quarters and, as he went in, he reminded
him of the matter he had communicated to him the day before.
Philotas replied that he was seeing to it — but even then he failed
to disclose to the king what he had heard.

Cebalinus had begun to suspect him. Thinking it inadvisable
to accost him again, he gave the information of the villainous plot
to a young nobleman called Metron who had charge of the
armoury. Metron hid Cebalinus in the armoury and immediately
revealed the informer's allegations to the king, who happened to be
taking a bath. Alexander dispatched guards to arrest Dymnus and
went into the armoury. Cebalinus was transported with joy. "You
are safe!" he said, "I see you delivered from the hands of criminals!"
Alexander then inquired into the pertinent details and, after he
was given a coherent account, made a point of asking how many
days it had been since Nicomachus brought him his information.
When Cebalinus admitted it had been two days, Alexander ordered
him to be clapped in irons because he thought that the fact that he
had taken so long to report what he had heard meant that his loyalty was questionable. Cebalinus, however, began to cry out that
he had run to Philotas the very moment he had heard of the plot,
and that Philotas had learned the details from him. The king asked
again if he had approached Philotas, if he had insisted that they
come to Alexander. When Cebalinus persistently reaffirmed his
story, Alexander held his hands up to the sky and, bursting into
tears, bemoaned the fact that he had been so repaid by one who
had formerly been the dearest of his friends.

Dymnus, meanwhile, well aware of the reason for his summons by the king, dealt himself a mortal wound with the sword he
happened to be wearing, but guards rushed up to restrain him and
he was carried into the royal quarters. Alexander looked at him.
"Dymnus," he said, "what is the vicious crime I have plotted against

you to justify your decision that Philotas deserves royal power more than I myself?" But Dymnus had already lost the power of speech. He groaned, turned his face away from the king's eyes, and immediately collapsed and died.

The king ordered Philotas to the royal quarters. "Cebalinus deserved the supreme penalty," he said, "if for two days he covered up a plot that had been hatched against my life. But he shifts the guilt for his crime to Philotas by his claim that he passed the information on to him immediately. Because of your closer ties of friendship with me, such suppression of information on your part is all the more reprehensible, and it is my opinion that conduct such as this suits Cebalinus more than it does Philotas. You now have a judge who is on your side — if there is any way of clearing yourself of what should not have happened."

Philotas was not in the slightest alarmed, if his emotions could be judged by his expression. In reply he said that, yes, Cebalinus had indeed reported to him his conversation with the catamite, but Philotas had set no store by it since the source was so unreliable — he feared that reporting a quarrel between a male prostitute and his lover would make him a laughing stock. However, Dymnus' suicide now revealed that the facts, whatever they were, should not have been suppressed. Philotas put his arms around the king and proceeded to entreat him to consider his past record rather than his present error — which, anyway, involved merely keeping silent, not committing an act. It would be difficult to say whether the king believed him or kept his anger concealed deep in his heart. He offered Philotas his right hand as a sign of reconciliation, and said that in his opinion it was a case of information not being taken seriously rather than being deliberately suppressed.

Even so, Alexander called a meeting of his friends, without inviting Philotas, and ordered Nicomachus to be brought before it. The latter repeated the whole story which he had brought to the king. Now Craterus, being an especially close friend of the king's, was consequently hostile to Philotas because of their competing for position, and he was not unaware that Philotas' excessively boastful talk about his courage and his services had often grated on the ears of Alexander, who therefore entertained the notion that while he was no criminal he was certainly self-willed. Believing there would be no better opportunity for crushing his opponent,

Craterus masked his personal animosity with feigned loyalty to Alexander and declared: "I wish you had also discussed this matter with us in the beginning! If you were set on pardoning Philotas, we would have urged you to keep him ignorant of how much he owed you. Rather that than that he now have cause to think more about his own danger — since he has been taken to the brink of death — than about your generosity. You see, *he* will always be able to plot against you, but you will not always be able to pardon Philotas. And you have no reason to suppose that a man whose daring has been so great can be changed by a pardon: he knows that those who have exhausted someone's clemency can expect no more in future. But even supposing penitence or your generosity induced him to take no further action, I for my part am sure that his father Parmenio will not be happy at being indebted to you for his son's life — he is the leader of a mighty army and because of his long-standing influence with your men holds a position of great authority not much inferior to yours. Some acts of kindness we resent. A man is ashamed to admit that he has deserved execution; the alternative is to foster the impression that he has been dealt an injury rather than granted a reprieve. So you can be sure that you must fight for your life against the men in question. The enemies we are about to pursue are still numerous enough. Protect yourself against enemies within our ranks. Eliminate those and I fear nothing from the foreigner."

Such were Craterus' words, and the others were also in no doubt that Philotas would not have suppressed evidence of the conspiracy if he had not been the ringleader or an accomplice. For, they reasoned, any loyal and well-intentioned person, even if he were of the lowest order and not a friend of Alexander, would have run immediately to the king on hearing the charges that had been brought to Philotas. But the son of Parmenio did not do that, commander of the cavalry and confidant of all the king's secrets though he was, not even when he had before him the example of Cebalinus who had reported to Philotas what he had learned from his brother. He had even pretended that the king had had no time to talk to him, intending thereby to prevent the informer from looking for a second go-between. Nicomachus had rushed to unburden his conscience in spite of the sacred obligation of his oath; Philotas, who had spent almost the entire day on frivolous amusements, was reluctant to insert into his lengthy and possibly inconsequential conversation a word or two vital to the king's survival. But, if he had felt no confidence in such a report from mere boys, why then would he have made the affair drag on for two days as if he believed their disclosures? He ought to have sent Cebalinus away if he rejected his charges. Being brave is appropriate when it is a question of one's own risk, but when there is concern for the life of the king one should be credulous and pay attention even to men who bring false information.

So the decision was unanimous that Philotas should be interrogated under torture to force him to name his accomplices in the crime. Then Alexander dismissed them, telling them to remain silent about their decision and, in order not to betray any hint of the course of action they had recently adopted, he had marching orders issued for the following day. Philotas was even invited to a banquet, which was to be his last, and the king was able not merely to dine with the man he had condemned but even to engage him in friendly conversation. Then, at the time of the second watch, when the lights were out, some of the king's friends, namely Hephaestion, Craterus, Coenus and Erigyius, met in the royal quarters with a few men, along with Perdiccas and Leonnatus from the bodyguard. Orders were issued by these for the men on guard at the king's tent to keep watch under arms. Cavalrymen had already been posted at all the entrances to the camp with orders also to block the roads so that no one could slip off secretly to Parmenio, who at that time was governor of Media and in command of strong forces.

Atarrhias had now entered the royal tent with 300 armed men. He was given ten attendants, each accompanied by ten armourbearers and, while these were sent in groups to arrest the other conspirators, Atarrhias and his 300 were dispatched to Philotas. With fifty of his best young men around him he set about forcing the door, which was closed, having ordered the others to cordon off the house entirely so that Philotas could not slip away by a secret entrance. Philotas was in a deep slumber, his relaxation the result of an easy conscience or else of exhaustion, and he was still half-asleep when Atarrhias grasped him. Finally he shook off the drowsiness and, as the shackles were placed on him, said: "Your Majesty, the bitter hatred of my enemies has triumphed over your kindness." This was all he said before they covered his head and took him into the royal quarters. The next day the king gave orders for a general assembly in arms.

Some 6,000 soldiers had arrived and a crowd of camp-followers and servants added to the total in the royal tent. Philotas was hidden by a column of men-at-arms so that he could not be seen by the crowd until the king had addressed the men. In capital cases it was a long-established Macedonian practice for the king to conduct the trial while the army (or the commons in peace-time) acted as jury, and the position of the king counted for nothing unless his influence had been substantial prior to the trial. So now, at the start, the corpse of Dymnus was brought in, the majority of the crowd having no idea of his plot or of how he had died.

Alexander marched into the assembly. His expression betrayed the anguish he felt, and the gloominess of his friends had charged the affair with considerable anticipation. The king stood for a long while with eyes fixed on the ground, looking dazed and nonplussed. Finally he pulled himself together and said: "Men! I was almost snatched from you by a criminal conspiracy: it is thanks to the gods' providence and mercy that I still live." . . .

Groans from the men interrupted him, and tears welled up in every eye. "I shall stir far deeper emotions in your hearts when I reveal to you the instigators of such villainy," the king continued. "I still shudder to mention them and I keep from naming them as though it were possible to save them. But the memory of my former intimacy with them must be expunged; a conspiracy plotted by treacherous citizens of ours must be exposed. How could I remain silent about such an outrage? Parmenio, despite his age and obligations from all the benefits he received from me and from my father; although he is the oldest of all my friends — it was he who offered to head this monstrous crime. His accomplice was Philotas, who suborned Peucolaus, Demetrius and Dymnus, whose body you see before you, and other equally insane individuals to assassinate me." Roars of pained outrage broke forth throughout the gathering, as typically happens in a crowd, and especially in a crowd of soldiers, when it is fired with enthusiasm or anger. Nicomachus, Metron and Cebalinus were now brought in. They repeated their various accounts, but the evidence of none of them marked Philotas as an accomplice in the crime and so, after the initial outburst of indignation from the crowd, the statements of the witnesses were received in silence.

Then Alexander said: "So what do you think were the intentions of a man who suppressed the actual information he was given about this affair? That there was some substance to it is shown by Dymnus' death. When the matter was still uncorroborated, Cebalinus reported it, undeterred by fear of torture, and Metron lost no time at all in unburdening himself of his information — going as far as to break into my bathroom! Only Philotas feared nothing and believed nothing. What a courageous fellow! Would a man like that be distressed at the thought of his king's peril? Would he alter his expression or feel anxiety as he listened to the bearer of such momentous news? Obviously some criminal intention lurks in his silence: it was greedy anticipation of the throne that sent his thoughts speeding towards the vilest of crimes. His father governs Media and, because of my support, Philotas himself exercised great influence with many of the officers — so that his aspirations exceed his ability to fulfil them. My childless state, the fact that I have no offspring, also arouses his contempt. But Philotas is wrong. In you I have children, parents, kinsmen, and while you are safe I cannot be childless."

He then read out a letter which had been intercepted, written by Parmenio to his sons Nicanor and Philotas. But it did not really contain evidence of some dangerous plot. Its gist was as follows: "First of all take care of yourselves and then of your people — that is how we shall accomplish our purpose." The king added that the letter was worded in this way so that if it reached his sons it could be understood by those involved in the plot whereas, intercepted, its meaning would escape those who were ignorant of it.

Alexander continued: "Dymnus, you will say, did not name Philotas despite designating the others involved in the crime. That is not evidence of Philotas' innocence but of his standing: he is so feared by the people who can betray him that, even when they confess their own guilt, they withhold his name. But Philotas' own record accuses him. When my cousin Amyntas engineered a treacherous plot against me in Macedonia, it was Philotas who made himself his ally and his accomplice. It was Philotas who gave his sister in marriage to Attalus, the worst enemy I have ever had! In view of our close association and friendship, I had written to him of the oracular response of Jupiter Ammon. It was Philotas who had the effrontery to reply that, while he congratulated me on being received among the gods, he nevertheless felt pity for people who would have to live under a man who was more than human. These are all indications that he has long been alienated from me and become envious of my fame. I have kept them locked in my heart for as long as I could, men, thinking that to bring down in my own estimation men to whose careers I had made such great contributions was like ripping away part of myself. But it is no longer mere words that call for punishment. Unbridled speech has led to the sword — which, if you believe me, Philotas has sharpened against me or which, if you believe him, he has permitted to be sharpened against me. Where am I going to turn, men? To whom am I to entrust my life? I made Philotas sole commander of the cavalry, the pick of my troops, the best of our young noblemen. To his loyalty and his protection I have entrusted my life, my hopes, and my victory. I have promoted his father to the same eminence in which you have placed me; I have set under his command and authority the richest of all countries, Media, along with many thousands of our citizens and allies. Where I looked for help I found only danger. . . . ”

Alexander then ordered Philotas to be brought in with his hands tied behind his back and his head covered with an old cloak. There was clearly an emotional reaction to the pitiful condition of a man who shortly before had been regarded with envy. The men had seen him as cavalry commander on the previous day, and they knew he had attended the king's banquet. Suddenly they saw him not merely on trial but condemned — even in fetters! They also began to reflect on the misfortunes of Parmenio: a great general and an illustrious citizen, he had recently lost two sons, Hector and Nicanor, and now in his absence he would be on trial with the only son his calamitous fate had left him. Consequently, since the assembly was inclining towards pity, Amyntas, one of the king's generals, stirred it up again with a speech attacking Philotas. They had been betrayed to the barbarians, he said. None of them would have returned to his wife and his parents, but they would have been like a decapitated body devoid of life, without a name, an object of ridicule to the enemy in a foreign land. Amyntas' words were not at all as pleasing to the king as he had hoped — reminding the men of their wives and country merely decreased their enthusiasm for tackling the jobs that remained.

Coenus spoke next and, although he had married a sister of Philotas, he attacked him more fiercely than anyone, loudly proclaiming him a traitor to his king, country and army. He then picked up a stone which happened to be lying before his feet to throw at Philotas — from a wish to save him from torture, many thought — but the king stayed his hand, declaring that the defendant must first be given an opportunity to make his defence and that he would not permit the case to proceed otherwise. Philotas was then instructed to make his defence. Distracted and nonplussed, either from a guilty conscience or because of the magnitude of his peril, he did not dare to lift his eyes or open his mouth. Then he burst into tears and fainted into the arms of the man holding him. He gradually recovered both his breath and his voice and, using his cloak to wipe his eyes, seemed to be about to speak. Alexander fixed his gaze on him. "The Macedonians are going to judge your case," he said. "Please state whether you will use your native language before them."

"Besides the Macedonians," replied Philotas, "there are many present who, I think, will find what I am going to say easier to understand if I use the language you yourself have been using, your purpose, I believe, being only to enable more people to understand you."

Then the king said: "Do you see how offensive Philotas finds even his native language? He alone feels an aversion to learning it. But let him speak as he pleases — only remember that he is as contemptuous of our way of life as he is of our language." So saying, Alexander left the meeting.

Then Philotas spoke. "When a man is innocent, finding words is easy," he said, "but when he is in trouble, limiting them is difficult. . . . I do not understand, quite frankly, of what crime I stand accused. None of the conspirators names me; Nicomachus said nothing about me; and Cebalinus could have known no more than what he had been told. And yet Alexander believes I headed the conspiracy. Then could Dymnus have omitted to mention the man whose lead he followed? . . . I ask you, my comrades: if Cebalinus had not come to me, if he had wanted me to know nothing about the conspirators, would I be on trial today — when no one names me? . . . I must turn to the one real charge against me, which goes: "Why did you remain silent about the matter that was reported to you? Why so little concern when you heard?" Alexander, wherever you are, I confessed to this misdemeanour, such as it is, and you pardoned me. I clasped your right hand, a gesture of our reconciliation, and I attended your banquet. If you believed me, I was declared innocent; if you forgave me, I was given a reprieve. Just abide by your decision. What was it that I did last night after leaving your table? What new crime has been reported to you to make you change your mind? I was in a deep sleep when, as I rested unperturbed by misfortune, my enemies put the fetters on me and woke me. How does a murderer and a traitor achieve such deep, relaxed sleep? Criminals cannot get to sleep because their consciences will not let them: they are hounded by the Furies not just after committing a crime but even after planning one. But I had gained a feeling of security, first from my innocence and then from your right hand, and I felt no apprehension that the cruelty of others would influence you more than your own merciful inclinations.

"But (not to have you regret that you believed me) the matter was reported to me by a mere boy. He was unable to produce any witness or any corroboration for his charges and, if he had begun to be heard, he would have filled everybody with alarm. Unfortunately for me, I thought that what was coming to my ears was a quarrel between lover and boyfriend, and my doubts about Nicomachus' reliability arose from the consideration that he did not bring the information in person but induced his brother to bring it. I was afraid he would deny having given instructions to Cebalinus and I myself would then appear responsible for having put many of the king's friends in jeopardy. . . .

"But Dymnus committed suicide, you will say. Surely you do not think I could have foreseen that he would? Of course not. So the one thing supporting this charge — that thing could not possibly have had any effect on me when I was accosted by Cebalinus. My god! Suppose I *had* been Dymnus' accomplice in such a horrible crime. I ought not to have hidden for those two days the fact that we had been betrayed — and Cebalinus himself could have been eliminated without difficulty. Then, after the information which I was going to suppress had been brought, I went into the king's bedroom alone, actually wearing a sword. Why did I postpone the deed? Was it that without Dymnus I didn't dare do it? Then it was Dymnus who was the leader of the conspiracy! I was merely lurking in his shadow — I, Philotas, who have eyes on the throne of Macedon! Was any one of you suborned with bribes? To what general or what officer did I pay undue attention? . . .

"Another charge: I wrote that I felt sorry for people who had to live under anyone who believed himself to be Jupiter's son. Ah, loyalty in friendship! Ah, perilous candour in giving honest advice! It was you who let me down! It was you who urged me not to conceal what I felt. I admit I wrote this *to* the king — but not *about* the king. I was not trying to generate animosity against him — I was afraid for him. . . . So, dearest father, you are going to die along with me as well as because of me. . . .

"The reference to my father reminds me of how necessary my timidity and hesitation really were in disclosing the information that Cebalinus had brought to me. After Parmenio heard of a plot to poison the king by the physician Philip, he wrote a letter because he wished to deter Alexander from drinking the potion which the doctor intended to give to him. My father wasn't believed, was he? His letter had no influence, did it? In my own case, how often have I reported things I have heard only to be snubbed and laughed at for being over-credulous! If we face unpopularity when we report things and suspicion when we remain silent, what must we do?" And when one of the crowd of onlookers exclaimed, "Don't hatch plots against your benefactors," Philotas said: "You're right, whoever you are. So if I have hatched a plot, I do not ask to be excused punishment, and I conclude my speech since my last words were apparently offensive to your ears." Then he was led away by the men acting as his guards.

Among the officers was a certain Bolon, a good fighter but a man of no refinement or cultivation, an older soldier who had risen from the ranks to his present position. The rest now fell silent but Bolon, with boorish impudence and in a brazen manner, began to remind them all of the time they had each been ejected from quarters they had taken over so that the scum of Philotas' slaves might have the places from which they had thrown out their colleagues. . . . The king returned to the assembly and adjourned the hearing to the following day, either to subject Philotas to further torture in prison or to conduct a more thorough investigation of the entire episode and, though the day was drawing on towards evening, he nevertheless called a meeting of his friends. The general feeling was that Philotas should be stoned to death according to Macedonian custom, but Hephaestion, Craterus and Coenus declared that torture should be employed to force the truth out of him, and those who had advocated other punishment went over to their view. So, when the council was adjourned, Hephaestion, Craterus and Coenus got up together to conduct the interrogation of Philotas. The king summoned Craterus and, after some conversation with him, the contents of which were not made public, withdrew to the inner section of his quarters. There, dismissing all who were present, he awaited the outcome of the investigation till late in the night.

The torturers laid out before Philotas' eyes all the instruments used to inflict pain. Philotas, on an impulse, asked: "Why hesitate to execute your king's enemy, a confessed assassin? What need is there for interrogation under torture? I planned the crime; I wanted it to succeed." Craterus insisted that he also make his confession under torture. Philotas was seized, blindfolded and his clothes stripped from him, while all the time he invoked the gods of his country and the laws of humanity — to no avail, for their ears were deaf. He was racked with the most cruel tortures: not only was he a condemned man but his torturers were personal enemies trying to please the king. . . . But Philotas began to beg for time to get his breath back, after which he was prepared to tell all he knew.

In the meantime word of the torture of Philotas had got around, and this spread panic among the cavalry, the men from the best families and especially those closely related to Parmenio. What they feared was the Macedonian law which provided the death penalty also for relatives of people who had plotted against the king. Some, therefore, committed suicide and others fled into remote mountains and desert wastes as sheer terror spread throughout the camp. Finally, the king learned of the consternation and proclaimed that he was suspending the law relating to the punishment of relatives of the guilty.

Whether Philotas told the truth or whether he lied from a wish to deliver himself from torture is debatable, for the end in view of both those who confess the truth and those who lie is termination of the pain. "You are aware of the close friendship my father had with Hegelochus," said Philotas. "I mean that Hegelochus who died in combat — he was the cause of all our problems. When the king first commanded that he be addressed as the son of Jupiter, Hegelochus was indignant and said: 'Well, do we recognize this man as our king? He disclaims Philip as his father. If we can stand that, we're done for. A man who demands to be believed a god shows contempt not only for men but for the gods as well. We have lost Alexander, we have lost our king! We have come up against an arrogance that can be tolerated neither by the gods, to whom he considers himself an equal, nor by men, from whom he excludes himself. Have we spilt our blood to make a god who despises us, who balks at attending a meeting of mere mortals? Listen to me: if we are true men, we also will be adopted by the gods! Who avenged the murder of this man's ancestor Archelaus, of Alexander after that, and of Perdiccas? But this man granted a pardon to his father's murderers.'

"Such were Hegelochus' words over dinner. The next day at dawn I was sent for by my father. He was in low spirits and could see that I was also dejected; for what we had heard was enough to strike anxiety into our hearts. So, to see whether Hegelochus had poured out those ideas under the influence of drink or whether they were spawned of some deep conviction, we decided he should be summoned. He came and without prompting spoke again in the same terms, adding that if we dared take the lead he would stand right behind us, but if we lacked the heart for it he would keep silent about the plan. With Darius still alive, Parmenio thought the plan premature, since killing Alexander would benefit the enemy, not themselves, whereas with Darius removed the reward of killing the king that would fall to his assassins would be Asia and all of the East. The plan was approved and pledges given and accepted on it. As for Dymnus, I know nothing. I realize, though, that after this confession it does me no good that I am entirely unconnected with his crime."

Once again they applied the instruments of torture, now themselves also using their spears to strike him in the face and eyes, and they extracted from him a confession to this crime as well. Then they demanded the full programme of the crime they had contrived. Philotas replied that it appeared as though Alexander would be detained in Bactria for a long time and he had feared that his father might die in the meantime, since he was seventy years old. Parmenio was then leader of a great army and in charge of a large quantity of money; if he, Philotas, were deprived of such great resources, killing the king would serve no purpose. Accordingly he had made haste to execute the plan while he still had the prize in his hands. If they did not believe his father took no part in it, he did not refuse further torture, even though he could no longer endure it. . . .

After conferring, his tormentors concluded that the interrogation had gone far enough. They went back to the king, who gave orders for Philotas' confession to be read out the next day and for Philotas himself to be carried to the assembly because he was unable to walk. Since Philotas admitted everything, they brought in Demetrius, who was accused of complicity in the most recent conspiracy. With vigorous protestations and with the confidence which he felt showing in his expression, he denied any plot against the king, going so far as to demand torture for himself. Then Philotas' eyes shifted round, falling eventually on one Calis who stood close by. Philotas told him to come closer and, when Calis showed agitation and refused to come over to him, he said, "Are you going to permit Demetrius to lie and me to be tortured again?" Calis was left speechless and pale. The Macedonians began to suspect that Philotas wished to incriminate the innocent, for the young man had been named neither by Nicomachus nor by Philotas himself under torture but, when he saw the king's officers around him, Calis confessed that he and Demetrius had planned the crime. Thereupon all those named by Nicomachus, when the signal was given, were stoned to death in the traditional Macedonian manner.

Alexander had been saved from great danger, danger to his popularity as much as to his life. Parmenio and Philotas had been his principal friends and their condemnation would have been impossible without causing personal indignation among the troops, unless they were demonstrably guilty. So attitudes to the interrogation shifted. While Philotas denied the crime his torture was thought cruel, but after his confession he no longer won pity even from his friends. . . .

Arrian

The Conspiracy
of Philotas

Arrian's account of the Philotas conspiracy is the closest to what may
have been the court's official version of the affair.

It was there too that Alexander learnt of the conspiracy of Philotas
son of Parmenio. Ptolemy and Aristobulus say that it had already
been reported to him earlier in Egypt, but he did not think it credible because of their long friendship, the honour he had shown to
Parmenio, Philotas' father, and the trust he had reposed in Philotas
himself. Ptolemy son of Lagus gives the following account. Philotas
was summoned before the Macedonians, Alexander vigorously accused him, Philotas made his defence; then those who had denounced the plot came forward and convicted Philotas and his associates with clear proofs; in particular, they showed that while
Philotas himself admitted that he had heard of some sort of plot
being laid against Alexander, he was convicted of having said nothing of it to Alexander, though he visited Alexander's tent twice
daily. Philotas was shot down with javelins by the Macedonians,
along with all his accomplices. As for action against Parmenio,
Polydamas, one of the Companions, was sent with a letter from
Alexander to the generals in Media, Cleander and Sitalces and
Menidas, who had been posted to the force under Parmenio's command. At their hands Parmenio perished, possibly because Alexander could not believe that when Philotas was conspiring, Parmenio
had no share in his own son's design, possibly because, even supposing he had no such share, it had now become a danger for
Parmenio to survive his son's execution, on account of the high

Reprinted by permission of the publishers and the Loeb Classical Library from
Arrian: *History of Alexander*, 3.26–27, vol. 1, translated by Peter A. Brunt,
Cambridge, Mass.: Harvard University Press, 1976.

honour which he enjoyed with Alexander himself and in the view of the army too — not only the Macedonian but the foreign troops also, whom he had often commanded with popularity both in and out of turn by Alexander's order.

They also say that Amyntas son of Andromenes was brought to trial at the same time, together with Polemon, Attalus and Simmias, his brothers, on the charge that they too had joined in the conspiracy against Alexander as loyal comrades of Philotas. Moreover the conspiracy seemed more credible to the masses, because Polemon, one of Amyntas' brothers, deserted to the enemy as soon as Philotas was arrested. However, Amyntas at least with his (other) brothers stood his trial, made a vigorous defence before the Macedonians, and was acquitted of the charge; and the moment he was acquitted, he asked leave to go and bring Polemon back again to Alexander; the Macedonians agreed. He departed that very day and brought him back; and thus his own innocence appeared much clearer than before. Soon after, however, when besieging a village, he received an arrow wound of which he died; so that all he gained from his acquittal was that he died with his good name unsmirched.

Alexander now put two hipparchs [cavalry commanders] in charge of the Companions, Hephaestion son of Amyntor and Clitus son of Dropides, and after dividing the Companions' brigade into two parts, since he would not have wished a single man, though his closest friend, to command so large a body of cavalry, especially as it was the best of all his mounted force in reputation and valour. . . . He arrived among the people formerly called Ariaspians. . . . There he sacrificed to Apollo, arrested Demetrius, one of the bodyguards, suspecting that he had a hand in Philotas' conspiracy, and appointed as bodyguard Ptolemy son of Lagus in his place. . . .

Ernest Badian

The Death of Parmenio

Ernst Badian is the John Moors Cabot Professor of History at Harvard University. His works include *From Plataea to Potidaea: Studies in the History and Historiography of the Pentecontaetia* (Johns Hopkins Univ. Press, 1993), among other writings. Badian argues that what occurred behind the scenes of the Philotas affair was more important than the official version of the conspiracy and posits the key participants' aims and roles.

No aspect of the career of Alexander the Great should be more important and constructive to the historian than the series of executions and assassinations by which he partly crushed and partly anticipated the opposition of Macedonian nobles to his person and policy. Yet no aspect has, on the whole, been less studied in modern times. Tarn, by acceptance of the favorable and rejection of the unfavorable sources, came to the conclusion that Alexander committed two murders, but only two. Of these two, one (that of Clitus) can be regarded as manslaughter under some provocation, while the other (that of Parmenio) can at least be mitigated by various legal, social and political considerations. This procedure is part of an attitude towards Alexander the Great of which Tarn was the most distinguished (though by no means the only) exponent, an attitude which has made the serious study of Alexander's reign from the point of view of political history not only impossible, but (to many students) almost inconceivable. Yet there is no plausible reason why the autocracy of Alexander the Great should not be as susceptible of political analysis as that of Augustus or Napoleon, for the grim and bloody struggle for power that went on almost unremittingly at his court is amply documented even in our inade-

"The Death of Parmenio" by Ernst Badian from *Transaction of the American Philological Association* 91 (1960), pp. 324–338. Copyright © 1960, American Philological Association. Reprinted with permission.

quate sources. . . . It is in this spirit that this paper attempts to direct attention to an acknowledged turning-point in the reign, the execution of Alexander's friend Philotas and the assassination of Philotas' father Parmenio.

Alexander's reign had opened with a reign of terror; whatever be the truth about the death of Philip II — and this can hardly be established with certainty, since it paid no one to speak or write the truth after the event — officially a father's death had to be avenged by the successor. We need not dwell on this initial massacre; it is enough to recall that ultimately no male heir of the royal blood survived Alexander except for the imbecile Arrhidaeus. This terror, however, had affected only those who, directly or indirectly, might make a bid for the throne. With the new king firmly established, the remaining nobles (except for those who preferred to escape to Asia and join the King of Persia) appeared to have no grounds for anxiety. The case of Alexander son of Aëropus of Lyncestis, not long after the invasion of Asia, will, on balance, have seemed reassuring rather than alarming. This man, prompted by his father-in-law Antipater (who had engineered Alexander's immediate recognition as king), had been one of the first to do homage to his namesake. He had consequently escaped the fate of the rest of his family and, in fact, had been entrusted with positions of responsibility. But he was of too high a lineage to be left unmolested for long. At some time before the battle of Issus (the details are not clear) he was relieved of his command on suspicion of aiming at the throne with Persian help, and in due course he was put under guard and made to accompany the expedition as a prisoner. It is unlikely that anyone (except perhaps Antipater) cared very much. This was, in a way, only the logical conclusion of the initial massacre; and the very fact that he was not executed, in spite of his high birth and the charge of treason, would seem evidence that the terror of the first days was over. We, who have seen similar happenings in our own day, can easily understand how relief might predominate over alarm among those not immediately concerned: men need no longer fear death for political reasons. That they did not fear it is clear. When Alexander's old friend Harpalus, in mysterious circumstances, was relieved of his post and decided to leave the king, he settled at Megara, clearly in no fear for his personal safety; and before long he secured his recall on his own terms.

All this must be borne in mind when we come to examine the so-called conspiracy of Philotas, which led to the death of Parmenio. Lulled into false security and convinced that the spirit of the régime had changed, the victims had no chance of escape when the thunderbolt struck them.

The story of the "conspiracy" is well known and can be briefly summarized. Philotas had made no secret of his disapproval of the king's oriental affectations ever since the visit to Ammon and had consequently been suspected and disliked for years. His enemy Craterus had worked against him at court, and his mistress Antigone had been suborned to spy on him, so that evidence of disloyalty might be collected. Plutarch, in fact, very justly speaks of a conspiracy *against* Philotas. It was realized that an attempt to remove Philotas would lead to a major trial of strength, not to be undertaken unless the loyalty of the army was secure. For this, a charge of treason was the obvious weapon, provided that enough evidence could be produced to build up a *prima facie* case. This seems to have proved difficult. But by 330 a time was approaching when Alexander could not afford to wait any longer. The Hellenic crusade, kept up — more and more perfunctorily — as a propaganda *motif* as long as Greece had to be conciliated, had been officially abandoned after Agis' defeat (Arr. 3.19.5.f.); Alexander had declared himself the lawful successor to the Achaemenids; but since he failed to capture Darius alive, he now had to assert his claim against the pretender Bessus, who called himself Artaxerxes (Arr. 3.25.3). The war was bound to be difficult, and to the Macedonians it would seem unnecessary. The men wanted to go home, especially when they saw the Greek allies dismissed (Curt. 6.2.15.f.); and both they and the nobles disliked the *Persici apparatus* that were the symbol of Alexander's new status and the corollary of his intention to make his rule over Iran permanent (see, e.g., Curt. 6.6). It was precisely in Parthia, just before the "conspiracy of Philotas," that Alexander first dressed and behaved undisguisedly as Great King (Curt. *loc. cit.*; Diod. 17.77.4; cf. Plut. 45). Of the attitude of Philotas and his father Parmenio there could be no doubt; typical of the proud Macedonian nobility, they were of those who equally despised Greeks and Orientals. The showdown was bound to come soon. With the men behind them, these nobles could feel confident of their power to enforce their views. To understand this confidence, we must go far back into the past.

Parmenio, firmly entrenched at Philip's court, seems to have had connections with both the factions contending for the succession in the last years of the reign. Towards the end, swimming with the tide, he turned towards that of Attalus and Cleopatra, who appeared to be overcoming the faction of Olympias and her son Alexander. Attalus married one of Parmenio's daughters and accompanied him when he took charge of the invasion of Asia before Philip's death. Philotas, known as a friend of Alexander, tried to reconcile him to Philip after the mysterious affair of the negotiations with Pixodarus (Plut. 10). It is significant that he did not (like Harpalus and other friends of Alexander) go into exile; he clearly placed good relations with the king above excessive loyalty to a discredited crown prince. As we have seen, the mystery of Philip's death cannot be penetrated; but in any case the faction of Olympias and Alexander profited by it. The rival faction of Cleopatra was exterminated. Parmenio adapted himself to the changed conditions and helped to eliminate his own son-in-law Attalus (Curt. 7.1.3). At Alexander's crossing into Asia, Philotas is found in command of the Macedonian cavalry (the *hetaeri*); but even earlier he appears as a cavalry commander, and there is no real reason to doubt that he commanded the whole of that force from the beginning. Nicanor, another son of Parmenio, had the corresponding infantry command (the hypaspists); and again there is good reason to date it further back. Parmenio's brother Asander probably commanded the light cavalry and certainly received the key satrapy [province] of Sardis as soon as it was conquered. Parmenio's clients and noble adherents — men like the brothers Coenus and Cleander, and the four sons of Andromenes — were firmly entrenched in positions of importance; while Parmenio himself, in nominal command of the whole infantry, in fact served as Alexander's chief of staff and second-in-command. It is clear that Parmenio had not lost by sacrificing Attalus.

The next few years saw the decline of his influence and the increase in Alexander's own stature in the army's eyes. Not *all* our stories of the occasions on which Alexander successfully ignored Parmenio's advice will be true. But some go back to good sources

(Ptolemy or even Callisthenes) and show that this kind of interpretation was *meant* to be spread; Alexander wanted his genius recognized as superior to the trained prudence of the general. The facts bear out this interpretation: in the battles, Parmenio was assigned the defensive part, while Alexander reserved the decisive advance for himself: success belonged to the king. . . . Parmenio was even more unfortunate in another way. His youngest son Hector, destined for high command, died in Egypt. In Aria another son, Nicanor (the commander of the hypaspists), died. This proved disastrous.

By this time Alexander, in addition to undermining Parmenio's reputation, had also made considerable progress in extricating himself from the stranglehold of Parmenio's family and adherents. His brother Asander, put in charge of the satrapy of Sardis after the battle of the Granicus, had justified the king's confidence by a great victory. Yet after Issus he was superseded by Menander and sent on a harmless mission to collect reinforcements (which he later brought to Alexander at Bactria). Adherents could be won over by persuasion and success: loyalty was not the outstanding virtue of Macedonian nobles. Just as Parmenio had betrayed Attalus, his own son-in-law Coenus turned out to be one of Alexander's chief assistants in his action against Philotas; while Coenus' brother Cleander, Parmenio's second-in-command at Ecbatana, later managed the murder of the general himself. Clearly, these attested changes of allegiance will have been neither unprepared nor unique. Finally Parmenio himself was removed from front-line service; he was left behind at Ecbatana to guard the imperial treasure and communications. It was at this time that fortune took a hand with Nicanor's death — as we have seen, precisely when Alexander had reached a point in the development of his policy, where an open clash with his Macedonian opponents could not be postponed much longer. The king seems to have taken advantage of the opportunity offered; this speed of decision was always the secret of his success. Philotas was left behind to see to his brother's funeral (Curt.6.6.19). For the moment, Parmenio and his family were out of the way.

It seems to have been during this time that the plot against Philotas was hatched. We are not told precisely when he rejoined the court, but the sequence of events strongly suggests that it was not long before the plot. The king, known to be marching towards the capital of Drangiana, was temporarily deflected from his route by the revolt of Satibarzanes. This was quickly dealt with (it appears to have been a matter of days rather than months) by swift marching and campaigning that kept the royal party constantly on the move in unknown country. . . . We may take it that Philotas only rejoined the king in the capital of Drangiana. And it was eight days after the royal party arrived there that the conspiracy came to a head. It is not unreasonable to suggest that something had been hatched during Philotas' absence.

On the "conspiracy of Philotas" itself, as it was now "discovered," no words need be wasted. Fortunately, scarcely any scholar in recent times has taken it seriously, naturally enough, since even Alexander (and Ptolemy) did not succeed in proving Philotas' guilt. The facts can therefore be stated quite briefly. An obscure Macedonian probably called Dimnus was the lover of a boy Nicomachus. This boy now suddenly confined to his brother Cebalinus that Dimnus, with the support of some others, was plotting against the life of Alexander. Cebalinus reported this to Philotas, who showed little interest. Finally, after some cloak-and-dagger scenes lovingly described by Curtius — with Cebalinus, for no very clear reason, hiding in a cupboard while the king was bathing — the whole story was reported to Alexander, and after careful preparations he ordered the arrest of Philotas and some others. Dimnus conveniently killed himself (or was killed while resisting arrest), and the others were put on trial for their lives before the army. Alexander himself demanded the death penalty for Philotas. Philotas admitted that he had heard of the plot but claimed that he had simply not taken it seriously. Since Dimnus is nowhere assigned a motive for his plot, nor was any evidence (except for his favorite's word) advanced against him or anyone else, we need not hesitate to agree with Philotas in this estimate. Against Philotas himself, not a scrap of evidence suggesting complicity could be produced. Even the prolonged espionage by his mistress seems to have been ineffective. Alexander merely proved (what was admitted and explained) that he had failed to pass on information about the plot. Speakers had been briefed to support the demand for a death sentence, and the army, seeing that Alexander made it a question of confidence as between himself and Philotas, agreed. It has been claimed that the army gave a fair trial according to its lights. This, up to a point, may be true. But if it is taken to imply that, because the army voted the death penalty, Philotas deserved it, this is surely putting too much trust in the perspicacity of these simple soldiers in what must have been an utterly bewildering situation.

Philotas was tortured before his execution, in the hope that evidence could be obtained against other men, notably his father Parmenio. It is unlikely that any was in fact obtained. We cannot be certain, since the sources that mention the incident, for their various purposes, elaborate it far beyond credibility. Curtius (6.11.22 f.) has a story of a plot between Parmenio and Hegelochus (then dead), which Philotas is said to have divulged under torture. Since no charge was in fact brought against Parmenio, it is almost certain that none could be: the plot with Hegelochus must be an effort of later *apologia* [attempt at defense].

In fact, the judicial murder of Philotas was at once followed by the undisguised assassination of Parmenio himself. . . . There was nothing in Macedonian custom, or indeed in Alexander's own, that called for the murder of Parmenio as the "only known alternative" to letting him rebel. Moreover, since Philotas' "treason" was a transparent fabrication, the assassination of his father was not a panic-stricken reaction to an unforeseen emergency; it must be regarded as an integral part of the same scheme, and indeed, in view of Parmenio's position, as its culmination. The careful preparation, the detailed planning (so well exemplified in Curtius' account of Philotas' arrest — the crucial and most dangerous step), finally the quick and decisive blow when fortune offered the chance — these will be recognized at once as the hallmarks of Alexander's genius, both military and political. He was to use the same technique in the reign of terror after his return from India, and then against the very men who had helped him strike down Parmenio. Political assassination — with or, if necessary, without observation of legal forms — was as much a normal weapon in his arsenal as the calculated military aggression in which he was so conspicuously successful. It is due entirely to a peculiarity of our own tradition — one that future historians may find as incomprehensible as we ourselves find the ancients' acceptance of slavery — that our historians, while willing to admire successful aggression, have shied away from its

equivalent in internal policy. In fact, it has sometimes been regarded as nothing short of sacrilege to notice it. Yet the historian
must not shut his eyes to the facts for the sake of an idealized
image.

The death of Parmenio was not quite the end of the matter.
For one thing, his brother Asander was still collecting reinforcements for Alexander. He brought them to the king at Bactra in the
following year, and he is never heard of again. . . . But the mere
number of important men involved in Parmenio's fall at least helps
to underline the extent of the faction and the pervasiveness of
Parmenio's influence even at the time of Alexander's *coup*. One of
these men, Demetrius (otherwise quite unknown to us), was a
Bodyguard, one of the highest nobles in the realm. He indignantly
denied complicity in the "conspiracy of Philotas," and Alexander
did not insist on his conviction. A little later, when the fuss had
died down, he was quietly eliminated and Ptolemy (the later king
and historian) was appointed in his place (Arr. 3.27.5). Amyntas son
of Andromenes, also named by the informer, was put on trial together with his three brothers. His case was made immeasurably
worse by the fact that Polemo (one of the brothers) attempted
flight before the trial. Yet Amyntas defended himself and his
brothers, and after a touching scene of reconciliation they were all
acquitted (Arr. 3.27.1 f.; Curt. 7.1.10 f.). Amyntas died in action
soon after, and two of his brothers are never heard of again under
Alexander, even though at least one of them survived the king.
The third, Attalus, in due course rose to a high position in the
army, clearly owing to a marriage connection with Perdiccas.
Though we cannot date the connection, it is tempting to conjecture that it already existed at the time of the trial and that it was, in
fact, Perdiccas who helped to secure the acquittal of Attalus and
his brothers in 330. Perdiccas' own loyalty was known to Alexander
and proved by the part he played in the arrest of Philotas (Curt.
6.8.17), so that he himself had nothing to fear.

Tarn uses the acquittal of these men as evidence of the fair-
ness of *all* the trials; yet Alexander could not afford (and had hardly
intended) to engage in wholesale slaughter of the Macedonian nobility. The extreme caution used in the arrest of Philotas (Curt. *loc.
cit.*) and, even more clearly, the case of Demetrius the Bodyguard,
show that he had to tread warily and not try the army's loyalty too

far. It is known — not that we need have doubted it — that Parmenio's own army did not take kindly to the murder of their commander. Dissatisfaction became so obvious that it had to be suppressed by forming the offenders into a special regiment of the "disorderly." Years later, in the reign of terror after the return from India, the destruction of Parmenio's murderers was greeted with joy (Curt. 10.1.1. f.). Although, after careful preparation, Alexander had been able to use the army against Philotas (not, as we have seen, against Parmenio himself), it had been a close thing. As a great general, Alexander was satisfied with the attainment of his objective (the destruction of Parmenio and his family) and knew where to call a halt, just as he knew where to call off pursuit after victory. Both in politics and in warfare the mind of Alexander followed the same unmistakable lines.

However, there was one man against whom the army could now be used without fear. Alexander son of Aëropus, the last survivor of the Lyncestian dynasty, had (as we have seen) been under guard for several years and, since he had taken no part in the great victories, had won no affectionate loyalty. . . . Accused of the treason for which he had been arrested years before — not, of course, of a part in the "conspiracy of Philotas," during which he had been under guard — he was now condemned by the army and at once executed (Curt. 7.1.5 f.). Nothing shows better than this cold-blooded execution of a harmless man how little point there is in attempts to find a moral justification for Alexander's acts of political terrorism.

It had been a close thing. But the king, possessed of the initiative and laying careful plans against unsuspecting victims, had won. He had not eliminated *all* of Parmenio's supporters: on the contrary, nobles and army now had to be conciliated by a display of forgiveness towards those members of the widespread faction who could (at least for the moment) safely be deemed innocent. The practical effects of forgiveness varied from complete reinstatement (as in the case of Attalus son of Andromenes) to a mere slight postponement of vengeance (as in the case of Demetrius the Bodyguard). One further measure of political conciliation followed at once. Having rid himself of Philotas, the king would not entrust anyone, not even his dearest friend, with the command of the whole of the *hetaeri*. The command was divided between Hephaestion and Clitus (Arr. 3.27.4). Hephaestion had been active in the plot against Philotas and thus earned his first important post. He was to rise, partly by the same methods, until he became the first of the king's subjects. Clitus was a man of entirely different stamp; second to none in bravery, he was also second to none in the frankness with which he criticized the king's oriental affectations. His elevation was an interesting concession, another measure of conciliation, to neutralize the elevation of the unpopular Hephaestion and show Alexander's attachment to dour Macedonians. In fact, Clitus' own hour had almost struck. But that is a different story, and one that was still in the future.

More lasting than the promotion of Clitus were the rewards of those who had cooperated with the king against the family of Parmenio. Craterus had always hated Philotas. It was he who had initiated the plan to spy on Philotas through the services of his mistress, and he had been prominent in the final stages of the affair: with Hephaestion, Coenus, Erigyius, Perdiccas and Leonnatus he had arranged the decisive step, the arrest of Philotas (Curt. 6.8.17). One of these six men, Erigyius (of Mytilene, it seems), was a Greek who could hardly expect to rise to the very highest rank in the army. Yet he was given independent commands of increasing importance and at the time of his premature death ranks *inter claros duces* [among the distinguished generals] (Curt. 8.2.40). This term could not have been applied to any other Greek in the army (except, later, Nearchus). Another of the six, Leonnatus, seems to have incurred the king's displeasure by contributing to the ridicule that killed the attempt to introduce *proskynesis* [prostration] among the Macedonians. This must have retarded his advancement. When he rehabilitated himself by outstanding courage and loyalty, his rise was rapid, culminating in the great honor he received at Susa.

These two are special cases. The other four enjoyed uninterrupted advancement. Finally, in the great army reform, they — Hephaestion, Perdiccas, Craterus and Coenus — were raised to the four chief hipparchies. We may call them, in the full sense, the marshals of the empire. The fact that those who assisted Alexander at this crucial moment later became the greatest men in the empire is far from mere coincidence: they had shown themselves "Alexander's men" in the decisive test. After the death of

Hephaestion and of Coenus, Perdiccas and Craterus survived the king himself, to become (whatever their exact rank and functions) the chief men among the Successors after his death. It is a fitting climax to the story that begins with the plot against the house of Parmenio.

Waldemar Heckel

The Conspiracy
Against Philotas

Waldemar Heckel is a professor of ancient history at the University of Calgary. His works include *The Marshals of Alexander's Empire* (Routledge, 1992), among other writings. Heckel shares Badian's opinion about the importance of behind-the-scenes developments in the Philotas controversy, but he disagrees with his colleague about the key participants' aims and roles.

Few problems in the history of Alexander the Great have been a greater vexation to the historian than the execution of Philotas and the murder of his father, Parmenio, events that shed an unfavourable light on Alexander's character and on the relationships of his younger Macedonian generals. For scholars such as W. W. Tarn and C. A. Robinson Jr., the Philotas affair became a moral issue, its discussion, ultimately, a conscious effort to exculpate Alexander. So it is with understandable regret that Tarn concludes that Parmenio's death was "plain murder and leaves a deep stain on Alexander's reputation." But in the last two decades the gentleman scholar and the gentleman conqueror have fallen out of favour, yielding to a new breed of sceptics. From this group E. Badian

"The Conspiracy *Against* Philotas" by Waldemar Heckel from *Phoenix* 31 (1977), pp. 9–21. Copyright © 1977. Reprinted by permission of *Phoenix*, the Journal of the Classical Association of Canada.

emerges as one of the most sound but, as I think, unduly suspicious in the case of the Philotas affair.

Badian's persuasive thesis, although many of its details have met with objections, has had a marked effect upon subsequent scholarship — as indeed has his entire characterization of Alexander as the ruthless, calculating opportunist — and, since it is the most recent specialized study, it warrants a detailed examination. In Badian's view, the murder of Parmenio was not the result of the Philotas affair in that it was a reaction to it, but the "culmination" of a greater scheme aimed at the destruction of Parmenio's house. . . . The view presupposes that Alexander had long desired the destruction of Parmenio and his adherents, that Parmenio was the ultimate target of the Philotas affair, that the actual conspiracy *of* Philotas did not exist, and that the conspiracy of Dimnos was a fabrication.

I propose to show that Badian's treatment of the affair is unsatisfactory on the matters of Alexander's motives and methods; that a study of the careers of Alexander's younger generals will show that they (Hephaistion not the least of these), and not Alexander, were primarily responsible for the fall of Philotas; that the latter's own position of prominence and arrogant nature gave rise to the ill-feeling against him; and that, far from being victimized by a "fabricated conspiracy" in the Dimnos affair, Philotas, through his foolish handling of the matter — for it did in fact exist — gave his enemies the perfect opportunity to move against him. Consequently, this view precludes the theory that the murder of Parmenio was the culmination of Alexander's "reign of terror," which began after Philip's assassination, and that Philotas was the object of a protracted conspiracy, contrived by Alexander himself.

Let us begin with Parmenio, allegedly the target of Alexander's smouldering hostility. It is true that Parmenio recognized the growing power of Attalus and his faction and, in an effort to bring himself into closer alliance with Philip (as was only fitting for the foremost commander of the army to do), married one of his daughters to Attalus. But we should not read too much into Parmenio's relationship with him; political marriages are not made in heaven. Nor was Parmenio so great a fool as to fail to realize that, when Philip's assassination had brought about the fall of Cleopatra and her adherents, it was politically expedient to sacrifice his new son-in-law to Alexander's vengeance. This was Parmenio's token of loyalty to the new king and there is no reason to doubt that Alexander was satisfied.

What we know of Parmenio's actions after Alexander's accession to the throne suggests that he had opted for conciliation with the king, nor is there any evidence that, before the Philotas affair, Alexander had viewed him with greater distrust than any other of Philip's generals. Certainly there are stories that cast Parmenio in an unfavourable light, but they do so for two obvious reasons: pro-Alexander propaganda and *apologia* [attempt at justification]. But to say [as Badian does] that some of these stories "go back to good sources (Ptolemy or even Callisthenes)" does not mean that they are true and, unless they can be proved to derive from Callisthenes, they were surely written after Parmenio's death. Furthermore, any such story that derives from Callisthenes (and only one can be assigned to him with certainty) need not be attributed to a deliberate attempt to undermine Parmenio's reputation. Callisthenes, as official historian of the crusade (Alexander's salesman to the League of Corinth, as many suggest), wrote with aim of enhancing the reputation of a young and ambitious king who was eager to win credit for himself and not appear to be winning battles through the skill of his father's general. Thus it was Callisthenes' function to impress the brilliance of Alexander's personality and military skill upon the *Greeks*; in order to undermine the reputation of Parmenio, he ought to have been writing for the Macedonian soldiery, to whom alone this will have been a major concern. More likely, any notable anti-Parmenio propaganda was written after Parmenio's death. *Apologia* and the history of Alexander are inseparable; what greater need than to justify the murder of Parmenio?

Badian charges that Alexander, while he was steadily "undermining Parmenio's reputation, had also made considerable progress in extricating himself from the stranglehold of Parmenio's family and adherents." The decline in power of Parmenio's house in the years that followed the crossing into Asia is evident. But is it fair to attach the blame for this to Alexander? Parmenio's sons, Hector and Nicanor, had died of natural causes, while a third member of the family, Asander, Parmenio's brother, had received the honour of the satrapy of Sardis. Can this really have been part of a scheme to weaken Parmenio's power in the army? If Berve is correct, all this occurred after Alexander had strengthened the family's position by appointing Philotas commander of the Companion cavalry. Asander was replaced in his satrapy [province] by Menander, under what circumstances we do not know. But how could Alexander have known that Parmenio's sons would die of natural causes? It is useless to speculate what he would have done had they not met such ends.

So, while fortune had taken two of Parmenio's sons, the most devastating move, as far as Philotas was concerned, was dictated by military sense. The events that followed Gaugamela made it clear that the nature of the war was to take a drastic change: the pursuit of Darius and Bessus would require vigour and mobility. Since Parmenio's seventy years made him ill-suited for this type of warfare and since the young, and extremely capable, Crateros had been groomed by a series of commands of ever-increasing importance as Parmenio's eventual successor, the latter was sent to Ecbatana with the imperial treasures. On account of the nature of the campaign, he was never recalled and took what we might today call a "desk job" at Ecbatana, entrusted with the securing of east-west communications. The appointment, while not a demotion, meant a considerable "loss of *power*" in relation to the army, but at Parmenio's age such a change of position was inevitable. While he may have resented the change, just as any commander, after a lifetime of service, resents removal from active duty, it was his son, Philotas, who was to suffer most from it.

With Parmenio at Ecbatana, Philotas found himself isolated within the Macedonian army; this proved disastrous. As a young man he had risen to his position of prominence, no doubt, through the influence of his father. His prestige, coupled with his friendship with Alexander, gave rise in turn to arrogance and licence in speech. It is difficult to determine the precise nature of his relationship with Alexander, for, while the two are portrayed as boyhood friends by Plutarch (Plut. 10.3), Philotas' role in the Pixodarus affair and his outspoken opposition to Alexander's orientalisms could not have raised him in the King's estimation. Nevertheless, both Ptolemy and Aristobulus reported that the friendship and honour in which he held both Philotas and Parmenio at the time of the conspiracy in Egypt (332–331 B.C.) induced Alexander to overlook the former's sins.

The existence of this so-called conspiracy has not been seriously questioned. The conspiracy, related by Arrian (3.26.1), must certainly be the subject of the first part of Plutarch's account of the Philotas affair (Plut. 48.4–49.2). At this point Plutarch speaks of a "conspiracy *against* Philotas," but our correct interpretation of this remark is vital to our understanding of the true nature of the conspiracy. . . .

Plutarch's account deserves closer attention. Crateros had suborned Philotas' mistress, Antigone, to inform against her lover and had reported the latest developments to Alexander. He was motivated by his strong sense of loyalty to the king, for which characteristic he won the label "the king's friend," and by his own personal ambition. Perhaps his zeal had brought him into open conflict with Philotas, just as it did on later occasions with Hephaestion. But this "prolonged espionage" revealed little that was not already known: that Philotas had been voicing his objections to Alexander's orientalisms, particularly the recent "Ammon's sonship," and that he claimed a greater share of the credit for his own military achievements and those of his father. There is no question that, when Plutarch speaks of Philotas as being ignorant of the conspiracy against him, he is referring to the activities of Crateros and Antigone and not the Dimnos affair that immediately follows in chapter 49.3–12.

The details of Dimnos' conspiracy can be briefly stated. Dimnos, for an unknown reason, had plotted with several others against Alexander. . . . But Philotas, whether privy to the plot or merely favouring it, failed to pass on the information. Cebalinus, perceiving that his words had fallen on deaf ears, resolved to bring the matter to Alexander's attention himself. In his second attempt, he found a more receptive ear. Philotas and the conspirators were subsequently arrested.

Because Dimnos "conveniently killed himself (or was killed while resisting arrest)" [see Badian's essay above] and because Philotas' guilt could not be proved, Badian concludes that the Dimnos affair was actually a "fabrication" aimed at implicating Philotas, a plot that was hatched while he was attending to the funeral rites of his brother. I consider Hamilton's refutation simple and adequate: "how could Alexander *know* that Philotas would fail to pass on the information?" There are, of course, other almost equally devastating objections: the complexity of the plot would have made its successful execution extremely difficult. But the strongest argument against the "fabricated conspiracy" is the understanding of the true conspiracy *against* Philotas.

As we have seen, Philotas was reported to have been one of Alexander's boyhood friends. Yet it appears that he was somewhat of an outsider to this inner group, the very people who were later to rise to prominence through their jealous rivalry with one another for Alexander's affection. Perhaps Philotas' alienation from the group was due to the difference in age that, although it may not have been great, was sufficient to separate him "from the boys" at a critical time. Certainly his devotion to his father and his military position made it neither necessary nor desirable for him to go into exile when Olympias and her children fell out of favour. At that point he very likely incurred the enmity of those companions of Alexander who had.

It does not appear that Alexander himself bore Philotas a grudge, for at the outset of the expedition he either retained him as commander of the Companions or promoted him to the post. But what Philotas had not done as a youth to alienate several of Alexander's young companions, he did in the early years of the campaign. His prestigious command was coveted by the younger commanders, while his arrogance fanned the flames of their jealousies, giving rise to a "conspiracy" against him. Now the irony of the situation becomes apparent. For, while Parmenio, through the rejection of the party of Attalus — and this will have included the arrest of Alexander of Lyncestis — and his loyalty, had won a reprieve from Alexander, his son, Philotas, through his own folly and unpopularity, was to bring about their downfall. Opposition was to come from another quarter. When the news of Dimnos' conspiracy broke, the cards were stacked against Philotas; his licence in speech and the suspicion of earlier treason made his complicity in the affair all the more credible. It appears that Philotas himself did not fully understand his own predicament at the time when the events of what we call the "Philotas affair" began to unfold. Certainly, his foolish disregard of his father's advice, his arrogance, and his general unpopularity made his ultimate deposition only a matter of time. His political enemies, who had long before begun to work for his elimination, seized the opportunity presented by the Dimnos affair. Deep-rooted animosities manifested themselves in the form of vigorous prosecution and, in the face of adversity, Parmenio, through whose influence Philotas had escaped an earlier charge of treason, was no longer present to help him.

When Philotas was confronted with the charge of complicity in Dimnos' conspiracy, he replied that he had not passed on the information because he had not taken it seriously, a peculiar attitude in a court where intrigues were common and always potentially dangerous. . . .

Curtius' lengthy discussion of the proceedings that followed Philotas' arrest is often tiresome, offering little in the way of new details. Yet Curtius is by far our most valuable source for the Philotas affair; it is unfortunate that his imaginative speeches and the reputation of his source, Cleitarchus, have detracted from the quality of Curtius' history. Cleitarchus drew his information mainly from eyewitness reports, and this will explain some of the confused details in Curtius' narrative. But Curtius was more than a skilful rhetorician: he understood the inner workings of the Philotas affair, relating what the other *vulgate* writers did not perceive and what Ptolemy and Aristobulus would not disclose. Curtius' Roman background had educated him in the ways of court intrigue and factional politics. One remark strikes to the heart of the matter: Philotas pronounces that the bitterness of his enemies has overcome Alexander's goodwill (*vicit . . . bonitatem tuam, rex, inimicorum meorum acerbitas*, Curt. 6.8.22). Furthermore, Curtius portrays Craterus and Coenus as Philotas' chief opponents, Craterus thinking that no better opportunity would present itself for destroying a detested rival and Coenus, although married to Philotas' sister, being his most outspoken assailant (6.8.4; 6.9.30). The latter, for his involvement in the affair, has been stigmatized by modern scholars as one of the most unsavory characters in the history of this period. Yet it is likely that the most serious blows to Philotas' hopes of acquittal were struck behind the scenes.

The years that intervened between the beginning of the expedition and the Philotas affair were marked by a conspicuous lack of achievement on the part of Alexander's dearest friend, Hephaestion. . . . Nevertheless, it is clear that at some time very early in the campaign Hephaestion began to exert an increasingly great influence upon Alexander. Certainly it would be naïve to believe that

Hephaestion's sudden rise from relative obscurity to command of one-half of the Companions was not in some way related to his role in the Philotas affair.

What we know of Hephaestion's later relationships with Alexander's commanders reveals that he was of a particularly quarrelsome nature and not reluctant to malign others to Alexander. His influence is evinced by his contribution to the fall of Callisthenes and the great alarm that Eumenes felt at Hephaestion's death, lest his former enmity toward him should bring about serious consequences. If any man had the power to persuade Alexander that Philotas was expendable, that man was Hephaestion. But Hephaestion's own military record provides an even greater cause for suspicion. As we have seen, his contribution to the war effort before 330 had been almost negligible. . . .

[More] important, however, is Hephaestion's failure to display, during the remainder of the campaign, those qualities of military skill and leadership that would warrant his unprecedented promotion. In fact, he is never reported exercising that command. Instead he appears to have been tactfully demoted whenever the actual command of military units was concerned.

We must therefore view Hephaestion's rise with suspicion. This is especially true in view of his vehement advocacy of the use of torture against Philotas, behaviour that is not out of character and that reflects a rivalry with Philotas on both a personal and official level (Curt. 6.11.10). Not only did he advocate torture but he took a personal lead in the act itself; Plutarch (Plut. 49.12) speaks of Philotas' tormentors as "those with Hephaestion." Even more suspicious is the nature of Arrian's account (3.26.2. ff.), which derives from Ptolemy. Here we are told of Hephaestion's promotion and of Ptolemy's own replacement of Demetrius the bodyguard, yet the account of the actual trial of Philotas is abbreviated to the point of uselessness. The Arrian-Ptolemy tradition has often been interpreted as official *apologia* for Alexander, but, as Schwahn and Errington have pointed out, it protected on numerous occasions Ptolemy's own interests and, very likely, those of his friends. . . .

The conspiracy *against* Philotas was not a "transparent fabrication," an invented conspiracy by an obscure individual named Dimnos, Alexander's means of trapping Philotas and eliminating Parmenio. It was, in fact, the Macedonian court at work, the struggle for power among Alexander's young and ambitious commanders. It entailed the undermining of Philotas' character and reputation by his most dangerous enemies: Hephaestion, Craterus, Coenus, Ptolemy, Erigyius, and others. These men realized that Philotas' isolation and his failure to pass on the information of Cebalinus presented the best opportunity for his destruction. Alexander had to be convinced that Philotas' involvement could not be overlooked or excused. When Alexander personally called for the death sentence before the Macedonian soldiers, the enemies of Philotas won the day. Their efforts had secured for them commands of major importance, positions that were to bring them into conflict with one another shortly afterward. The success of their conspiracy against Philotas only helped to encourage this factional rivalry and no other individual was more prone or better able to seek promotion by winning Alexander's ear than Hephaestion. It becomes clear that Alexander has been too much the centre of the history of his period, with the result that a hybrid, biographical-historical literature has developed. It is all too easy to view the Philotas affair and similar events from Alexander's vantage point, to assume that all things were initiated by Alexander. Should it be unreasonable to expect that Alexander was himself influenced, even manipulated at times, by those people who were closely associated with him?

There is no doubt that Alexander was not acting against his will when he allowed himself to be persuaded that Philotas must be removed. . . . We need not belabour the fate of Parmenio, nor indeed ought we to take into consideration its moral implications. Parmenio's death was outright murder, quite conceivably a "regrettable necessity," which not even Arrian-Ptolemy attempted to disguise. Alexander realized that, once Philotas' death had been demanded, Parmenio's murder was inevitable: the father would not endure the son's execution. It became apparent that Parmenio must die before the news of his son's death reached him and that the murder must in some way be justified. For the immediate purpose, the alleged confession of Philotas under torture proved adequate. The army, indignant at the audacity of the proposed crime, remained loyal; disciplinary measures were taken against a small dissident faction. Polydamas was sent with all haste to Sitalces, Cleander, and Menidas, who struck Parmenio down as he read the news of his son's execution and the charges against himself. It was an act of fearful desperation. The process had advanced to the point of no return.

The fates of the "fellow conspirators" need be treated only briefly. They are, in fact, not a part of the conspiracy *against* Philotas but of the Dimnos affair, the catalyst that brought about the destruction of Philotas and the subsequent murder of Parmenio. Demetrius the bodyguard remains an obscure figure; Curtius is certainly incorrect in claiming that he was executed together with Philotas and those named by Dimnos and Nicomachus (6.7.15; 11.38). Alexander of Lyncestis ended his imprisonment as the victim of a lynching, a thing characteristic of the mob when passions are aroused. Amyntas and his brothers were reprieved and, despite Amyntas' death shortly afterward, their futures cannot be linked with their roles in the Philotas affair with any certainty. As for the other conspirators (Peucolaus, Nicanor, Aphobetus, Theoxenes, Iolaus and Archepolis), their existence and identities, owing to their obscurity, cannot be determined. It is true that, at that time, Alexander could ill afford a "wholesale slaughter of the Macedonian nobility," but it is also doubtful that he wished even as much as actually came about.

A silver tetradrachm, 300–298 B.C.E., of Lysimachus, Alexander's general and one of his successors, now in the Boston Museum of Fine Arts. It depicts on the obverse Alexander wearing the horn of Ammon and a fillet. (Ronald Sheridan's Photo-Library)

VII Alexander's Divinity

The Visit to the Temple of Ammon

Arrian

The Road to Ammon

A number of events in Alexander's life revealed his quest for superhuman status. His visit to the oracle of the god Zeus Ammon at Siwah (in today's Libya) in 331, as well as his attempt to persuade his followers to perform *proskynesis* (prostration) before him ca. 327, illuminates especially well his perception of himself as equal to his supposedly divine ancestors.

Regardless of what contemporaries thought of Alexander's claim to be the son of the god Zeus Ammon, he took the belief very seriously

Reprinted by permission of the publishers and the Loeb Classical Library from Arrian: *History of Alexander*, 3.3–4, vol. 1, translated by Peter A. Brunt, Cambridge, Mass.: Harvard University Press, 1976.

himself. He received confirmation of his origins during a visit to the god's temple at Siwah. Whereas Strabo (see Part I) cites Callisthenes for the revelations made to Alexander at the temple, Arrian focuses on the journey itself and on the king's motives in going to Ammon, but is cryptic about the oracle's responses.

After [receiving a report in Egypt on affairs in Asia Minor], a longing seized Alexander to pay a visit to Ammon in Libya, for one reason to consult the god, since the oracle of Ammon was said to be infallible, and to have been consulted by Perseus, when he was sent by Polydectes against the Gorgon, and by Heracles when he was on his way into Libya to find Antaeus, and into Egypt to find Busiris. Alexander sought to rival Perseus and Heracles, as he was descended from them both; and in addition he himself traced his birth in part to Ammon, just as the legends traced that of Heracles and Perseus to Zeus. In any case he set out for Ammon with this idea, hoping to secure more exact knowledge of his affairs, or at least to say he had secured it.

As far as Paraetonium [Mersah Matruh] he went along the coast through country which, though desert, is not wholly waterless, a distance of sixteen hundred stades [ca. 187 miles] as Aristobulus tells us. There he turned into the interior, where the oracle of Ammon lay. The route is desolate; most of it is sand, and waterless. Alexander, however, had plenty of rain, and this was attributed to the divinity. And so was the following incident. Whenever a south wind blows in that country, it makes a great heap of sand on the route and obscures its marks, and one cannot get one's bearings in a sort of ocean of sand, since there are no marks along the route, no mountain anywhere, no tree, no solid hillocks standing up, by which the wayfarers might judge their proper course, as sailors do from the stars; in fact Alexander's army went astray, and the guides were in doubt as to the route. Now Ptolemy son of Lagos says that two serpents preceded the army giving voice, and Alexander told his leaders to follow them and trust the divinity; and the serpents led the way to the oracle and back again. But Aristobulus agrees with the more common and prevalent version, that two crows, flying in advance of the army, acted as guides to

Alexander. That some divine help was given him I can confidently assert, because probability suggests it too; but the exact truth of the story cannot be told; that is precluded by the way in which different writers about Alexander have given different accounts.

The district [Siwah] in which the Temple of Ammon lies is desert all round, covered with sand, and without water. But the site in the centre, which is small (for its broadest stretch only comes to about forty stades), is full of garden trees, olives and palms, and of all the surrounding country it alone catches the dew. A spring, too, rises from it, not at all like other springs which rise from the ground. For at midday the water is cold to the taste and even more to the touch, as cold as can be, but when the sun sinks towards evening it is warmer, and from evening on it grows warmer and warmer till midnight, and at midnight it is at its warmest; but after midnight it cools off in turn, and from dawn onwards it is already cold, but coldest at midday. This change occurs regularly every day. Then there are natural salts in this district, to be obtained by digging; some are taken by priests of Ammon to Egypt. Whenever they are going off to Egypt, they pack the salt into baskets woven of palm leaves, to be conveyed as a present to the king or to someone else. The grains of this salt are large, some of them have been known to be more than three fingers' breadth, and clear as crystal. Egyptians and others who are particular about religious observance use this salt in their sacrifices, as being purer than the sea-salts. Now Alexander surveyed the site with wonder, and made his enquiry of the god; he received the answer his heart desired, as he said, and turned back for Egypt, by the same route according to Aristobulus, but according to Ptolemy son of Lagos, by a different way, direct to Memphis. . . .

Arrian

The Introduction of *Proskynesis*

Even Arrian, who usually portrays Alexander in a favorable light, cen-
sures the king's request that people perform *proskynesis* before him.
The request evoked opposition made vocal by the historian Callisthenes, who ultimately paid for his position with his life. The following
account describes the failed attempt to introduce *proskynesis*, as well as
the competition in court for the king's ear and favors.

Some say that Anaxarchus the Sophist came by summons to Alexander to offer consolation [to Alexander, who regretted his killing
of Clitus], and finding him groaning on his bed, laughed at him and
said that he had not learnt why the old philosophers made Justice
sit by the throne of Zeus, because whatever is determined by Zeus
is done with Justice; so too the acts of a great King should be held
just, first by the king himself and then by the rest of mankind.
These words are said to have consoled Alexander for the time, but
I say that he did Alexander even greater harm than the affliction he
then suffered from, if indeed he gave this opinion as that of a sage,
that the duty of the king is not to act justly after earnest consideration, but that anything done by a king in any form is to be accounted just. The fact is that the report prevails that Alexander
desired people actually to do him obeisance, from the underlying
idea that his father was Ammon and not Philip, and as he was now
expressing his admiration for the ways of the Persians and Medes,
both in his change of dress and in addition by the altered arrange-

Reprinted by permission of the publishers and the Loeb Classical Library from
Arrian: *History of Alexander*, 4.9–19, vol. 1, translated by Peter A. Brunt, Cambridge,
Mass.: Harvard University Press, 1976.

ments for his attendance, and that even as to obeisance there was no lack of flatterers to give him his wish, among whom the most prominent were Anaxarchus and Agis of Argos, an epic poet, two of the sophists at his court.

It is said that Callisthenes of Olynthus, a past pupil of Aristotle, and with something of the boor in his character, did not approve of this, and here I myself agree with Callisthenes; on the other hand I think Callisthenes went beyond reason, if the record is true, in declaring that Alexander and his exploits depended on him and his history; it was not he who had come to win fame from Alexander, but it would be his work to make Alexander renowned among men; and again, that Alexander's share in divinity did not depend on Olympias' invention about his birth, but on the account he would write and publish in Alexander's interest. Some too have recorded that Philotas once asked him whom he thought to be held in highest honour by the Athenians; and he replied, Harmodius and Aristogiton, because they slew one of the two tyrants, and destroyed the tyranny. . . .

As to Callisthenes' opposition to Alexander regarding obeisance, the following story is also prevalent. It had been agreed between Alexander and the Sophists and the most illustrious of the Persians and Medes at his court that mention of this topic should be introduced at a wine party. Anaxarchus began the subject, saying that it would be far more just to reckon Alexander a god than Dionysus and Heracles, not so much because of the magnitude and nature of Alexander's achievements, but also because Dionysus was a Theban, and had no connection with Macedon, and Heracles an Argive, also unconnected with Macedon, except for Alexander's family, for he was descended from Heracles; but that Macedonians in their turn would be more justified in paying the respect of divine honours to their own king; in any case there was no doubt that when Alexander had departed from men they would honour him as a god; how much more just, then, that they should give him his due in life rather than when he was dead and the honour would profit him nothing.

When Anaxarchus had said this and the like, those who shared in the scheme approved his argument and were actually ready to begin doing obeisance, but the Macedonians for the most part were opposed to it, though silent. Callisthenes broke in and said:

"Anaxarchus, I declare Alexander unworthy of no honour appropriate for a man; but men have used numerous ways of distinguishing
all the honours which are appropriate for men and for gods; thus
we build temples and erect images and set aside precincts for the
gods, and we offer them sacrifices and libations and compose
hymns to them, while eulogies are for men; but the most important
distinction concerns the matter of obeisance. At greeting men receive a kiss, but what is divine, I suppose because it is seated above
us and we are forbidden even to touch it, is for that very reason
honoured by obeisance; dances, too, are held for the gods, and pae-
ans sung in their praise. In this distinction there is nothing surprising, since among the gods themselves all are not honoured in the
same way; and what is more, there are different honours for the
heroes, distinct again from those paid to gods. It is not, therefore,
proper to confuse all this, by raising mortals to extravagant propor-
tions by excesses of honour, while bringing the gods, as far as men
can, down to a demeaning and unfitting level by honouring them
in the same way as men. So Alexander himself would not endure it
for a moment, if some private person were to thrust himself into
the royal honours by unjust election or vote, and the gods would
have far better cause to be displeased with any men who thrust
themselves or permit others to thrust them into divine honours.
Alexander both is and is thought to be above all measure the brav-
est of the brave, most kingly of kings, most worthy to command of
all commanders. As for you, Anaxarchus, you above all should have
expounded these arguments and stopped those on the other side,
as you are attending on Alexander as philosopher and instructor. It
was improper for you to take the lead in this topic; you should
rather have remembered that you are not attending nor advising a
Cambyses or Xerxes [i.e., a Persian despot] but a son of Philip, a
descendant of Heracles and of Aeacus, whose forefathers came
from Argos to Macedonia, and have continued to rule the
Macedonians not by force but in accordance with custom. Even
Heracles himself did not receive divine honours from the Greeks in
his own lifetime, nor even after his death till the god of Delphi gave
his sanction to honouring him as a god. If, however, we must think
like barbarians, as we are speaking in their country, even so I appeal
personally to you, Alexander, to remember Greece, on whose behalf you made your whole expedition, to annex Asia to Greece.

Consider this too; when you return there, will you actually compel the Greeks as well, the freest of mankind, to do you obeisance, or will you keep away from the Greeks, but put this dishonour on the Macedonians, or will you yourself make a distinction once for all in this matter of honours and receive from Greeks and Macedonians honours of a human and Greek style, and barbarian honours only from barbarians? But if it is said of Cyrus son of Cambyses that he was the first of men to receive obeisance and that therefore this humiliation became traditional with Persians and Medes, you must remember that this very Cyrus was brought to his senses by Scythians, a people poor but free, Darius too by other Scythians, Xerxes by Athenians and Lacedaemonians, and Artaxerxes by Clearchus, Xenophon and their Ten Thousand, and Darius by Alexander here, who does not receive obeisance."

By these and the like words Callisthenes greatly provoked Alexander, but pleased the Macedonians, and realizing this, Alexander sent and told the Macedonians to think no more of obeisance. When, however, a silence fell after these words, the senior Persians arose and did obeisance one by one. Leonnatus, one of the Companions, thinking that one of the Persians made his obeisance ungracefully, mocked his posture as abject; Alexander was angry with him at the time, though reconciled later. The following story has also been recorded. Alexander sent round a loving cup of gold, first to those with whom he had made an agreement about obeisance; the first who drank from it rose, did obeisance, and received a kiss from Alexander, and this went round all in turn. But when the pledge came to Callisthenes, he rose, drank from the cup, went up to Alexander and made to kiss him without having done obeisance. At the moment Alexander was talking to Hephaestion, and therefore was not attending to see whether the ceremony of obeisance had been carried out by Callisthenes himself. But as Callisthenes approached to kiss Alexander, Demetrius son of Pythonax, one of the Companions, remarked that he was coming without having done obeisance. Alexander did not permit Callisthenes to kiss him; and Callisthenes remarked, "I shall go away short of a kiss."

In these incidents I do not at all approve either of Alexander's arrogance at the time or of Callisthenes' tactlessness, but in fact I think it enough for a man to show moderation in his own individual conduct, and that he should be ready to exalt royalty as far as practicable, once he has consented to attend on a king. So I think that Alexander's hostility to Callisthenes was not unreasonable in view of his untimely freedom of speech and arrogant folly, and on this account I infer that Callisthenes' detractors were readily believed that he had a part in the plot laid against Alexander by his pages. . . .

Alexander's Divinity

Lowell Edmunds

The Religiosity of Alexander

Lowell Edmunds is a professor of classics at Rutgers University. Among his works is *Approaches to Greek Myth* (edited, Johns Hopkins Univ. Press, 1990). In the selection below, Edmunds tries to explain what moved Alexander to ask for recognition of his divine status by examining his religious background and his attempts to realize contemporary heroic ideals.

Between the time when Alexander crosses the Hellespont with his army (334 B.C.) and the time of the invasion of India (327 B.C.), the nature of his enterprise obviously changes. To the extent that this change is not merely the result of external circumstances, it is a change in Alexander himself. The attempt to connect such an inner change with one event is intriguing but futile. It is better to look for a period in which various events all indicate that Alexander has formed a new plan or is embarking on a plan already formed but as yet unrevealed. "An acknowledged turning-point" in the reign of Alexander is the execution of Alexander's friend, Philotas, which was soon followed by the assassination of Philotas' father,

"The Religiosity of Alexander" by Lowell Edmunds in *Greek, Roman, and Byzantine Studies* 12 (1971), pp. 363, 368–391. Copyright © 1977. Reprinted by permission of the publisher.

Parmenio. This turning-point in fact suggests a period, the year 330 B.C., in which a general alteration in the campaign becomes apparent. The Graeco-Macedonian phase of the campaign ends, and what I should like to call the heroic phase begins. The heroism of Alexander, his belief in and emulation of mythical heroes, is an aspect of his religiosity, a matter that has been overlooked or underestimated in much recent scholarship on Alexander. . . .

Most Observant of Religion

In the list of superlatives in which he sums up the character of Alexander, Arrian calls him "most observant of religion" (7.28.1). Alexander in fact believed wholeheartedly in divinity. This belief is the presupposition of belief in the possibility of heroic *arete* [excellence], through which the hero attained a certain divinity of his own. Without this belief, Alexander's ambition to surpass the deeds of Achilles, Heracles and Dionysus must be fundamentally meaningless, or understood as a fabrication by the sources. But it can be shown to be neither of these.

In the past two decades we have been made more aware of how much we are in the grip of the prejudices, literary and other, of our sources and of the sources of our sources. . . . For example, Tarn complained that Clitarchus and certain poetasters "made" Alexander an "imitative character." Still in the fourth century, however, to praise a man is, just as it was for [the poet] Pindar, to compare him with the great heroes of the past. Aristotle's *Hymn to Arete*, with its praise of Hermeias, is sufficient evidence for this point. To see Alexander in such a way was hardly original with Clitarchus. Furthermore, in Alexander's case, the encomiastic convention perfectly suited the psychological and factural realities of the man who was to be praised. Alexander deliberately imitated heroes. It is not a poetaster or a novelist but the sober Arrian himself who says (7.14.4) that Alexander imitated Achilles from boyhood.

This imitation of heroes should be seen as religious in origin; but the religiosity of Alexander is now usually reduced to a problem of his divinity, the problem of whether or not Alexander really believed himself to be divine. The problem of his divinity is in turn reduced to the interpretation of two or three isolated events, e.g., to the question of whether he really sent a proclamation to the

Greek cities in 324 B.C. demanding divine honors. Another way in which the fundamental and consistent religiosity of Alexander has been lost to view is in the treatment of all his religious acts as really political in intent, as propaganda. Again, Alexander's emulation of heroes has been associated with his seizures by *pothos* [longing] and thus reduced to an irrational, romantic quirk.

In order to grasp the religiosity of Alexander one must first realize that the spiritual ambience of his youth was not the philosophic schools, the oratory and the comedy of Athens, but a Macedon that had more affinities with sixth-century or even Homeric than with fourth-century Greece. If Alexander gained anything from his study with Aristotle besides an admiration of Pindar and Homer, not a trace of it is reflected in his life. The aristocratic and heroic ideals of these poets did not have to be inculcated by argument. Homeric kingship lived on in Macedon. The king was preeminent amongst the aristocratic chiefs on account of his own wealth and power. His power consisted in his own *arete*. The same Philip who demonstrated such cunning in his dealings with the Greeks also fought in the forefront of battle. To the elevated sensibilities of an Athenian statesman, he was simply a one-eyed barbarian.

But Macedonian kingship is of interest to the present study above all because of its religious character. The Macedonian king was the chief priest. It was his duty, for example, to purify the army, should the occasion arise, by the sacrifice of a dog (Curt. 10.9.11–12). Even when he had to be carried on a litter, Alexander continued to perform the daily sacrifices according to ancestral custom (Arr. 7.25.2; Curt. 4.6.10). But it is needless to repeat the long list of the sacrifices to various divinities mentioned in our sources.

The Macedonian king kept a staff of seers. . . . Thus Aristander, who had been a member of Philip's court, accompanied Alexander on his expedition and interpreted many a dream and omen. . . . It is difficult to believe that Alexander ever abandoned the seers who belonged to his office any more than he abandoned the custom of daily sacrifice. On the contrary, one detects a mounting extravagance of religiosity in the last year of Alexander's life.

Alexander's religiosity is not, of course, a matter simply of the traditions of Macedonian kingship. His preoccupation with religious matters goes beyond any formal requirements of his office. In this connection the influence of Olympias, with her well-known enthusiasm for Dionysus, has often and no doubt correctly been mentioned, in the same way that Alexander's claim to divinity is referred to Philip's own similar though less extensive venture in having his statue carried in a procession along with those of the twelve gods. Strong though such influences may have been, they are insufficient to account for Alexander's vehement and rather eclectic piety.

Consider, for example, the matter of temple building. He ordered a temple of Zeus to be built at Sardis (Arr. 1.17.5–6). In his disappointment at the Ephesians' refusal to allow him to dedicate their temple of Artemis, to which he had caused to be paid the levy previously paid to the Persian king, he dedicated the temple of Athena Polias at the next city he came to, Priene. Temples to Isis and Greek gods were among the provisions for Alexandria in Egypt. . . .

The preceding observations on the religiosity of Alexander have been set forth in order to indicate a dimension of his character usually overlooked in recent scholarship and to serve as an introduction to the analysis of the main dynamic of his character, the striving for divinity through heroic *arete*. The heroes whom Alexander emulated were principally Achilles and Heracles. The other principal object of his emulation was Dionysus. . . . With Heracles, Achilles and Dionysus, it was a lifelong preoccupation with surpassing their great achievements.

Alexander claimed descent from Achilles on his mother's side through Neoptolemus (Plut. 2.1; Curt. 4.6.29). When Alexander landed in Asia Minor, after setting up altars to Zeus, Athena and Heracles, he went up to Ilium, where, in the temple of Athena, he dedicated his own armor and took in exchange armor dating — so Arrian says and so, as will appear, Alexander believed — from the Trojan War (Arr. 1.11). He also made an offering at the tomb of Achilles (Arr. 1.12.1; Diod. 17.17.3; Plut. 15.7). These and other ceremonies of Alexander's first days in Asia Minor have been interpreted as propagandistic. They were intended to symbolize the pan-Hellenic and vengeful character of the campaign. Undoubtedly, as has been argued above, Alexander intended to give his campaign this character in its early years and thus would have wished to exploit the propagandistic value of these ceremonies. But much later, long after Alexander needed to concern himself with what the Greeks thought, he still had the sacred shield from the temple at Ilium carried before him into battle. It was this shield with which Peucestas protected him in the city of the Malli (326 B.C.) (Arr. 6.9.3, 10.2; cf. 1.11.7). This fact shows that Alexander's imitation of Achilles was not mere romanticism, if we define romanticism as insubstantial and uncreative, since Alexander's attachment to the shield and his absorption in the spirit represented by the shield were obviously the source of ever-renewed strength. As Arrian observed, Alexander's imitation of Achilles was a lifelong pursuit (7.14.4). Even his grief for Hephaestion was expressed in Achillean form.

In this connection one should record the finding of W. B. Kaiser that Alexander's helmet on the decadrachms (the so-called Porus medallion) in the British Museum is not a combination of Greek and oriental styles but Homeric, as is the motif of the duel with Porus. In fact there are numerous examples of Alexander's delight in man-to-man combat. It was expected of the Macedonian king, but here again Alexander's deeds are obviously more than *pro forma*. His motive is fundamentally heroic, and the inspiration comes from Homer. One might wish to describe Alexander's well-known attachment to Homer as romantic; but could a merely romantic interest in heroism have caused Alexander to risk his life so many times and to suffer so many wounds (cf. Arr. 7.10.1)?

Alexander also claimed Heracles as an ancestor and felt the same pious envy of him as of Achilles (Arr. 3.3.2; cf. 4.10.6, 5.26.5). On one occasion Heracles is set alongside the gods to whom he customarily made sacrifice (Arr. 6.3.2), while elsewhere sacrifices of thanksgiving to Heracles with Zeus Soter and other gods are mentioned several times. En route to Tyre Alexander told envoys of that city that he wished to sacrifice to Heracles (Arr. 2.15.7). When the Tyrians subsequently refused him admission to the city, he decided to lay siege to it. In the speech on this occasion reported by Arrian, Alexander explains to his officers the strategic importance of the city (Arr. 2.17). But the siege obviously had a personal meaning for Alexander. He had a dream in which he saw Heracles leading him to the walls of the city (Arr. 2.18.1). One should not, by the way, assume that such a rationalistic interpretation of the Tyrian

Heracles as Arrian gives (2.16) would have meant anything to Alexander. To him Heracles-Melcarth was Heracles, just as Ammon was Zeus under another name. When, after a siege of seven months (Diod. 17.46.5; Curt. 4.4.19) — the most difficult single operation of his career — Alexander captured the city, he spared only the Tyrians who had taken refuge in the temple of Heracles, selling the rest into slavery. He sacrificed to Heracles at last, and held a parade and naval review in Heracles' honor. He rededicated with an inscription the Tyrian ship sacred to Heracles (Arr. 2.24.5–6). On his return to Tyre from Egypt he again sacrificed to Heracles (Arr. 3.6.1). He set up altars to the twelve gods at the limit of his eastern campaign in imitation of Heracles.

Though Arrian does not believe the story that Heracles tried and failed to capture the rock of Aornos, he does believe that Alexander's desire to capture the rock was influenced by this story. We see here the same rivalry with Heracles that was part of the motivation for the visit to Siwah (Arr. 3.3.2). Callisthenes is the source for this motive. Now in the case of Callisthenes' account of Alexander's visit to the oasis, one might plausibly explain the reference to Heracles as flattery of Alexander or as propaganda directed toward a Greek audience. But when one finds Alexander thousands of miles from Greece besieging impossible places in emulation of Heracles and building altars in imitation of him, long after Alexander has ceased to be seriously concerned with what the Greeks think and after indeed Callisthenes is dead, can one still reduce his concern with Heracles to an invention of the sources? It is not a flattering source or even a favorable one but the hostile Ephippus* who records that Alexander often imitated the dress of Heracles.

The coinage of Alexander provides confirmation of his preoccupation with Heracles. The traditional ancestor of the Macedonian kings (Arr. 3.3.2; Plut. 2.1), Heracles appears on Macedonian coins from the fifth century, but comes to predominate on Alexander's coinage. For present purposes the most important conclusion that can be drawn from the study of these coins is that the traditional Heracles head begins to acquire the features of

---

*Ephippus of Olynthus wrote "On the Death of Alexander and Hephaestion," which was very hostile to Alexander.

Alexander between 330 and 320 B.C., in particular the leonine brow, and that this change is due to Alexander himself. This coinage is thus taken to represent a change in Alexander, dating from the siege of Tyre, from imitation of Achilles to imitation of Heracles, a change confirmed by study of the portraits. In line with this attempt to connect imitation of certain heroes with certain stages in Alexander's life, Schachermeyr argued that in the course of the Indian campaign, Dionysus replaced Heracles as the prime object of Alexander's *philotimia* [love of distinction]. But Alexander imitated the hero whom circumstances suggested. Towards the end of his life, at the time of the death of Hephaestion (324 B.C.), Alexander shaved his head in imitation of Achilles' grief for [his closest friend] Patroclus (Arr. 7.14.4). This fact does not mean that Alexander had ceased to imitate Heracles and Dionysus. He emulated an ideal, emulating the representative of the ideal demanded by the occasion.

Dionysus has suffered more than either Achilles or Heracles from source criticism. Nearly everything that is said of Dionysus is attributed to fabrication, exaggeration or flattery by the sources. For this reason it is well to begin the discussion of Alexander's emulation of Dionysus with a piece of evidence that goes back to Aristobulus. In explanation of Alexander's motives for a campaign against the Arabs, Arrian states [7.20]:

> There is a story current that he heard the Arabs honoured only two gods, Uranus (the sky) and Dionysus: Uranus because he was actually visible to them and contained within himself all the stars including the sun, from which were derived the greatest and most obvious benefits for all human needs, and Dionysus because of the fame of his expedition to India. Alexander therefore considered himself not unworthy to be regarded as a third god by the Arabs, a god who has performed deeds not less splendid than Dionysus, if indeed he conquered the Arabs and then allowed them like the Indians to live in accordance with their own customs.

Thus when the poetasters Agis and Cleon compare Alexander to Dionysus, "opening heaven to him" (Curt. 8.5.8), it is not a matter of flattery that shows nothing about Alexander. In order to succeed as flattery, flattery must be accurate. Agis and Cleon associate Alexander with Dionysus because they know it will please him. Alexander, after all, had let his reverence for Dionysus be known. He was not unwilling to have the murder of Clitus referred to the wrath of Dionysus on account of a neglected sacrifice (Arr. 4.8.1, 9.5–6) or on account of the sack of Thebes, to which he also attributed the mutiny on the Hyphasis (Plut. 13.3). It sounds, then, like a kind of mockery of Alexander when Ephippus attributes Alexander's fatal illness to overindulgence in wine caused by Dionysus. . . .

Alexander's emulation of heroes is the sign of his belief in the possibility of his own divinity. His heroism is the fulfillment and attainment of the divinity that was vouchsafed him at Siwah. But before undertaking to describe the psychology of these beliefs, one must say something of the visit to Siwah (332 B.C.) and the supposed request for divine honors from the Greek cities (324 B.C.) Though the *proskynesis* [prostration] episode need not form part of the discussion of Alexander's divinity, its religious overtones are well attested.

The detour to Siwah was nonstrategic and had nothing to do with Alexander's pharaohship. It was a personal matter. The preceding events which bear most directly on the consultation of the oracle are the cutting or untying of the Gordian knot (spring 333 B.C.) and the victory at Issus (Nov. 333 B.C.). The oracle associated with the knot, that the man who could undo it would be lord of all Asia, would have affected Alexander deeply, since he believed that the god at Gordium was Zeus, and since he thought he had received divine signs of his fulfillment of the oracle. His victory at Issus was a partial confirmation of what he had come to believe at Gordium. There followed the long siege of Tyre and the invasion of Egypt. Meanwhile Darius, whose offers of peace Alexander had twice refused, remained to be conquered. The immediate motive for the visit to the oasis is the uncertainty that had grown upon Alexander in the period since the victory at Issus. One should remember that Alexander is not self-confident. His fearfulness is often alluded to; he showed dubiety about the grand strategy of the campaign against Darius. His confidence in his superiority is not self-confidence but a belief in the revelation of this superiority — such a revelation, for instance, as had come at Gordium and had been confirmed at Issus. This belief needed to be renewed by oracles and divine signs, just as it needed to be tested continually in action. The consultation of the oracle at Ammon is not a vagary but perfectly consistent with Alexander's religiosity. In particular, the consultation of the oracle of Ammon should be seen as following from the promise of lordship over all Asia made by Zeus Basileios at Gordium. It was easy for contemporaries to believe that this was precisely the subject of Alexander's consultation: thus the tradition, probably originating with Callisthenes, that Alexander asked the priest of Ammon if he was granted rule over the whole earth (Diod. 17.51.2; Curt. 4.7.2).

The visit itself is the most vastly discussed episode in Alexander's life. The fact that most concerns the present study is the incontestable importance to Alexander of the revelation, no matter how or in what terms it came. The deep religiosity of Alexander is the grounds of the strong effect of this revelation. Its importance is seen in Alexander's heroism, in the push eastward after the death of Darius, in the ruthlessness with which he dealt with his men, and his carelessness of his own life. But since at the time of the consultation of the oracle of Ammon Alexander is still in the Graeco-Macedonian phase of the campaign, one cannot expect him to emphasize his divine sonship — for such were the terms in which he understood the revelation — at least not to Macedonians. Other oracles came to Alexander from Miletus concerning his origin from Zeus. These oracles must reflect what Alexander believed he had learned from Ammon. Later, before the battle of Gaugamela, in a prayer uttered before the Greek contingents, Alexander alluded to himself as the son of Zeus. Plutarch's report of the prayer is from Callisthenes but is not to be discredited for this reason. Ephippus tells us that Alexander used sometimes to wear the purple robe, slippers and horns of Ammon. But the divine sonship remains for the most part unstated throughout the years of campaigning, for the reason that the promise of divinity is being tested and fulfilled as Alexander becomes what he is. There is, however, one other piece of evidence for Alexander's belief in his divine sonship: the letter quoted by Plutarch (Plut. 28.2), in which Alexander refers to his "so-called father" Philip. If, as Hamilton stoutly argued, the letter is genuine, then there is no reasonable doubt about this aspect of Alexander's religiosity.

The date of the letter is uncertain. If, as Hamilton thought, 323 B.C. is the date, then the letter would fit with Alexander's dying request that his corpse be conveyed to Ammon (Curt. 10.4.4) and also with the many indications of a new, fanatical religiosity: the decision to deify Olympias; the order for the pyre of Hephaestion, to cost 10,000 talents; the consultation of Ammon as to whether Hephaestion might be worshipped as a hero; the pardon of Cleomenes on condition of the satisfactory completion of the shrines in Egypt (Arr. 7.23.6–8); the last plans, which, even if distorted by Perdiccas, reflect what the army would have believed of Alexander; and the overblown pomp of Alexander's court. It was at this time, according to Plutarch, that Alexander became excessively superstitious, and the palace was full of sacrificers, purifiers and seers (Plut. 75.1).

Against this background a request for divine honors from the Greek city-states in 324 B.C. appears not incredible. The contemporary evidence for the awarding of such honors is Dinarchus (Dem. 94) and Hypereides (Dem. fr.8 col. 31). In Athens the pro-Macedonian Demades made the proposal for Alexander and was fined for his efforts. There are many satirical quips on the subject preserved in later writers. As at so many other points in Alexander's life, a political motive may well be bound up with the religious. Though the request (if there was one) was surely not legalistic in intent, it was still a way of reminding the Greeks of the authority of the man who had promulgated the decree for the return of the exiles. But far more than this, a request for divine honors would have issued from a new fanatical development of the lifelong religiosity of Alexander. The early Greek view of divinity is markedly ambiguous. On the one hand, the gods are remote, harsh and vengeful; in comparison with them, man can feel only self-contempt. Zeus regrets that he gave immortal horses to Peleus, to a mortal, which is the most pitiable thing on earth (*Il.* 17.443). Apollo warns Diomedes that "the tribe of deathless gods and of men who go upon the earth is never the same" (*Il.* 5.441–42). On the other hand, the opposite of Apollo's statement could be maintained, as in [the poet] Hesiod's line, "From one origin are begotten gods and mortal men," a notion amplified in Pindar's well-known lines, "One is the race of men, one is the race of gods, and from one mother do we both derive our breath; yet a power that is wholly sundered parteth us, in that the one is naught, while for the other the brazen heaven endureth as an abode unshaken forever. Albeit, we mortals have some likeness, either in might of mind or at least in our nature to the immortals. . . ." Thus divinity is far and near.

The hero is the embodiment of this theology. In him the two sides of the antithesis are combined and reconciled, though uneasily. He is a mortal subject to his mortality, but through a divine *arete* within him he surpasses the ordinary limits. He is not a god, but from the mortal point of view he is half-divine.

Heroism and Divinity

The complex of beliefs associated with heroism was never systematized. The heroes of poetry are spoken of as half-divine; the heroes of cult are often closely connected in worship with deities; some cult figures were worshipped as either heroes or gods. If we set Alexander against the background of such beliefs, what is most striking is that he never sought heroic honors. Our sources contain many references to emulation of heroes but nothing concerning heroization. Alexander sought heroism as distinct from heroization, since heroism implied divinity. Alexander's feelings in these matters can be seen in the fact that he wished to heroize his friend Hephaestion. A hero cult would suffice a lesser man than Alexander. He himself sought something more.

For the broader heroic ideal persisted even into the fourth century B.C. Aristotle, in the so-called *Hymn to Arete*, associated his patron, Hermeias of Atarneus, who had been treacherously executed by the Persian king, with Achilles, Heracles and other heroes:

> *Arete, you whom the mortal race wins by much toil,*
> *the fairest prey in life,*
> *for the beauty of your form, maiden,*
> *it is an enviable lot in Hellas both to die*
> *and to endure toils violent and unceasing.*
> *On such fruits do you set the mind:*
> *equal to the Immortals, better than gold,*
> *and noble ancestors and languid-eyed sleep.*
> *For your sake Heracles, the son of Zeus, and Leda's youths*
> *endured much in their deeds*
> *hunting after your power.*
> *Through longing for you, Achilles and Ajax came to the house*
>   *of Hades.*

Because of the gracious beauty of your form the nursling
*   of Atarneus forsook the sun's rays.*
Therefore the Muses will exalt him, famous in song for
*   his deeds and immortal,*
The daughters of Memory, exalting reverence for Zeus
*   who guards the rights of hospitality, exalting the*
*   gift of honor that is faithful friendship.*

The heroic life remains the model of the highest achievement, and heroism still means the possibility of divinity. *Arete* is "equal to the Immortals." The mortal who can attain *arete*, i.e., the mortal who already has within him the capacity for *arete*, attains to an immortal, a divine quality.

The notion that the display of *arete* could bring one divinity was also often alluded to by Isocrates, and his example was, of course, Heracles (Isoc. 1.50, 5.132). He also says that "if any of those of former times became immortal through their *arete*," he thinks that [the Cypriot king] Evagoras deserves this gift (9.70). To Philip, Isocrates held up Heracles as the example of the mortal who had achieved a reputation equal to a god by his campaign against Troy (Isoc. 5.145). How literally Philip received this suggestion, one does not know. But it is obvious that Isocrates was serious about his policy for Greece and thus would have used the most persuasive arguments possible. If he holds up Heracles as an example to Philip, he must think that Philip can be so inspired. As for Alexander, there is no reason to doubt that rivalry with heroes was a passion of his. What the *Hymn* and these statements of Isocrates add to an understanding of heroism is that still in the fourth century B.C. heroism was associated with divinity, as it had been from the beginning. Clearly Aristotle and Isocrates did not offer Alexander a program for the attainment of divinity, and Alexander cannot be shown to be following any definite plan to that end. But he can be shown to be animated by an ideal of *arete* that appears in Isocrates and Aristotle and was thus part of the spiritual ambience in which Alexander grew up.

The contemporaneity of the notion of the possibility of an heroic and divine *arete* is illustrated also in a passage at the beginning of Book 7 of Aristotle's *Nicomachean Ethics:*

to say that it is superhuman virtue, a kind of heroic and divine excellence; just as Homer has Priam say about Hector that he was of

> *surpassing excellence: "for he did not seem like one who was a child*
> *of a mortal man, but of a god." Therefore, if as is said, an excess of*
> *virtue can change a man into a god, the characteristic opposed to brut-*
> *ishness must evidently be something of this sort.*

Note here again the coupling of the heroic and the divine, and especially the illustration from the *Iliad*, where superhuman *arete* appears as divine sonship. In just this way did Alexander conceive of
his own *arete*. . . . Aristotle does not mean that men can literally
become heroes or gods, but only that a superhuman *arete* would be
the opposite of brutishness. Alexander, on the other hand, might
have taken literally the human possibility of heroism and divinity
achieved through toilsome *arete*.

The *Hymn to Arete* is of use to us in suggesting how Alexander
might have understood the requirements of such an achievement.
The hero must already have in him the *arete* that will signify his
heroism, but the potentiality is far from sufficient. Rather, the very
potentiality of such *arete* means a life of toil beyond what the ordinary mortal can endure. The life of the hero is in allegiance to, and
is a ceaseless unfolding of, his *arete*. As Wilamowitz said of the
Hymn, "The heroes did not offer up their lives in order to gain
arete, but rather offered to the *arete* they possessed the life they led
and the death they died."

In Alexander's life the cutting of the Gordian knot and the oracle at Siwah might have served as guarantees of the *arete* which
Alexander had, from our point of view, already revealed, but
which, from his point of view, had been revealed to him and therefore needed the confirmation of oracles. Furthermore, in accordance with heroism as understood by Aristotle in the *Hymn*, the
condition of such a revelation as had come from Ammon was that
Alexander spend his life in the fulfillment of it. One is reminded of
Socrates' lifelong confirmation of the response of the Pythia concerning his wisdom. Alexander could measure the accomplishments of his *arete* and thus the attainment of the divinity that lay
in store for the hero only by the standard of the great heroes known
in legend and poetry: thus his emulation of them.

The relation of heroism and aspiration to divinity is in fact expressed on the coins: " . . . the obverse and reverse of Alexander's
tetradrachms function as a unity in such a way that the thought of

Alexander as Heracles and son of Zeus can hardly be avoided. What especially contributes to this effect is the unusual appearance of the enthroned Zeus as the counterpart to Heracles."

The Debate of Anaxarchus and Callisthenes

Two of our sources, Arrian (4.10.6ff) and Curtius (8.5.5ff), contain a debate on the subject of deification in general and the deification of Alexander in particular. This debate is a well-known kind of Alexander story, which could be labelled "Alexander and the philosophers." But this debate may contain the residue of something historical, and, in any case, it clearly presents the fundamental theological alternatives in the matter of deification as they would have appeared to Alexander's contemporaries. Thus the debate provides a scheme according to which we can define Alexander's own attitude toward the possibility of his divinity.

The context of the debate in Arrian and Curtius is the *proskynesis* episode. . . . No matter how good or bad the tradition is here, the debate is of interest to the present discussion since it outlines so clearly the theological issues that would have been provoked by Alexander's pretensions if they were expressed as explicitly at this time as they were later.

The participants in the debate are, in Arrian, Callisthenes and Anaxarchus; in Curtius, Callisthenes and a Cleo who is not mentioned elsewhere. Since the position of Anaxarchus in Arrian, which corresponds perfectly to the position of Cleo in Curtius, can be shown to agree with everything else we know about Anaxarchus, the mysterious Cleo can be discounted as a figure invented by Curtius for his own reasons. Furthermore, Anaxarchus and Callisthenes appear elsewhere as rival philosophers in Alexander's court, and there is no reason to doubt the historical reality underlying these stories, especially considering the bitterness with which the philosophical schools of the day opposed one another. Plutarch records that Callisthenes and Anaxarchus gave Alexander different sorts of consolation after the murder of Clitus (Plut. 52.3–7; cf. Arr. 4.9.7ff); and implies that there was enmity between them (Plut. 52.8). Strabo (13.1.27) says that Alexander read Homer with Callisthenes and Anaxarchus (cf. Plut. 8).

No matter who should be considered the winner of the debate

at a theoretical level, Anaxarchus was the winner as regards the practical consequences. Our sources associate the death of Callisthenes with his philosophical position as well as with his personality. Anaxarchus, on the other hand, remained the king's favorite until the end. . . . Yet Anaxarchus, as in the debate, encouraged Alexander's pretensions to divinity. Once the philosophical basis of Anaxarchus' position becomes clear, it will be seen that there was for him no contradiction between his encouragement and his irony. Anaxarchus has two arguments for deifying Alexander (Arr. 4.10.6; cf. Curt. 8.5.10–11). The second of these maintains that, since the Macedonians will surely honor Alexander as a god when he is dead, it is juster to honor him thus when he is alive, when it is of use to him. We turn from the dubious piety of this to the first argument, which shows more clearly Anaxarchus' philosophical assumptions. He says that the Macedonians would with greater justice honor Alexander as a god than Heracles or Dionysus, since the former is an Argive and the latter a Theban. Anaxarchus here assumes first that divinity is strictly local. A people should honor gods of its own creation. Second, he assumes that gods can in fact be created by fiat, and thus that they exist only by convention. In short, Anaxarchus' position is conventionalist, and this is what our scanty sources would lead us to expect, no matter what label — sceptic, eudaemonist, Democritean — we should apply to him.

Callisthenes opposes the conventionalism of Anaxarchus, maintaining the old triad of man, hero and god (Arr. 4.11.3). The distinctions within the triad are not to be tampered with by mortals (Arr. 4.11.4), who cannot create gods (Curt. 8.5.18). For Callisthenes, who is arguing against *proskynesis,* the distinctions are especially expressed in the different kinds of honors paid to gods, heroes and mortals (Arr. 4.11.3–4; Curt. 8.5.19). Callisthenes admits that mortals can be deified — Heracles is the example — but only after death and only by the pronouncement of Delphi (4.11.7) — "divinity sometimes follows a man, but never accompanies him" (Curt. 8.5.16).

Neither of the two sides of the debate would have found favor with Alexander. The conventionalism of Anaxarchus would have rendered meaningless Alexander's heroism, the aim of which would thus have been not the revelation of Alexander's *arete* but his people's admiration. Clearly, however, Alexander cared less for the honors the world could bestow than for the continual campaigning by which he could prove his superhuman greatness. In imitating heroes Alexander did not aim at heroization after death or during life but at the divine *arete* that was out of reach of all but a few mortals. This sort of thing is not provided for in the views of Anaxarchus, who does not grant gods or heroes any but a conventional existence. But Anaxarchus' views presented no real threat to Alexander's enterprise, and Anaxarchus knew how to be pleasing, both by flattery and favors.

But Callisthenes' views did present a threat. If, as he said, the gap between men and gods was unbridgeable, and if any superhuman status could be attained only after death, then Alexander's personal enterprise was futile. As the heroic phase of the campaign progressed, it did not please Alexander to have someone with Callisthenes' views and austere personality in his retinue.

Conclusion

In the life of Alexander myth becomes history only to become myth again, not only because his contemporary historians inevitably see him in terms of myth, but also because he saw himself in, and wanted to be seen in, those terms. Thus our sources do not altogether conceal the "real" Alexander; rather, Alexander consciously and willfully gave himself a certain ideality through conceiving of his life as a reenactment of myth. His individuality is, then, not a matter of originality and peculiarity but of the spectacular degree to which he could fulfill the heroic ideal of the myths.

But the fulfillment, as in the myths, meant overstepping the limits. As he returns from the east to Babylonia, the march through the Gedrosian desert, the reign of terror, and perhaps the proclamation of his own divinity, as well as other matters already touched upon, mark a change in his character, a fanatical development of his religiosity. And all the while his heroism has been meaningless to a Diogenes and laughably pretentious to a Menander.* His divinity soon becomes the butt of satire in the Greek cities. Alexander's

---

*Diogenes was a Cynic philosopher who led a very simple life. Menander was a comic poet.

heroism could seem then not the sacred reenactment of myth he intended, but a performance, even a masquerade, as he dresses for dinner in the lion-skin of Heracles. One recalls Hegel's saying that Achilles, the ideal youth of poetry, commences the Greek achievement, and Alexander, the ideal youth of reality, concludes it. Alexander is this ideal youth not simply analogously to the ideal youth of epic but because of Achilles. Achilles, or the heroic life, is the formal cause, as it were, of Alexander's life. But in willing an imitation of the heroic life and in fulfilling it with his boundless energy, Alexander breaks the mould.

Ernst Badian

The Deification of Alexander the Great

In the selection below, Badian considers what the sources actually tell us about Alexander's wish for deification, contemporary reactions to it, and whether his request was exceptional in the context of the Greco-Macedonian and Asian world of the fourth century B.C.E.

Let us start with a theoretical discussion of the deification of mortals that we find in an Alexander context and that ought perhaps to be more seriously considered than it usually has been. When the historian Arrian comes to speak of Alexander's attempt to introduce *proskynesis* [prostration] for Greeks and Macedonians (4.10.5 — we shall have more to say about the incident as such), he begins by reporting, as a *logos* [tale] not from his main sources, a debate

From Ernst Badian, "The Deification of Alexander the Great," in *Ancient Macedonian Studies in Honor of Charles F. Edson*, ed. Harry J. Dell, (Thessaloniki: Institute for Balkan Studies, 1981), 27–71. Reprinted by permission.

between Anaxarchus and Callisthenes as to whether Alexander ought to be worshipped as a god. . . .

Anaxarchus, for various reasons based on Alexander's descent and achievements, claims that the time has come to worship him as a god — why not now, in his lifetime, rather than uselessly after his death? It is in reply to this that Callisthenes sets out (11.2 ff.) the classic theory of religious demarcations within the spheres of the divine, and between it and the human. There is a line drawn between gods and men that has never been crossed (the exception of Heracles proves the rule, as this was after his death and at the command of Delphic Apollo) and never must be. There is also a line between gods and heroes, which is an equally strict boundary; and indeed, different gods have different forms of worship, appropriate to the particular case of each.

It would be rash to claim that the great debate is a trustworthy account of the actual *proskynesis* affair; even though it was clearly the *accepted* account, knowledge of which among educated men could be taken for granted. However, it must not (at the other extreme) be written off as a late historical figment, a mere rhetorical invention. . . .

Arrian gives it as a *logos* obtaining. Although he may have adapted it stylistically for his own purposes, we have no right whatever to accuse him of merely making it up himself or of inserting it from an extraneous source: his *logoi* [tales] come from the main Alexander tradition, though on the whole from outside his two proclaimed main sources. We are not entitled to place this *logos* in a special class, or to disbelieve that it is Hellenistic and part of the Alexander "vulgate"; and indeed, this is confirmed by its appearance in Curtius and the way it is treated by Plutarch.

In fact, we may go further and (I believe) assign it to Alexander's lifetime. Christian Habicht has pointed out that as early as twenty years after the *proskynesis* trouble, at the time of the *Hymn to Demetrius*, opposition to the deification of mortals was already expressing itself in political and not in religious form. Habicht has also carefully examined the characteristic forms of phrase that mark a statement concerning deification as late: all forms of speech that refer to "making" a god or "voting" a mortal to be a god, as opposed to recognising the fact of his divinity. Now, such phrases are totally absent from the debate, and it is surely

unlikely that they would have been accidentally avoided, in a passage of such length, at a late date, or that anyone composing the
passage at a late date would have known the facts that Habicht has
disengaged. I can see no plausible alternative to the view that the
debate (and particularly Callisthenes' part in it — for it can be held
that Anaxarchus is a lay figure, a man of straw set up for Callisthenes to overthrow) belongs to the age of Alexander and was inserted
at this point of the Alexander "vulgate" at a very early date. Of
course, Callisthenes does not speak as a philosopher — indeed, he
was not a philosopher, though some of his acquaintances were. His
opposition is not based on philosophy, as (e.g.) similar opposition
under the Empire was. It is firmly based on the religion of the common man: his belief in a status society (as we might call it) of gods,
heroes and men, and his fear of disturbing it and "throwing everything into confusion." The idea appears in Pindar's *Sixth Nemean*;
it was still the belief of the men who convicted Socrates, and —
quite recently — of those who had felt qualms about Aristotle's
hymn to Arete on the death of Hermias and had launched a sacrilege suit against him (Athen. 15.696). . . .

No one would deny that for an ancient Greek the boundary
between human and divine, between mortal and immortal, was not
where it is for a believing Jew or Christian. In Greek myth (which
was to some extent regarded as ancient history) gods consorted
with mortals in various ways and could father mortal sons born by
mortal women — sons who, after death, might (like Heracles) be
admitted to the circle of the gods, or (like most others) might not;
in which case they became heroes, with their own forms of cult,
differing from that due to gods. Within fully historical times, mortal men had attained heroic status after death — especially found-
ers of cities and those made equal to them. No doubt this was usually done with the approval of Delphic Apollo, who watched over
religious practice in general and over the founding of cities in particular. Now, this is precisely the kind of well-regulated world that
we find in Callisthenes' speech. Modern Jews and Christians, or
modern rationalists, from their different points of view, have always found it difficult to believe that the ancient Greeks took their
religion seriously, since it seems so patently absurd. Among other
misunderstandings and misinterpretations caused by this attitude,

they have tended, in particular, to deny the existence of the status boundaries set out by Pindar and Callisthenes (among many others), and especially their validity in the fourth century B.C. — the very century which, in the most "enlightened" city in Greece, saw the incidents of Socrates and the Hermias hymn that we have mentioned.

[Badian proceeds with an examination of the evidence for deification of living Greeks before Alexander and concludes:]

It follows that, on careful scrutiny, not one of the instances of deification of a living man alleged in the standard work as coming between that of Lysander and that of Alexander the Great is securely attested. . . .

There is no secure evidence for any exception to Callisthenes' statement regarding deification of living men before Alexander: each of the cases alleged fails to pass the test of the usual criteria of scholarship. We may now proceed to Alexander himself, reasonably assured that our suspicion based on the vast disproportion of the evidence cited has turned out to be correct: that it was indeed his case that set the precedent, that opened the floodgates. It is a revelation that, in view of our knowledge of Alexander's life and career, should in any case not excessively surprise us. But we must now all the more try to gain precision about his own deification. Let us again proceed by looking at the various incidents that have been associated with it by modern scholars. The first of these — although there is in fact not much that can be confidently asserted about it — is the visit to Ammon.

Whether Alexander had some idea of his "divine birth" before the visit — in particular, whether Olympias had already been spreading the story of her intercourse with the serpent, which does seem to go back to her own account — we simply cannot tell: the sources are too bad and not worth discussing at length. Arrian seems to hint at such prior knowledge (3.3.2) in giving Alexander's reasons for visiting the oracle. That passage has been taken far too seriously. It is merely a reflection of his own, interposed in the story, and does not claim to be derived from any source. Since on a point of this kind Arrian's opinion is not worth more than ours, no great care need be devoted to elucidating that opinion where it is (perhaps deliberately) obscure. Nor can we be sure what Alexander was told by the oracle, since — despite Callisthenes' apparent claim that something was known to his companions (Strabo, 17. 1, 43, 814) — it seems fairly clear that no one heard the communication except Alexander himself; and he did not choose to say much about it. So far, most present-day scholars would probably agree.

The chief outcome of the visit was the god's declaration, or confirmation, of Alexander's divine sonship. It is often said that as Pharaoh he would be *ex officio* Ammon's son. Strictly speaking, this assumes not only the identification of the god of Siwah with the Pharaoh's divine father, but Alexander's coronation as Pharaoh before the visit. The former point, Egyptologists will have to decide. As to the latter, none of our sources . . . mentions a coronation at any time. We cannot be sure that he was crowned Pharaoh at all. Naturally, he appears as the rightful king with the proper titles in Egyptian documents; but who would expect him not to? Perhaps the incident is omitted because our Greek sources were embarrassed by it; yet it is odd that Clitarchus, with his love for ceremonial and display, should have failed to pick it up. If he was in fact crowned, it was more probably on his return from Siwah, when he spent a long time at Memphis, rather than on his first short stay there. It adds up to another reason why, in the state of our information, it is inappropriate to devote much discussion to the visit to Ammon.

One or two points related to the visit should, however, be made at this stage. First, the divine sonship was at once confirmed by another oracle and also (we do not know when) by a prophetess, both in Ionia; and this was publicised by Callisthenes. Strabo is explicit, and Plutarch (e.g. Plut. 33.1: the Gaugamela prayer) confirms that the sonship was at least part of the official image, as propounded by Callisthenes. Ammon had long been identified with Zeus, as most scholars have recognised. Hence the content of the Ionian revelations, making Alexander a son of Zeus, coincided with that of Ammon's. . . .

Another coincidence must be noted. The oracle at Branchidae had been mute since Xerxes' day (perhaps, more accurately, since Darius' destruction of Miletus) until it was reactivated for precisely this prophecy and others related to it. Similarly, there had been no sibyl prophesying at Erythrae for a long time (perhaps the same length of time), until a priestess who was *not* a sibyl now received a similar inspiration. The conclusion that both were stimulated to prophesy for Alexander's benefit and (as is almost an inevitable conclusion for Branchidae) inspired precisely by Ammon's relevation is almost inevitable. Taeger long ago saw it. Once discovered, the divine sonship of Alexander had to be hammered home. . . .

There can be no doubt that Alexander was deeply moved by Ammon's revelation. It must be added that the god came to mean more and more to him in the course of his campaign. We are entitled to deduce that, at least in general terms, what Ammon had prophesied in that secret consultation was gradually fulfilled before the King's eyes. The most striking evidence of his attachment to Ammon was to come just before the end of his life, when Ammon denied his request that the dead Hephaestion be given divine honours and Alexander dutifully scaled the honours down to heroic, much against his own deepest feelings. And there is at least a good chance that Alexander's reported request that he be buried in the great oasis (Curt. 10.5.4) is good tradition. Rationalist historians will have to come to terms with the mystical element in Alexander.

We shall have to return to Ammon, at least briefly. For the moment, let us move on to *proskynesis*, which has already, by necessary anticipation, engaged our attention. It was early in 327 that Alexander tried to introduce that court custom and to make it a regular part of his official protocol. The sources leave no doubt that the idea was his own, though the staging was naturally left to his friends, chiefly (it seems) Hephaestion. There has been much debate on the actual nature of the ceremony: did it consist in merely blowing a kiss or did it involve more, e.g., prostration? Fortunately, this does not greatly concern us. What concerns us here is the interpretation; and whatever the nature of the ceremony, this is no less debated. Among the usual attempts at scholarly originality, two points of fairly general agreement may perhaps be picked out, though I know that even here there are exceptions. First, that *proskynesis* was mandatory before the King of Persia; secondly, that Greeks regarded it as confined to divine cult. Most scholars would add that there was no implication of divinity in the Persian ceremony: indeed, though the King of Persia was hedged with it as few rulers have been, neither what we know of Iranian religion nor the explicit language of the royal Achaemenid documents leaves any room for a divine king. I shall henceforth take all these points for granted.

On the actual events at Bactra we have two different accounts, both (it seems) known to all our main literary sources. These sources, in fact, show remarkable agreement, at least in outline. The first . . . is a story based on Chares, the Court Chamberlain. . . . In fact, Chares' story is quite unsophisticated — it is (we may say) *deceptively* simple. At a banquet arranged for the purpose of introducing the ceremonial, each of the guests received the cup from Alexander, stood up by the hearth, drank his wine and performed *proskynesis*. He then received a kiss from Alexander (he may also have given the King one — the versions vary) and returned to lie down on his dining-couch. When Callisthenes' turn came, he went through the routine without performing the *proskynesis*. Alexander was talking to Hephaestion and did not notice (whether in fact or from policy we are left to guess); but a busybody among the courtiers drew his attention to the omission, forcing him to treat it seriously. He then declined the kiss. Callisthenes left, with the remark that he had merely lost a kiss.

Chares was in a position to know the facts, on this as on other events at the court. The question is whether he told them. Even in the few fragments we have, he appears far from truthful and reliable: thus he reports that at Issus Alexander personally wounded Darius. Worse still, he not only flatters the king in this positive way, but he tries to make excuses for him (he is, in the true sense, an apologist), and he appears to be hostile to Callisthenes. The story of Callisthenes' end will illustrate both features. Ptolemy reports, matter-of-factly, that Callisthenes was guilty of instigating some page-boys to plot against the king, was denounced, and was executed after torture. He naturally assumes his guilt, as he does that of Philotas, and sees no reason to disguise the punishment (Arr. 4.14.1–3). Chares, however, says that Callisthenes was merely imprisoned, to be tried in due course by the Council of the Hellenic League, and that after seven months he died a natural death, of lice and disease. Here too Chares must have known the facts. That he did not choose to tell them is shown not only by Ptolemy's version (and on a matter of such importance and general interest Ptolemy cannot have been wrong — he might have lied in order to whitewash the king, but it is clear that it never occurred to him that the king needed whitewashing); even if we did not have this, the story as such would be suspect. First, Callisthenes could easily have been sent to Greece for trial, under guard. He had no connection with the army, and it was most unlikely that he would be able to escape, let alone start a rebellion. Secondly, we do not know that the Council of the League had any business acting as a court to judge high treason: it had certainly shown in the case of Sparta after Agis' War that it had no intention of exercising any relevant powers it might have theoretically had.

Chares' *proskynesis* story, as far as Callisthenes' part is concerned, cannot be as lightly believed as it usually has been. Note that there is no open opposition: Callisthenes becomes involved by chance. Nor was Alexander eager to punish: he either did not or would not see the omission until he was forced to act — and then he behaved with exemplary moderation, and it was Callisthenes who made the provocative remark. How, then, did he later come to be accused (and, we must think, executed) on a charge that can be proved to have been trumped up? How did he come to acquire the reputation of the steadfast opponent, who prevented the introduction of this humiliating practice for Greeks and Macedonians? The reputation of a martyr may always be exaggerated. But if Chares' story is true, we must assume it pure fiction; which, where so many people knew, is difficult. The execution, soon after, tells its own story. He cannot have merely omitted a gesture he personally disliked, in the hope that the omission would not be noticed; nor is Alexander's reaction likely to have been so unusually moderate. Chares does not even say that the practice was dropped. (Or if he does, our sources do not report it.) The point of his story was — perhaps in opposition to the version that may already have been circulating in Alexander's lifetime, well before Chares wrote — to *trivialise* Callisthenes' action and to exculpate the king.

Proskynesis — the events at Bactra and the literary garb in which they have reached us — must remain much more of a puzzle than has generally been allowed. The set debate on deification, which the ancients seem, at least some centuries later, to have accepted as the true account, obviously cannot be as readily accepted by modern scholars. It reads too much like a pamphlet. Moreover, Anaxarchus' part seems lightly sketched in, merely to provide a target, as in a Platonic dialogue. On the other hand, that Ptolemy and Aristobulus (if we may judge by the fact that Arrian uses a *logos*) wholly omitted the affair serves, if anything, to underline its importance: their bias and their techniques are well known. We must therefore take it that Callisthenes did speak out in opposition: that much, surely, ought to be believed, even if we reject the set debate. His refusal to perform the ceremony cannot have been as clandestine, or its discovery as accidental, as Chares tries to make us believe. That is perhaps all we can hope to know about the actual occasion.

However, the last part of the main version, once the speeches are done, is worth taking seriously: certainly, Chares does not contradict it. When various Persian nobles went on to perform the act, one of them looked so funny doing it that Leonnatus, one of the senior Macedonian officers and a friend of Alexander's, burst out laughing. Alexander, we are told, was angry at Leonnatus, though he later forgave him. I have pointed out that Leonnatus, although prominent in the fighting, did not advance as quickly to the highest command as the other five men who had assisted the king in the action against Philotas, and that his behaviour on this occasion must be thought to explain it. We may conjecture that it was perhaps only after his laughter revealed the Macedonians' opinion of the whole matter (and not, as the sources have it, after the great debate and Callisthenes' opposition) that Alexander realised that *proskynesis* for Macedonians was a lost cause — and that, in that case, there was no point in forcing it on the Greeks, even though they could not defend themselves. Inevitably, the effect was ascribed by Greek tradition to Callisthenes' philosophical arguments, not to Leonnatus' realistic demonstration.

The least we must accept from the tradition is that Callisthenes reminded Alexander — who surely did not need reminding — that *proskynesis*, for Greeks, implied deification, and that this would be thought offensive to at least *some* Greek sentiment. It will not do to claim, as has often been attempted, that all the king wanted to do was to unify court ceremonial: that he was surprised to find a purely technical reform so sadly misinterpreted. That the Greeks regarded the act as pertaining to cult cannot have been unknown to one brought up in the Greek tradition. . . .

Uniformity of ceremonial would obviously be an advantage —

though, as it turned out, Alexander continued to manage well enough without it. Moreover, as he grew into his role of Great King, he must have found the simplicity of "Homeric" kingship irksome. Since he well knew Greek attitudes, the least we must assert is that, if Greeks and Macedonians were to consider the gesture he demanded an act of worship, he did not find the prospect displeasing. His anger at Callisthenes, and (less fatally) at Leonnatus, was not over a mere failure to simplify court ceremonial.

Callisthenes deserves a final word. He, of course, had spread the story that Alexander was the son of Zeus. He can hardly have literally believed it. It must be seen as an allegory, a noble lie — a myth to make Alexander more acceptable to the Greeks, as well (of course) as an attempt to please the king himself by turning him into a fully Homeric hero. Objection to *proskynesis*, on the premiss we have been examining, was by no means inconsistent with this, as critics from Timaeus to Tarn have charged. Divine sonship was precedented and was fully acceptable: it did not, during a man's lifetime, confer even heroic status, let alone divine. Indeed, the worship of a Great King that (as Callisthenes interpreted it) he was now asked to accept implied the total extinction of what his myth had meant to convey — so far from (as critics have alleged) being merely another step in the same direction. The noble lie is a reprehensible device at best: one of many by which, in all ages, an élite has tried to control those it considered its inferiors. Let no one acquit Callisthenes of this. But he also has a right to be properly understood within the context of his age; and he deserves credit for opposition with the risk of martyrdom, of which Chares tried to deprive him.

In the autumn of 324 there began a protracted debate in Athens on whether Alexander should be declared a god. A decree to that effect was introduced by [the orator] Demades, and much opposition is attested. Demosthenes, at first opposed, finally changed his mind and was never forgiven for this grudging conversion by more inflexible men like Hyperides. The debate took place against a major political crisis: Athens was hard hit by Alexander's order to restore all exiles, if (as seemed likely) this was interpreted as restoring Samos to the Samians, who had been expelled from the island a generation earlier for the benefit of Athenian colonists. Negotiations with Alexander were in progress, and Demades at one point reminded the Athenians that in their concern over heaven they were likely to lose the earth.

This must have been the consideration that convinced Demosthenes, and (it seems) most Athenians. The arrival and escape of Harpalus added immense complications: the atmosphere of crisis and suspicion can hardly be exaggerated. At some time after Hephaestion's death (perhaps October 324), heroic honours for him were accepted at Athens — we cannot be quite sure whether as an obvious consequence of making Alexander a god or as a less repulsive substitute. I personally agree with those who, like Habicht, believe that a cult of Alexander was in fact instituted. Obviously, it did not survive long enough to leave any traces we could expect to recognise.

The debate is amply attested. All we hear shows that it moved on a religious as well as on a purely political plane. It was sacrilege that a man like [the Athenian orator] Lycurgus (possibly even Hyperides) was concerned about. For Sparta, there is only the famous aphorism reported by Plutarch: "Since Alexander wishes to be a god, let him be a god." That, plus the story of events in Athens, is all the direct evidence we have for the discussion of Alexander's deification in Greece. But an order to all the Greeks, demanding worship as a god, has been construed out of this and other material, sometimes embroidered by irrelevant matter. It centres, however, on one passage in Arrian, which must be scrutinised in detail.

In the spring of 323 (Arr. 7.23.2) envoys (*presbeis*) from Greek cities in Europe came to Alexander, wearing wreaths and offering him golden crowns. Arrian says of them that they came "as if on a sacred embassy," to honour a god, although the king's end was in fact at hand. The question is: were they *really theoroi* [sacred envoys] or did they come *as though* they were *theoroi*, although in fact they were not. . . . It seems to me that we ought to read the passage as the arrival of embassies from Greece, whose members were so fulsome in the honours they bestowed and in the way in which they bestowed them that (Arrian ironically observes) *you might have thought* they were *theoroi*. And that, he goes on, for a god whose death was in fact imminent. I do not think the passage implies anything about a cult of Alexander in cities in Greece (not, of course, that it implies its absence any more than its presence) and that Arrian has made it fairly clear, by his usual careful choice of words, that he is here ridiculing those who encourage the divine pretensions of mortals.

It follows, if this is accepted, that the passage remains irrelevant to any presumed order to the Greek cities to deify Alexander; what is more, that there is then no evidence for any such positive request. No source mentions or implies any such request, let alone order, nor its execution. That theory (we must remember) was chiefly developed in order to fill a need felt by some modern scholars. It could be used (as by Eduard Meyer and by Tarn) to "explain" Alexander's very real, and amply attested, order to the cities to receive their exiles back. Deification could be said to provide the legal basis for the order, which was patently contrary to the oaths of the Hellenic League. In other words, it could be argued that Alexander used sacrilege to mask perjury. As so often, Alexander's apologists did him no service. His real faults were at least heroic, not those of a shady lawyer. But that theory is in any case stone-dead now, on grounds of chronology no less than of law and of character. For the exiles decree, in our sources, precedes the first mention of deification by several months. . . .

[Following an examination of the archaeological and literary evidence on cults of Alexander in his lifetime, Badian concludes as follows:]

To sum up: in the present state of our evidence we can be fairly sure that there were no cults of Alexander in Asia in the winter of 332–331; and we are not entitled, without positive evidence, to assume that there were any in 327. Only new evidence or a new and irrefutable argument will be able to change these conclusions. It therefore seems necessary, for the present, to assume (for nothing can be firmly proved) that any cults in Asia instituted during Alexander's lifetime began in approximately the last four years of his life.

It is not the purpose of this study to speculate on Alexander's psychology: to argue about *why* he wanted to be worshipped as a god or *why* he considered himself a god. However, we must conclude by stressing that he did so. This has often been denied by "rationalist" historians, who assume (in Peter Green's words) that men "of whom they approved were reasonable in the same way as themselves." The attempts of that class are on record in the pages of Tarn and Kraft, to mention no others. They have often been refuted, yet they are unlikely to cease, as long as historians still adopt these naive and anachronistic attitudes. It is of some interest to note that similar attempts may have been made by "defenders" of Alexander in antiquity. Let us look at a well-known anecdote.

Aristobulus reports that Dioxippus, a well-known Athenian athlete and Olympic victor who was for a time a member of Alexander's court, quoted a line of Homer meant to imply that Alexander's blood was divine *ichor* [blood]. Whether it was flattery or irony we cannot tell, for Dioxippus, long a court favourite, finally got into trouble and ended by committing suicide. The way in which the report is quoted suggests that it may belong to the first period of his life at court and was a piece of flattery. But we also have another version of the story, which we find in Plutarch (Plut. 28) and other sources. . . . In that version, Alexander himself quotes the line, ironically, when he was bleeding from a wound; and he quotes it in a negative form: his blood was blood and not *ichor*. There can be no doubt which was the original version: Dioxippus is no fictitious or even obscure person. It is difficult to imagine for what purpose this story, centered in a well-known athlete, was stood on its head and the speaker changed to the king himself, unless it was precisely to "acquit" Alexander of the charge that he believed in his own divinity.

Yet the facts seem clear, at least basically, in modern times as they did in ancient. In a careful scholarly discussion of the question whether Athens instituted a cult of Alexander, E. J. Bickerman pointed out that the answers to this and similar questions do not affect what we know of Alexander's desires: what was taken for granted all along, in the debate at Athens, was the *fact* that Alexander intensely wanted to be deified — that his attitude on an important political question like Samos might depend on whether it was done. This obvious fact tells us, with irrefutable contemporary authority, all that really matters. The reported wording of the Spartan statement on the matter ("Since Alexander wishes to be a god, let him be a god") lends further support. And if (admittedly) its authority must be regarded as less, what helps to inspire some confidence in its authenticity is the very fact that there is no mention of an "order" by Alexander — merely of a wish. . . .

We have seen that, at least as early as 327, Alexander wanted to introduce a ceremony that he well knew the Greeks would regard as implying deification, and that his failure to enforce that ceremony rankled. We have also seen that, probably after that date, some Greek cities began to offer cult to Alexander. It is an obvious suggestion (at present it cannot be more) that that strange and (at least to some) unacceptable idea was born out of those very events at Bactra.

Let us end with another suggestion that, from the nature of our evidence, can again be no more than that. I think, however, that it can be advanced with a high degree of plausibility.

We have noted that Alexander seems to have been increasingly impressed by the secret revelations he had received from Ammon in his oasis. Some ancient writers, inevitably, tried to guess what he had been told: most obviously, a prophecy of universal dominion was asserted. His retreat from India and his decision to give up part of his conquests there did not affect his faith in Ammon, and that makes this particular guess unlikely. Invincibility is a more likely part of the revelation: no doubt Alexander always continued to feel that this had been fulfilled. But there is another question that is surely intriguing.

When his dearest friend Hephaestion died, Alexander conscientiously sent an embassy to Ammon to ask what posthumous honours he might legitimately bestow upon him; and he as conscientiously obeyed the response, even though it permitted much less than he had hoped and desired. How, then, is it that Alexander seems to have accepted, indeed wished for, divine cult in his lifetime without ever asking Ammon for permission? Surely that was a far graver infraction of precedent (and, even if the argument of this paper be wholly rejected, at least a far more serious matter) than whatever posthumous honours he had planned for his friend. I can see only one answer. The permission was unnecessary. Among the mysteries communicated to Alexander by his divine "father" at Siwah there must have been an explicit promise that (at whatever time and in whatever form) he would become a god in his lifetime.

A sixteenth-century Persian miniature portraying Alexander as a contemporary horseman. Alexander's fables became an integral and permanent part of local traditions in Iran and other parts of his empire. (The Granger Collection)

PART

VIII The Policy of Integration

Arrian

The Susa Marriages and the Opis Mutiny

Alexander's role as king of both Macedonia and the Persian Empire could create conflicting demands and expectations, especially because the conqueror claimed to be the heir of the Achaemenid dynasty that he had replaced. To what extent did Alexander remain a Macedonian conqueror, and what did he need to do to become an effective and legitimate king of Asia? The king and the Macedonians had different perceptions of the relationship between conqueror and conquered, a fact that opened a rift between them, especially in the last years of Alexander's reign.

In early 324, Alexander presided over a wedding ceremony in Susa

Reprinted by permission of the publishers and the Loeb Classical Library from Arrian: *History of Alexander*, 7.4–6, 8–12, vol. 2, translated by Peter A. Brunt, Cambridge, Mass.: Harvard University Press, 1983.

between the conquering and conquered elites. Arrian describes the elaborate celebrations that were intended to formalize the links between Macedonians and Persians. He then reports the measures that the king took to incorporate Iranians into his army and administration and the Macedonians' reactions to these steps. In the summer of that year, at Opis in Mesopotamia, Alexander proclaimed his intention to discharge veteran Macedonians from service and send them home. The announcement sparked a mutiny, which Arrian describes, in which resistance to Alexander's policy toward the subject population played a major part.

He [Alexander] also held weddings at Susa for himself and for the Companions; he himself married Darius' eldest daughter Barsine, and, as Aristobulus says, another wife as well, Parysatis, the youngest daughter of Ochus. He had already taken to wife Roxane, the daughter of Oxyartes the Bactrian. To Hephaestion he gave Drypetis, another daughter of Darius, sister to his own wife (for he desired Hephaestion's children to be cousins to his own); to Craterus, Amastrine daughter of Oxyartes, Darius' brother; to Perdiccas, a daughter of Atropates, satrap [governor] of Media; to Ptolemy the bodyguard and Eumenes the royal secretary, the daughters of Artabazus, Artacama and Artonis respectively; to Nearchus the daughter of Barsine and Mentor; to Seleucus the daughter of Spitamenes the Bactrian, and similarly to the other Companions the noblest daughters of Persians and Medes, numbering about eighty. These weddings were solemnized in the Persian style; chairs were placed for the bridegrooms in order, then, after the healths had been drunk, the brides came in and each sat down by the side of her bridegroom, and the men took them by the hand and kissed them, the king setting the example, for all the weddings took place together. None of Alexander's actions was thought to show more affability and comradeship. After receiving his bride each bridegroom led her home. Alexander gave them all dowries. All other Macedonians who had married Asian women had their names registered by Alexander's orders; they proved to be more than ten thousand, and Alexander gave them too wedding gifts.

He thought this a convenient moment to discharge all the

debts any of his soldiers had incurred and ordered each man to register what he owed, on the basis that they would receive the money. At first only a few registered their names in the fear that Alexander had merely tried an experiment, to see which soldiers had not lived on their pay and which had been extravagant; but when he was informed that most were not registering their names but concealing any bonds, he reproved the troops for not trusting him; the king, he said, must always speak the truth to his subjects, and none of the subjects must ever suppose that the king speaks anything but the truth. He set up tables in the camp with gold on them and instructed the persons who were to administer the grants to discharge the debts to all who produced a bond, without any further registration of names. As a result they actually came to believe that Alexander was speaking the truth, and they were more gratified by the concealment of their names than by the extinction of the debts. This grant to the army is said to have amounted to twenty thousand Talents. . . .

[Alexander] was also joined by the satraps from the new cities he had founded, and the other land he had conquered, bringing about thirty thousand boys now growing up, all of the same age, whom Alexander called Epigoni (Successors), dressed in Macedonian dress and trained to warfare in the Macedonian style. It is said that their arrival aggrieved the Macedonians, as if Alexander was actually contriving every means of reducing his dependence on Macedonians in future, that in fact they were greatly pained to see Alexander wearing the Median dress, while the marriages celebrated in the Persian style did not correspond to the desires of most of them, including even some of the bridegrooms, despite the great honour of being raised to equality with the king. They were also aggrieved at the adoption by Peucestas, satrap of Persia, of the Persian apparel and language because Alexander approved of him going barbarian; at the incorporation of the Bactrian, Sogdianian, Arachotian, Zarangian, Areian and Parthyaean cavalrymen and of the Persian troopers called Euacae in the Companion cavalry, in so far as they seemed to be specially distinguished by rank, physical beauty or any other good quality; at the addition to these of a fifth hipparchy [calvary unit], though it was not entirely barbarian, but when the whole cavalry force had been augmented, barbarians had been enrolled for the purpose; at the further enrolment in the *agema* [royal guard] of Cophen, son of Artabazus, Hydarnes and Artiboles, sons of Mazaeus, Sisines and Phradasmenes, sons of Phrataphernes, satrap of Parthyaea and Hyrcania, Itanes, son of Oxyartes and brother of Alexander's wife, Roxane, and Aegobares and his brother, Mithrobaeus, at the appointment of Hystaspes the Bactrian as their commander, and at the issue to them of Macedonian lances in place of barbarian thonged javelins. All this aggrieved the Macedonians, as they thought that Alexander was going utterly barbarian at heart, and treating Macedonian customs and Macedonians themselves without respect. . . .

On reaching Opis, [Alexander] summoned his Macedonians and announced that he was discharging from the army and sending home men unfit for active service because of old age or physical disability. He would give those who remained with him enough to make them objects of envy to those at home, and stir up the rest of the Macedonians to readiness for sharing the same dangers and hardships. Alexander said this, no doubt, to show his favour to the Macedonians. But they supposed that they were by now objects of his contempt and that he thought them wholly useless in his wars; they were, not without reason, aggrieved once more by the speech he had delivered. In the whole of their expedition they had had many sources of discontent; on many previous occasions they had been vexed by his Persian dress, which suggested the same thing, by the equipment of the barbarian Epigoni in Macedonian style and the introduction of foreign horsemen in the ranks of the Companions. Consequently, they did not endure in silence, but called on him to discharge them all from the army, and to campaign himself in company with his father, referring in mockery to Ammon. Hearing this Alexander, who had become by this time quicker-tempered and, courted as he now was in the barbarian manner, had ceased to be so kindly as in old times to the Macedonians, leapt down from the platform with the officers round him and ordered them to arrest the most conspicuous of the popular agitators, personally pointing out to the hypaspists [elite infantry] with his finger whom they were to arrest; they numbered about thirteen. He ordered them to be led away to execution but, as the others were stunned and remained in dead silence, he remounted the platform and spoke. . . .

[Alexander charges the Macedonians with ingratitude in view of the services rendered to them by his father and especially by himself. He argues that they are the major beneficiaries of the empire and concludes by stating the following:]

"And now it was my intention to send away only men unfit for war, to be the envy of those at home but, as you all desire to go, let all of you begone, return to your homes and report that your king, Alexander, defeated Persians, Medes . . . and that when you returned to Susa you deserted him and went off, handing him over to the protection of the barbarians he had conquered. This is a report that will perhaps win you a fine reputation with men and will doubtless be holy in the sight of heaven. Begone!"

After his speech he leapt down swiftly from his platform and, passing into the palace, paid no attention to his bodily needs, and was not seen by any of the Companions, not even on the following day. But on the third day he summoned inside the picked men among the Persians and divided the commands of the battalions among them and restricted the right to kiss him to those he declared his kinsmen. The Macedonians had been immediately stunned by his speech, and stayed in silence there by the platform, none following the king when he left except for the attendant Companions and bodyguards; but the mass, though they stayed behind, had nothing to say and yet were unwilling to depart. But when they heard about the Persians and the Medes, and the commands given to the Persians, and the Oriental force being drafted into the units, and the Macedonian names — an *agema* called Persian, and Persian "foot-companions," and *astheteroi* [royal guard] too, and a Persian battalion of "silver-shields," and the cavalry of the Companions which now included a new royal *agema* — they could no longer contain themselves, but all ran together to the palace and, throwing down their arms there before the doors as signs of supplication to the king, they themselves stood shouting before the doors begging to be let in. They said they would give up the instigators of the late disturbance and those who began the clamour; they would depart from the doors neither by day nor by night unless Alexander would have some pity on them.

When this was reported to Alexander, he quickly came out, and seeing them so humble, and hearing most of them lamenting loudly, he too shed tears. He came forward as if to say something, while they stayed there in supplication. One of them called Callines, a man distinguished by age and hipparchy in the Companions' cavalry, said something like this: "What grieves the Macedonians, Sire, is that you have now made some of the Persians your kinsmen and that Persians are called 'Alexander's kinsmen,' and permitted to kiss you, but no Macedonian has yet enjoyed this privilege." On this Alexander broke in: "But I regard all of you as my kinsmen, and from this time forth I shall give you that name." When he had said this, Callines approached and kissed him, and so did any other who wished. So they took up their arms again and returned to the camp shouting and singing their victory song. On this Alexander sacrificed to the gods to whom it was his custom to sacrifice, and gave a public banquet, seated all the Macedonians round him, and next to them Persians, and then any persons from the other peoples who took precedence for rank or any other high quality, and he himself and those around him drank from the same bowl and poured the same libations, with the Greek soothsayers and Magi initiating the ceremony. Alexander prayed for various blessings and especially that the Macedonians and Persians should enjoy harmony as partners in the government. The story prevails that those who shared the banquet were nine thousand, and that they all poured the same libation and gave the one victory cry as they did so.

And now such of the Macedonians as were unfit for service from old age or any other circumstance were ready to leave him; they numbered about ten thousand. Alexander gave them the pay due not only for the time already served but also for that of their journey home; in addition he also gave each man a gratuity of a Talent. If they had children by Asian wives, he ordered them to leave them behind with him, and not take home to Macedonia a source of conflict between foreigners and children of foreign wives and the children and mothers they had left behind them; he promised personally to see that they were brought up in the Macedonian way, particularly in military training; when they were grown to manhood, he would take them back himself to Macedonia and hand them over to their fathers. While making these vague and uncertain promises to them at their departure, he also thought fit to give them the most solid proof of his love and affection for them by sending with them Craterus, his most loyal follower, whom he loved as dearly as his own life, to protect and lead them on their march. So then having bidden them all farewell, with tears in his eyes, and tears in theirs, he dismissed them. Craterus was not only appointed to be their leader but, after conducting them back, he was to take charge of Macedonia, Thrace, Thessaly and the freedom of the Greeks, while Antipater was to bring drafts of Macedonians of full age to replace the men being sent home. He also despatched Polyperchon with Craterus, as the officer next in seniority to Craterus, so that in case of harm coming to Craterus on the way, since he was an invalid when sent off, they should not want a general on their route. . . .

Plutarch

The Mixing of Greeks and Barbarians

Plutarch states in a rhetorical composition that Alexander wished to mix Persians and Macedonians together in a bowl of love. Historians who claim that Alexander intended to unite Persians and Macedonians often repeat this metaphor.

Moreover, the much-admired *Republic* of Zeno, the founder of the Stoic sect, may be summed up in this one main principle: that all the inhabitants of this world of ours should not live differentiated by their respective rules of justice into separate cities and communities, but that we should consider all men to be of one community and one polity, and that we should have a common life and an

Reprinted by permission of the publishers and the Loeb Classical Library from Plutarch: *Moralia*, 329A–D, vol. 4, trans. by F. C. Babbitt, Cambridge, Mass.: Harvard University Press, 1972.

order common to us all, even as a herd that feeds together and shares the pasturage of a common field. This Zeno wrote, giving shape to a dream or, as it were, shadowy picture of a well-ordered and philosophic commonwealth; but it was Alexander who gave effect to the idea. For Alexander did not follow Aristotle's advice to treat the Greeks as if he were their leader, and other peoples as if he were their master; to have regard for the Greeks as for friends and kindred, but to conduct himself toward other peoples as though they were plants or animals; for to do so would have been to cumber his leadership with numerous battles and banishments and festering seditions. But, as he believed that he came as a heaven-sent governor to all, and as a mediator for the whole world, those whom he could not persuade to unite with him, he conquered by force of arms, and he brought together into one body all men everywhere, uniting and mixing in one great loving-cup, as it were, men's lives, their characters, their marriages, their very habits of life. He bade them all consider as their fatherland the whole inhabited earth, as their stronghold and protection his camp, as akin to them all good men, and as foreigners only the wicked; they should not distinguish between Grecian and foreigner by Grecian cloak and targe, or scimitar and jacket; but the distinguishing mark of the Grecian should be seen in virtue, and that of the foreigner in iniquity; clothing and food, marriage and manner of life they should regard as common to all, being blended into one by ties of blood and children. . . .

William W. Tarn

Alexander the Dreamer

Tarn's works (see Borza in Part I) include *Hellenistic Military and Naval Developments* (Cambridge University Press, 1930). In Tarn's

From William W. Tarn, *Alexander the Great,* Beacon Press, 1956 (reprint of University of Cambridge, 1948; Boston, 1956), pp. 115–117, 145–148. Reprinted with permission of Cambridge University Press.

view, Alexander was a visionary, picturing a world in which, under the king's fatherly guidance, occupier and occupied would be equal.

It was soon afterwards, at Opis, that the discontent in the army came to a head. Alexander was not trying to oust the Macedonians from their ancestral partnership with him, but they thought he was; he only wished to take it up into something larger, but they distrusted the changes entailed by a new world, and especially his Persian policy. The occasion was his proposal to send home with Craterus any veterans past service. The Macedonians took this to mean that he intended to transfer the seat of power from Macedonia to Asia, and the whole army except his Guard, the *agēma* [royal guard] of the hypaspists [elite infantry], broke into open mutiny; all demanded to go home, and told him to go and campaign with his father Ammon. Alexander's temper rose; after ordering his Guard to arrest the ringleaders, he passionately harangued the troops, and ended by dismissing the whole army from his service. . . . [Later, however,] the reconciliation was complete. Those veterans who desired (10,000) were then sent home with large presents under Craterus' leadership.

But before they went, Alexander's reconciliation with the army had been followed by a greater reconciliation. He made a vast banquet — traditionally there were 9,000 guests — to celebrate the conclusion of peace; at his own table there sat Macedonians and Persians, the two protagonists in the great war, together with representatives of every race in his Empire and also Greeks, who were part of his world though not under his rule. The feast ended, all at his table drew wine for the libation from a huge silver crater which had once belonged to Darius, the crater which Eratosthenes [a third century B.C.E. scholar] or his informant was to figure as a loving-cup of the nations, and the whole 9,000 made libation together at the sound of a trumpet, as was Macedonian custom, the libation being led by Greek seers and Iranian Magi. The libation led up to, and was followed by, Alexander's prayer, in which the ceremony culminated. A few words of summary, and a brief allusion, are all that have reached us; but he prayed for peace, and that Macedonians and Persians and all the peoples of his Empire might be alike partners in the commonwealth (i.e. not merely subjects), and that the peoples of the world he knew might live together in harmony and in unity of heart and mind — that *Homonoia* [concord] which for centuries the world was to long for but never to reach. He had previously said that all men were sons of one Father, and his prayer was the expression of his recorded belief that he had a mission from God to be the Reconciler of the World. Though none present could foresee it, that prayer was to be the crown of his career; he did not live to try to carry it out. . . .

The real impress that he left on the world was far different; for, whatever else he was, he was one of the supreme fertilising forces of history. He lifted the civilised world out of one groove and set it in another; he started a new epoch; nothing could again be as it had been. He greatly enlarged the bounds of knowledge and of human endeavour, and gave to Greek science and Greek civilisation a scope and an opportunity such as they had never yet possessed. Particularism was replaced by the idea of the "inhabited world," the common possession of civilised men; trade and commerce were internationalised, and the "inhabited world" bound together by a network both of new routes and cities, and of common interests. Greek culture, heretofore practically confined to Greeks, spread throughout that world; and for the use of its inhabitants, in place of the many dialects of Greece, there grew up the form of Greek known as the *koinē*, the "common speech." The Greece that taught Rome was the Hellenistic world which Alexander made; the old Greece counted for little till modern scholars re-created Periclean Athens. So far as the modern world derives its civilisation from Greece, it largely owes it to Alexander that it had the opportunity. If he could not fuse races, he transcended the national State; and to transcend national States meant to transcend national cults; men came to feel after the unity which must lie beneath the various religions. Outwardly, this unity was ultimately satisfied in the official worship of the Roman Emperor, which derived from the worship of Alexander after his death; but beside this external form there grew up in men's hearts the longing for a true spiritual unity. And it was Alexander who created the medium in which the idea, when it came, was to spread. For it was due to him that Greek civilisation penetrated western Asia; and even if much of the actual work was done by his successors, he broke the path; without him they would not have been. Consequently, when at last Christianity showed the way to that spiritual unity after which men were feeling, there was ready to hand a medium for the new religion to spread in, the common Hellenistic civilisation of the "inhabited world"; without that, the conquests made by Christianity might have been as slow and difficult as they became when the bounds of that common civilisation were overpassed.

But if the things he did were great, one thing he dreamt was greater. We may put it that he found the Ideal State of Aristotle, and substituted the Ideal State of [the Greek Stoic philosopher] Zeno. It was not merely that he overthrew the narrow restraints of the former, and, in place of limiting men by their opportunity, created opportunities adequate for men in a world where none need be a pauper and restrictions on population were meaningless. Aristotle's State had still cared nothing for humanity outside its own borders; the stranger must still be a serf or an enemy. Alexander changed all that. When he declared that all men were alike sons of one Father, and when at Opis he prayed that Macedonians and Persians might be partners in the commonwealth and that the peoples of his world might live in harmony and in unity of heart and mind, he proclaimed for the first time the unity and brotherhood of mankind. Perhaps he gave no thought to the slave world — we do not know; but he, first of all men, was ready to transcend national differences, and to declare, as St. Paul was to declare, that there was neither Greek nor barbarian. And the impulse of this mighty revelation was continued by men who did give some thought to the slave world; for Zeno, who treated his slave as himself, and [the Roman Stoic philosopher] Seneca, who called himself the fellow-slave of his slaves, would (though Alexander might not) have understood St. Paul when he added "there is neither bond nor free." Before Alexander, men's dreams of the ideal state had still been based on class-rule and slavery; but after him comes [the utopian] Iambulus' great Sun-State, founded on brotherhood and the dignity of free labour. Above all, Alexander inspired Zeno's vision of a world in which all men should be members one of another, citizens of one State without distinction of race or institutions, subject only to and in harmony with the Common Law immanent in the Universe, and united in one social life not by compulsion but only by their own willing consent, or (as he put it) by Love. The splendour of this hopeless dream may remind us that not one but two of the great lines of social-political thought which until recently divided the world go back to Alexander of Macedon. For if, as many believe, there was a line of descent from his claim to divinity, through Roman Emperor and medieval Pope, to the great despotisms of yesterday, despotisms "by the grace of God," there is certainly a line of descent from his prayer at Opis, through the Stoics and one portion of the Christian ideal, to that brotherhood of all men which was proclaimed, though only proclaimed, in the French Revolution. The torch Alexander lit for long only smouldered; perhaps it still only smoulders today; but it never has been, and never can be, quite put out.

A. B. Bosworth

Alexander and the Iranians

In the selection below, Bosworth differs sharply from Tarn in his assessment of the sincerity and historicity of the vision of Alexander as an advocate of unity of humankind. Instead, he examines the actual and symbolic manifestations of Alexander's policy toward the Iranians and concludes that the king planned to retain the preferred status of the Macedonians in his empire.

The last two decades have seen a welcome erosion of traditional dogmas of Alexander scholarship, and a number of hallowed theories, raised on a cushion of metaphysical speculation above the mundane historical evidence, have succumbed to attacks based on

"Alexander and the Iranians" by A. B. Bosworth from *Journal of Hellenic Studies* 100 (1980), pp. 1–20. Copyright © 1980, Society for the Promotion of Hellenic Studies. Reprinted with permission of the author and the publisher.

rigorous logic and source analysis. The brotherhood of man as a vision of Alexander is dead, as is (one hopes) the idea that all Alexander sources can be divided into sheep and goats, the one based on extracts from the archives and the other mere rhetorical fantasy. One notable theory, however, still flourishes and has indeed been described as one of the few certainties among Alexander's aims. This is the so-called policy of fusion. As so often, the idea and terminology go back to J. G. Droysen, who hailed Alexander's marriage to Roxane as a symbol of the fusion (*Verschmelzung*) of Europe and Asia, which (he claimed) the king recognised as the consequence of his victory. At Susa the fusion of east and west was complete and Alexander, as interpreted by Droysen, saw in that fusion the guarantee of the strength and stability of his empire. Once enunciated, Droysen's formulation passed down the mainstream of German historiography, to Kaerst, Wilcken, Berve and Schachermeyr, and has penetrated to almost all arteries of Alexander scholarship. Like the figure of Alexander himself the theory is flexible and capable of strange metamorphoses. In the hands of Tarn it developed into the idea of all subjects, Greek and barbarian, living together in unity and concord in a universal empire of peace. The polar opposite is an essay of Helmut Berve, written in the heady days before the Second World War, in which he claimed that Alexander, with commendable respect for Aryan supremacy, planned a blending of the Macedonian and Persian peoples, so that the two racially related (!) *Herrenvölker* [master races] would lord it over the rest of the world empire. On Berve's interpretation the policy had two stages. Alexander first recognised the merits of the Iranian peoples and placed them alongside the Macedonians in his court and army hierarchy. Next came the *"Blutvermischung"* [mixing of blood], the integration of the two peoples by marriage.

Most scholars have tacitly accepted Berve's definition and take it as axiomatic that Alexander did recognise the merits of the Iranians and did try to integrate them with the Macedonians. The extent of the fusion is disputed, some confining it to the two aristocracies, but few have denied that Alexander had a definite policy. The loudest voice crying in the wilderness has been that of Franz Hampl. Hampl has repeatedly emphasised the arbitrary and speculative nature of most discussions of the subject and the absence of concrete evidence in the ancient sources, and he categorically denies the existence of any policy of fusion. The protest is a valuable warning but in itself it is insufficient. The fact that there is no reliable ancient attestation of the policy of fusion does not prove that no such policy existed; it merely makes the case more complex. The attested actions of Alexander may still be explicable only on the assumption that he had some definite policy of integration. This is a viable hypothesis, but it must be tested rigorously. We need to examine precisely what the ancient sources say and not interpolate them with our own interpretations or wishful thinking; and above all the evidence needs to be treated in its historical context, not thrown together haphazardly to buttress some abstract concept which attracts us for sentimental reasons.

There are two passages in the sources that suggest that Alexander had some ideas of fusing together the Macedonians and Persians. Foremost comes the famous prayer of reconciliation after the Opis mutiny (late summer 324). According to Arrian, Alexander held a sacrifice at which all participants, Macedonians, Persians and representatives of other nations, sat around Alexander while he and his entourage poured libations from the same vessel. The king made a prayer whose main burden was "concord and community in empire for Macedonians and Persians." The two concepts, concord and community, are tied together grammatically and contextually. The background of the prayer was mutiny, a mutiny caused in part at least by Macedonian resentment of Persians and crushed by Alexander turning towards his Persians and creating a new court and army structure composed totally of Persians. The stratagem had been entirely successful and the Macedonians capitulated as soon as Alexander began his distribution of army commands to notable Persians. There was certainly Macedonian fear and resentment of the Persians around Alexander and the king played upon these emotions to destroy the mutiny. There was every reason under the circumstances for a ceremony of reconciliation and a prayer for concord. Concord is associated with community in empire, and there is no doubt that Arrian means the sharing of command in Alexander's empire. The terminology is vague and imprecise, as so often with Arrian, but there is no reason to give the prayer a universal significance. Alexander may be referring to the satrapies [Persian provinces] of the empire which had been and were to continue to be governed both by Macedonians and Iranians. There may even be a reference to the army commands recently conferred upon Persians and a covert threat that he would repeat his action if there were further trouble. The prayer and its context are primary evidence for bad blood between Macedonians and Iranians and Alexander's desire to use some at least of both races in the administration of the empire. They do not give any support for a general policy of fusion.

Diodorus is more explicit. In the context of the notorious *hypomnemata*, the alleged last plans of Alexander presented to the Macedonian army by Perdiccas, came a proposal to synoecise cities and transplant populations from Europe to Asia "to bring the continents to common unity and friendly kinship" by means of intermarriage and ties of community. We have here two things, a proposal to found cities and transplant populations, and an interpretation of that proposal. The interpretation is unlikely to have been embodied in the original plans submitted by Perdiccas, and like the puerile note a few sentences later (that the Pyramids were accounted among the Seven Wonders) it is most probably a comment either by Diodorus or his source. Now there is little or no evidence that Diodorus had a personal interest in Alexander as an apostle of international unity and the overwhelming probability is that the comment comes from his immediate source, Hieronymus of Cardia. Hieronymus was a contemporary of Alexander but his history was written towards the end of his prodigiously long life and covered events at least to 272. His recollections of Alexander were now distant and his views of the king's motives perhaps affected by fifty years of experience and reflection. He may have considered that Alexander's shifts of population were designed to bring about greater community between races, but nothing suggests that Alexander shared his views. What is more, the authenticity of the *hypomnemata* is a notorious crux. It is certainly possible that Perdiccas included fictitious proposals which he knew would antagonise the army in order to induce them to revoke the whole of Alexander's *acta* [records]. If so, those proposals would have been couched in the most provocative terms. There is, then, no certainty that even the original proposal to transplant populations emanates from Alexander, let alone the parenthetical comment. And the force of the comment is that Alexander envisaged a general spirit of unity among all his subjects, Greek and barbarian; it is not in any sense a plan to combine Macedonians and Persians as a joint ruling class. The only connection with the Opis prayer is the fact that the concept of *homonoia* [concord] occurs in both passages!

The next relevant observation comes from Eratosthenes, who observed that Alexander ignored advice to treat the Greeks as friends and barbarians as enemies, preferring to welcome all possible men of fair repute and be their benefactor. On the surface Eratosthenes' comment has nothing to do with any policy of fusion; it is merely the just observation that Alexander was catholic in his benefactions and did not treat the conquered peoples with hostility. There is no hint here of a proposed union of races. But discussion has been unforgivably confused by the belief that Eratosthenes lies at the base of Plutarch's exposition in the first of his speeches *On Alexander's Fortune*. As is well known, this essay is the prime source for the view of Alexander as the reconciler of mankind. In a famous passage of rhetoric Plutarch tells of the rejection of Aristotle's advice to treat the Greeks [as their leader]; Alexander blended all men together, mixing their lives, marriages and ways of life in a *krater* [mixing bowl] of friendship and making his only distinction between Greek and barbarian a man's virtue or vice. After the recent analyses by Badian and Hamilton there should be no question that the whole shaping of the passage is Plutarch's own, designed to show that Alexander achieved in fact the single polity which Zeno advocated. He may have drawn on Eratosthenes, but nothing suggests that the passage as a whole is an extract or summary. In particular there is no reason to believe that Eratosthenes used the metaphor of mixing.

There is still a tendency to argue that Eratosthenes described a policy of fusion. Two chapters later Plutarch explicitly cites him on the subject of Alexander's court dress, a mixture of Persian and Macedonian elements. He goes on to explain that the object was to win the respect of the subject peoples and further the aim of a single law and polity for all mankind. But there is nothing to suggest that Plutarch's interpretation of the mixed dress comes from Eratosthenes. The whole passage is designed to buttress the paradoxical thesis that Alexander was a philosopher in arms and seeking the reconciliation of mankind which was merely preached as an ideal by conventional philosophers. The concrete examples of the

Susa marriages and the adoption of mixed court dress are chosen as examples of his achievement of *koinonia* [community] and the choice is Plutarch's own. The reference to Eratosthenes seems thrown in as a passing remark, just as he interlaces his exposition with casual references to Onesicritus, Aristobulus, Anaximenes and Duris. Eratosthenes, we may be sure, described Alexander's court dress, but we cannot assume that he gave it an ecumenical significance. . . .

In these pieces of epideictic rhetoric it is the thesis adopted for debate which determines both the choice of material and the interpretation put upon it, and it is a possibility, if no more, that the whole topic of racial fusion in Alexander's reign was a creation of the rhetorical schools of the early Empire. In Plutarch himself there is only one reference in the *Life of Alexander* (Plut. 47.3) to Alexander's efforts to achieve *koinonia* and *anakrasis* [mixture], and the examples he chooses are different from those in the earlier speech — the creation of the *Epigoni* [successors] and the Marriage to Roxane. And there is virtually no reference to racial fusion outside Plutarch. Only Curtius places in Alexander's mouth a speech commemorating the Susa marriages as a device to remove all distinction between victor and vanquished. This speech was allegedly delivered to the Iranian soldiers during the Opis mutiny, and once again the circumstances determine the content of the speech. The subject matter, as often in Curtius, may be derived from his immediate source; but the speech is composed in generalities with none of the interesting points of authentic detail found in other Curtian speeches, and it seems to me that the observations on the fusion of Macedonian and Iranian tradition are most likely to be embellishments by Curtius himself.

We may begin with the assumption of Persian court ceremonial. This is most fully described by the vulgate sources, especially Diodorus who mentions five aspects. Alexander introduced court chamberlains of Asiatic stock and a bodyguard of distinguished nobles, including Darius' brother Oxyathres. Secondly he adopted some aspects of Persian court dress — the diadem, the white-striped tunic and the girdle. Next he distributed scarlet robes and Persian harness to his companions, and finally took over Darius' harem of 360 concubines. Curtius has much the same detail but adds that Alexander used Darius' ring for his correspondence in

Asia. The sources assess these moves variously. The vulgate sources unanimously regard them as a decline towards barbarian custom, as indeed does the normally uncritical Arrian (later he suggests on his own initiative that the adoption of mixed dress was a device to win over the barbarians). Plutarch in his life represents the mixed dress as either an adaptation to native custom or an anticipation of the introduction of *proskynesis* [prostration]. It is only in *On Alexander's Fortune* that he represents it as a means to bring about friendship between victor and vanquished. There is no indication that any of the ancient sources had direct information about Alexander's motives for the innovation.

It should be emphasised that the adoption of Persian court protocol was fairly extensive, not confined to Alexander's choice of a mixed court dress. On the one hand he used Persians in ceremonial positions, but he also issued his *hetairoi* [Companions] with the traditional purple robes of the Achaemenid courtiers. The new king had his courtiers, but they were Macedonians. As yet there was no attempt to integrate the two nobilities. Diodorus implies quite clearly that they formed separate groups. The Persians might be given posts as chamberlains and selected nobles formed into a corps of *doryphoroi* [spear-bearers], but Alexander showed clearly by his distribution of purple that the courtiers of the new Great King were his Macedonians. In his dress and court ceremonial Alexander adopted Achaemenid practices but he kept Persians and Macedonians distinct and the Macedonians were in a privileged position.

The date of the innovation is also important. Plutarch states explicitly that Alexander first assumed mixed dress during the rest period in Parthia after the Hyrcanian expedition, that is, in autumn 330. It is precisely at this point that the vulgate sources place the episode, and we cannot doubt the accuracy of the chronology. Now Alexander's claims to be the legitimate king of the Persian empire go back at least to the Marathus correspondence of early 332, when he demanded that Darius acknowledge him as overlord. After Gaugamela he was solemnly pronounced King of Asia and furthered his claims by solemnly occupying the throne of Darius in Susa. It is possible (though it cannot be proved) that Alexander was never formally consecrated in Pasargadae, and he seems never to have used the title "King of Kings" in his dealings with the Greek world. But his claims to be the legitimate king of the Persian empire were absolute. Yet, even so, Alexander did not adopt Achaemenid court protocol until at least six weeks after the death of Darius. What was the importance of the period in Parthia? The answer is that Alexander now had a rival. It was precisely at the time that he returned to Parthia that Alexander learned that Bessus had declared himself Darius' successor, assuming the jealously guarded royal prerogative, the *kitaris* or upright tiara, and also the regnal name Artaxerxes. . . . It was late 329 before Bessus was captured and the last rebels were brought from Parthia and Areia to meet the judgment of Alexander. There had been almost a year of challenge and insurrection, and it is difficult to believe that Alexander did not foresee trouble when he first heard of Bessus' usurpation.

The adoption of court protocol had an obvious propaganda value in these circumstances. Alexander demonstrated that he was genuinely King of Kings, not a mere foreign usurper, and the bodyguard of noble Persians was crucial to his claim. At his court in a position of high honour was none other than Oxyathres, brother of the late king. Not only was Alexander the self-proclaimed successor to Darius, but Darius' brother recognised the claim and supported Alexander's court ceremonial. This had been one of Alexander's assertions as early as 332, when he boasted that the Persians in his entourage followed him out of free choice. At the same time Alexander adopted some items of Persian court dress, not the more obtrusive regalia (the tiara, and the purple trousers and long-sleeved cloak), but the diadem, the royal tunic and girdle, which he wore with the broad-brimmed Macedonian hat (*kausia*) and the Macedonian cloak.

Even this caused serious discontent among the Macedonian army — and Macedonian resistance to things oriental is one of the persistent factors of Alexander's reign. All sources stress the hostility to Alexander's adoption of mixed dress and it is prominent in the list of grievances which led to the Opis mutiny in 324. The cleft widened among Alexander's officers, and the disagreements between Craterus and Hephaestion were notorious; Craterus, we are told, steadfastly adhered to Macedonian tradition. . . . The reason Plutarch gives (excerpting Hieronymus) is that Craterus often incurred Alexander's hatred by opposing his inclination to Persian excess and protecting ancestral customs from erosion. Now it is notable that in the latter years of Alexander's reign Craterus was sent repeatedly on lengthy missions away from court, almost assuming the mantle of [second in command] Parmenio. In particular he led the army division of Macedonian veterans first from India to Carmania in 325–324 and then from Opis to the coast. The veterans were the men most closely bound to him but his popularity was universal and the reason was his championship of ancestral custom. Macedonian kings were said to rule by custom rather than force and the sight of a Heraclid and Argead in the trappings of the Great King, the paradigm of despotism, must have been deeply shocking. All the more so since the march from Babylon, which had been a triumphal progress, marked by the sacking of Persepolis and the burning of the palace and finally the ignominious death of the last Archaemenid at the hands of his subjects. Now the victor was assuming the protocol of the vanquished, acting the part of Great King and declaring his intentions of remaining as lord of Asia — a matter of weeks after his troops had come near mutiny in their desire to end the campaign and return home.

The autumn of 330 was a time of crisis when Alexander was under strong and conflicting pressures. On the one hand the challenge from Bessus and his temporary shortage of troops forced him to propaganda, demonstrating to his subjects that he was not merely a foreign conqueror but the true Great King, supported by the old nobility of Darius. On the other he could not antagonise his Macedonians by too outrageous a breach of custom. The mixed dress was a compromise, taking on the very minimum of Persian attire compatible with his pretentions; and at the same time Alexander's Macedonian companions were given the purple robes of courtiers. This involved them in some of the odium of breach of custom and at the same time marked them out as the friends and satraps [governors] of the Great King. It was a limited experiment, and Diodorus is probably right that Alexander used the new ceremonial fairly sparingly. . . .

The court ceremonial was far more obtrusive after the return from India in 325–324. Alexander's mixed court dress figured prominently in the complaints made by his Macedonian troops before the Opis mutiny, and, far from confining it to his appearances before barbarian subjects, he now wore it every day, the Macedonian cloak with the Persian white-striped tunic and the Macedonian *kausia* with the Persian diadem. The source admittedly is Ephippus of Olynthus, who was markedly hostile to Alexander, but there is no reason to doubt what he says. In any case it is not the day-to-day costume of the king that he is out to pillory but the outrageous charades that he staged at banquets, dressing as Ammon, Hermes, Heracles and even Artemis. Ephippus' evidence moreover fits in well with what is otherwise known of the extravagance of Alexander's court during his last year. There is a famous description, deriving from the third century author, Phylarchus, which deals with the day-to-day splendour of Alexander's court. Three versions survive (in Athenaeus, Aelian and Polyaenus) and they are complementary. All these sources indicate that the court scene described was regular in Alexander's later days, but it is clear that the description refers primarily to the five-day period of the Susa marriages. The vast tent with its 100 couches and 50 golden pillars corresponds to the description of the Susa marriage hall provided by Alexander's chamberlain, Chares of Mytilene, and it is hard to see how such a mammoth structure could have accompanied Alexander on all his travels. Similarly Polyaenus refers to a group of 500 dignitaries from Susa who formed a group outside the tent and there is no reason why such a group should have been present when the court was not at Susa. The description, then, refers to a limited period, but the arrangements described are interesting. The court was arranged in concentric circles around Alexander and his *somatophylakes* [body guards], that is, the eight supreme marshals of the Macedonian nobility. The first circle comprised 500 Macedonian silver-shields, selected for their physique; next came 1,000 archers in multicoloured costumes, and on the outer circle of the tent 500 Persian *melophoroi*, the old infantry guard of the Achaemenid court with the distinctive golden apples on their spear butts. Alexander now had two royal guards, one the traditional Macedonian *agema* of hypaspists (the equation with silver-shields is certain) and the other the traditional Achaemenid guard, but the two forces were kept distinct — the Macedonians closest to the king and the Persians separated by a girdle of archers. The division was continued outside the tent where the *agema* of elephants was stationed together with 1,000 Macedonians in Macedonian dress and in the final outer circle 10,000 Persians in Persian costume and scimitars. This was a brilliant display of Persian and Macedonian ceremonial, but the two races were kept rigidly separated. There was no attempt at integration — nor even of *"Gleichstellung"* [equalization], for the Macedonians were invariably closer to the king. Again we have no reason to doubt the main details of this description. The arrangement with its concentric circles was clearly imitated in Peucestas' great state banquet at Persepolis in 317 B.C., only here it was the closeness to Philip and Alexander which was emphasised by the division and at the centre Persian dignitaries occupied couches alongside Macedonians.

Some degree of integration had taken place by the end of the reign. After the great mutiny of 324 Alexander introduced 1,000 Persians into the court guard of hypaspists. Both Diodorus and Justin agree on the fact but differ over whether it came after or during the mutiny. Either it was part of Alexander's moves to bring his Macedonians to heel or it was a consequence of the mutiny, a permanent reminder of his threat to recruit his guard from Persians alone. But even so there is no evidence that the two races were intermingled in the guard and some that they were not. . . .

It is clear that Alexander's court had become much more pretentious in the last two years of his life. The mixed dress was a more permanent feature and there was an increasing use of Persian *melophoroi* ["apple-bearers" — royal guard] as court guards. The pomp and circumstance fits well the increasing megalomania of Alexander's last years which, as is well known, rose to a climax after the death of Hephaestion. The increase in Persian ceremonial was doubtless caused by the fact that in 325–324 Alexander was travelling consistently between the old Achaemenid capitals (Persepolis, Susa, Ecbatana and Babylon) and needed to display himself to his oriental subjects as the new Great King. What is more, his absence in India between 327 and 325 had brought renewed insubordination and insurrection. The satraps of Carmania, Susiana and Paraetacene were executed when Alexander returned to the west and replaced by Macedonians. More seriously, when he reached Persia proper he discovered that Orxines, apparently a lineal descendant of Cyrus the Great who had commanded the Persian contingent at Gaugamela, had established himself as satrap without any authorisation by Alexander. There had also been trouble in the inner satrapies, for Craterus needed to arrest an insurgent, Ordanes, during his progress through southern Iran; and in Media a certain Baryaxes had assumed the upright tiara and laid claim to the throne of the Medes and Persians. Alexander must have felt that there was widespread reluctance among his Iranian subjects to accept his regal authority, and his parade of all the magnificence of the Achaemenid court including the old bodyguard of *melophoroi* is perfectly understandable. But while Alexander increased the Persian complement in his immediate entourage he appears to have reduced their political influence away from court. The end of the reign saw only three Iranians governing satrapies — Alexander's own father-in-law in distant Parapamisadae, the impeccably loyal Phrataphernes in Parthia/Hyrcania, and Atropates in Media, the satrapy with the most formidable garrison of Hellenic troops. There are many aspects to Alexander's behaviour. We may plausibly argue a desire to flaunt ostentatiously the splendour of his court, to impress his Iranian subjects with his military power and legitimacy as Great King; and there are signs that he used his promotion of Iranians to crush discontent among his Macedonian army. What we cannot as yet assume is any serious policy of assimilating and fusing the two races. The reverse seems the case.

We must now turn to the theme of mixed marriage, which was the original inspiration for Droysen's idea of the "policy of fusion." For almost the first ten years of his reign Alexander avoided marriage with remarkable success. After Issus the majority of the Persian royal ladies were in his power. Alexander scrupulously cultivated the Queen Mother, Sisygambis as his "Mother" and promised dowries to Darius' daughters. Taking over Darius' functions as son and father he buttressed his claims to be the genuine King of Asia. But he stopped short of actual marriage, contenting himself with a liaison with Barsine, the daughter of Artabazus and descendant of Artaxerxes II. This liaison was protracted and from it came a son, Heracles, born in 327, but there was no question of marriage until the last days of Alexander's campaign in Bactria/Sogdiana. Then came his meeting with Roxane and almost immediate marriage. The circumstances whereby Roxane came into his hands cannot be elucidated here, for they involve one of the most intractable clashes of authority between Arrian and the vulgate tradition, but fortunately there is unanimity about the date of the wedding (spring 327) and equal unanimity that it was a love match.

There is, however, no suggestion of a policy of fusion. Curtius merely accredits him with a statement that it was conducive to the stability of the empire that Persians and Macedonians were joined in marriage; the arrogance of the victors and shame of the vanquished would both be reduced. This is a far cry from the symbolic union of races which many have seen in the marriage.

There is, however, a point to be stressed. Alexander married Roxane whereas he had only formed a liaison with Barsine. If all that was at issue was physical attraction, there was no reason for a formal marriage, unless we believe that Alexander's chivalry had improved since Issus. There were undoubtedly political reasons as well. Roxane married Alexander in spring 327 on the eve of his march into India. The previous two years had seen unremitting warfare caused by repeated insurrections inside Bactria/Sogdiana and invasions from the Saka nomads of the steppes. Alexander's response had been increasingly savage repression. . . . At the same time Alexander founded a network of military settlements with a nucleus of Greek mercenaries and discharged Macedonian veterans together with settlers from the barbarian hinterland. The relationship between Greek and barbarian is hard to elicit in this instance, but both Curtius and Justin suggest that the barbarians involved in the foundation of Alexandria Eschate were survivors from the recently conquered cities, especially Cyropolis. . . . Hellenic military settlements dominated the bulk of the countryside and the hierarchy was exclusively Greco-Macedonian.

The marriage to Roxane marks the final act of the settlement, and Curtius may be justified in viewing it as an act of conciliation after two years of warfare and devastation. But there is another aspect. The taking of a bride from the Iranian nobility of Bactria underlined Alexander's claims to be the legitimate lord of the area. . . . It was natural that after demonstrating his military supremacy to the Bactrians and Sogdians he married one of their princesses, cementing his rule by the wedding. There is a tradition moreover that Alexander also persuaded some of his friends to marry Bactrian ladies. If it is true (and there is no contrary evidence), his fellow bridegrooms may well have been the satrap and garrison commanders left behind after the march on India. The new lords of the region would now have native wives.

Finally we come to the palladium of Alexander's alleged policy of fusion — the mass marriage at Susa at which Alexander and 91 of his Companions took Iranian brides. The weddings were celebrated with the utmost splendour in the Iranian mode and Alexander commemorated the event by distributing gifts to Macedonian soldiers who had taken native wives, to the number of 10,000. Without doubt this was a ceremony of unparalleled pomp with important political implications, but the sources leave us totally uninformed of those implications. In the speech *On Alexander's Fortune* Plutarch represents the marriage as a means of uniting the two imperial peoples, as does Curtius in the speech he attributes to Alexander; but, as we have seen, both statements reflect the rhetorical interpretations of the first century A.D. rather than any authentic tradition from the time of Alexander. But if we look at the recorded facts, one feature stands out starkly — so starkly that it is incredible that it was first noted by Hampl in 1954. The marriages were totally one-sided. Persian wives were given to Macedonian husbands, but there is no instance of the reverse relationship. Admittedly Alexander's court was not well endowed with noble ladies of Greek or Macedonian extraction, but, if his aim was really to place the two imperial races on an equal footing, it would have been relatively easy for him to import the necessary brides from mainland Greece and delay the ceremony until they arrived. In fact there is nothing attested except Persian women married to Greco-Macedonian men. The names as recorded are striking. Alexander and Hephaestion both married daughters of Darius, Craterus a daughter of Darius' brother, Oxyathres. The other wives whose names are recorded came from prominent satrapal families — daughters of Artabazus, Atropates of Media, and even Spitamenes, the leader of the insurgent Sogdians during 329 and 328. This was an integration of sorts, but its effect was to mark out Alexander's Companions as the new rulers of the Persian Empire. They already had the scarlet robes of Persian courtiers; now they were married into the most prominent satrapal families. Nothing could have made it clearer that Alexander intended his Macedonians to rule with him as the new lords of the conquered empire.

It is also debatable how far Alexander intended his Macedonians to be assimilated into Persian ways. The traditional view is that Alexander wished the Macedonian nobles to adapt themselves to Persian customs but was frustrated by the Macedonians' tenacious adherence to their ancestral tradition. This theory rests primarily upon Arrian's account of Peucestas' installation as satrap of Persis in early 324. As soon as he was appointed he affected Median dress and became the only Macedonian to do so and learn the Persian language. Alexander commended him for his actions and he became popular with his Persian subjects, correspondingly unpopular with the mutinous Macedonian rank-and-file. Peucestas' adoption of Persian customs is an unchallengeable fact, . . . but Diodorus gives another perspective when he explains Peucestas' popularity with his subjects in 317 B.C. Alexander, so it was said, made a concession. Only Peucestas was *allowed* to wear Persian dress, so that the favour of the Persians could be secured. If we accept the text as it stands (and nothing in Arrian contradicts it) we must conclude that as a general rule Macedonian nobles were not permitted to assume the full Persian dress. The satrap of Persis was the one exception. Doubtless Alexander had laid to heart the lesson of Orxines' usurpation and concluded that in Persis his satrap had to conform and be seen to conform to the local *mores*. And in the case of Peucestas there was no reason to suspect his personal loyalty; he had saved the king in the Malli town and owed his promotion to Alexander's favour. He could therefore be encouraged to adapt himself to Persian tradition and ingratiate himself with his subjects. In other satrapies Alexander might have felt it prudent to drive a wedge between the satraps and their subjects. The rulers were marked out by their dress as aliens and were accordingly most unlikely to develop the accord with their subjects which they would need to revolt from the central authority. The evidence of Diodorus suggests that Peucestas was not meant to be a paradigm for other governors but rather an exception to the general rule.

It is difficult to trace any admission of Persian nobles into the Macedonian court hierarchy. Before 324 the only certain example is Oxyathres, brother of Darius, who was admitted to the ranks of the *hetairoi* [Companions] immediately after his brother's death. It is hazardous to argue from silence, given the defective nature of all Alexander histories, but there is some evidence that Persians were initially excluded from the court hierarchy. . . .

By 324 there were more Iranians among the *hetairoi*. Arrian gives the names of nine nobles who were drafted into the élite cavalry *agema*, the king's guard. The list is intended to be exhaustive, and what makes the first impression is its brevity. Not only is the list short but the families are well known — a group selected by Alexander for especial distinction. There is a son of Artabazus, two sons of Mazaeus, two of Phrataphernes and finally Itanes, brother of Alexander's wife Roxane. The fathers were all satraps and their loyalty was impeccable throughout the reign. Two names, Mithrobaeus and Aegobares, are totally unknown, but the leader of the group, Hystaspes of Bactria, was connected by marriage to the house of Artaxerxes III Ochus, and he may have been a descendant of the son of Xerxes who ruled Bactria in the fifth century. The lineage of these nobles was beyond reproach and, given their small numbers, one may assume that Alexander was forming an élite within the Persian nobility. One can only guess at his motives, but there were two clear results from his actions. The small group of nobles incorporated in the *agema* were effectively isolated from their father's satrapies. They were trained and armed in Macedonian style and doubtless identified with the conquerors by their people. At the same time they acted as hostages for their parents, as did the Macedonian pages around Alexander's person. These additions to the *agema* seem a parallel phenomenon to Alexander's satrapal appointments. The Iranian satraps were reduced to a handful — Phrataphernes, Oxyartes and Atropates — and their sons were attached to Alexander's own court, separated by distance and culture from their roots in the satrapies.

The evidence so far has produced little or nothing that suggests any policy of fusion. Alexander's actions when viewed in their historical context seem rather to indicate a policy of division. There was no attempt to intermix the Macedonian and Persian nobilities, if anything an attempt to keep them apart. In particular the Macedonians seem to have been cast as the ruling race. It is they who monopolise the principal commands, civil and military, they who marry the women of the Persian aristocracy, they who dominate court life. Even when Alexander adopted Persian ceremonial his Macedonians were marked out as his courtiers and his chiliarch (or grand vizier) was no Persian but his bosom friend Hephaestion. By contrast apart from a small, carefully chosen élite the Persians had no positions of power at court and the Iranian satraps were inexorably reduced in numbers as the reign progressed. The factor which dominated everything was Alexander's concept of personal autocracy. From early 332 to the end of his life he declared himself King of Asia. He acknowledged no equal and all were his subjects. Against that background the traditional recalcitrance of the Iranian satraps was totally unacceptable and, I believe, Alexander's actions can largely be explained as a demonstration of the fact of conquest. His court ceremonial underlined that he alone was the Great King and the mass marriages made it patently obvious that he and his nobles were the inheritors of the Achaemenids. As for the Persians, they were gradually extracted from the satrapies in which they had been prematurely confirmed in the years after Gaugamela and only a small group was left, tied by marriage to the Macedonian conquerors and with sons virtual hostages at court. This is a far cry from any policy of fusion. The only counter evidence comes from the Opis mutiny, when Alexander turned to his Iranians in order to crush disaffection among the Macedonians. Afterwards Alexander was able to pray for community of command, but the prayer was demonstrably affected by the recent events. In effect there is no hint that Alexander gave positions of power to Iranians during his last year; the hierarchy of command remained stubbornly Macedonian.

If there is no trace of any planned integration of the Macedonian and Persian aristocracies, it might be thought that the fusion took place at a lower level. By the end of his reign Alexander certainly possessed a mixed army, in which Persians and Macedonians fought side by side both in the phalanx and Companion cavalry. But did the mixture come about by policy or by military necessity? And how rigorous was the fusion? Were the two races divided into separate subunits or did they fight side by side in integrated companies and with common weaponry? These questions are fundamental and once again require close examination of the evidence.

According to orthodox dogma Alexander began to use oriental cavalry at an early stage. In his description of the Hyrcanian campaign (late summer 330) Arrian notes that the king now had a body of mounted javelin-men. These troops were used repeatedly in the campaigns in central Iran and Bactria, and it is universally assumed that they were a select Iranian squadron, recruited to give extra flexibility to his cavalry. But there is no hint in any of the ten references in Arrian that these troops were Iranians. In fact they are invariably grouped with regular units of the Macedonian army, the Agrianians, and the Companions. . . .

The first unequivocal reference to use of oriental troops comes in the Sogdian revolt of 328–327, when we are told that Bactrians and Sogdians fought in the satrapal forces of Amyntas. When he left Bactria for India Alexander had with him large numbers of Iranian cavalry, from Bactria, Sogdiana, Arachosia and Parapamisadae. There were also Saka cavalry from the northern steppes. These troops fought alongside the Macedonians at the Hydaspes but they were brigaded in separate formations and outside the battle narrative they are not individually mentioned. There is one exception, the squadron of horse-archers which first emerges during the march on India and is mentioned repeatedly in Arrian's campaign narrative. . . . These horse-archers seem to have been recruited from the Dahae, who are specifically designated the horse-archers at the Hydaspes, and it looks as though they formed a *corps d'élite* corresponding to the Agrianians in the infantry. The first appearance of these Iranian troops is significant. After the protracted campaign in Bactria/Sogdiana Alexander was leaving the area altogether and moving to invade India. The Iranian cavalry were being employed outside their home territory where there was little chance of disaffection. Alexander could safely draw upon them to strengthen his own cavalry, and at the same time they served as a great pool of hostages, exactly as had the troops of the Corinthian League during the first years of the campaign. They fought in national units and there was as yet no attempt to combine them with his Macedonian troops.

The combination took place, in the cavalry at least, after Alexander's return to the west in 325. The only evidence unfortunately is a single passage of Arrian which is at best unclear and most probably corrupt. In his list of Macedonian grievances at Susa Arrian gives superficially detailed information about the use of barbarians in the cavalry (7.6.2–5); this he summarises two chapters later as an admixture of heterogeneous cavalry into the ranks of the barbarians. What kind of admixture is meant? Arrian divides the Macedonians' grievance into three parts. In the first place he mentions that certain Iranians, selected for their social distinction and physique, were assigned to the Companion cavalry. There were three categories, carefully marked off: first Bactrians, Sogdians and Arachosians; next Drangians, Areians and Parthyaeans; and finally an obscure group of Persians termed the "Euacae." As Brunt saw, these groups correspond to the cavalry taken from Bactria in 327, the troops which arrived in Carmania in late 325, and finally cavalry levied in Persis in early 324. The incorporation of the last two groups was a relatively recent occurrence, but it is possible that the Bactrian cavalry had been integrated with the Companions as early as the campaign in Southern India. . . . Arrian makes the situation clearer in his next phrase. Besides these Iranians assigned to the Companion cavalry there was a fifth hipparchy [calvary unit] which was not entirely barbarian. The phrase implies clearly that there were four hipparchies consisting wholly of Iranian cavalry and a fifth which was only partially so. It must be emphasised that the passage says nothing about the number of Macedonian hipparchies at this period (although it has frequently been taken to do so). What is at issue is the reaction of the Macedonians to Persian involvement in the Companion cavalry, and their grievances are presented in ascending order. First comes the objection that the Iranians were organised in separate hipparchies within the cavalry body, next the more serious complaint that there was a mixed hipparchy, in which Iranians and Macedonians served together and finally the crowning outrage that there was a troop of Persian nobles inside the élite *agema*. The organisation of the Macedonians was irrelevant to the grievances, and we must assume that there was an unspecified number of Macedonian hipparchies *in addition to* the four Persian hipparchies and the mixed hipparchy. The total number at this period cannot even be guessed at. . . .

If the evidence of Arrian is strictly interpreted, it indicates that, apart from one hipparchy, Macedonians and Iranians served in separate units within the body of the Companion cavalry. In other words, the Iranian cavalry shared the title of *hetairoi*. This has often been doubted, but Arrian's terminology seems unambiguous: they were assigned to the Companion cavalry. Alexander's actions at Opis are not contrary evidence. There he began to create new formations of Persians bearing the Macedonian names, including a fresh cavalry *agema* "and the cavalry of the Companions." This does not imply that all Companions had previously been Macedonians, rather that in future he intended to have a corps of

Companions who were exclusively Persian. That is quite compatible with a situation before the mutiny in which Macedonians and Iranians served together in a single body of Companions. And the single reference in Arrian to Macedonian Companions does not exclude there having been Persian Companions also. A curious picture therefore emerges. The Iranian cavalry largely served in separate hipparchies, and they retained their national weapons (it is only the group of nobles in the *agema* who are said to have exchanged their javelins for Macedonian lances). Nevertheless they served in the Companion cavalry and presumably bore the title *hetairoi*. It would seem that Alexander was using the traditional policy of Macedonian kings. The title *pezhetairoi* (Foot Companions), as a name for the entire phalanx infantry, appears to have been introduced as a deliberate measure to place the infantry on terms of equality with the cavalry. The King named all his infantry his Companions and emphasised their close ties to him, thus setting them up as a group parallel and opposed to the aristocratic cavalry, the group which had previously monopolised the title of Companion. Alexander, it seems, did the same with his cavalry, establishing a body of Iranian Companions in the same organisation as the Macedonians. This development fits well into the period after the Hyphasis mutiny, when Alexander was faced with disaffection or, at best, lack of enthusiasm among his own troops. The admission of Iranian Companions made it clear that he was not limited to his Macedonians and could find support elsewhere. It was an implicit threat, which was nearly fulfilled at Opis. There is, then, no trace of a policy of fusion. Once again the tendency seems to have been to keep Iranians and Macedonians separate and even mutually suspicious. Each served as a check and balance on the other.

The pattern is further exemplified in Alexander's use of Iranian infantry. First and foremost is the formation of 30,000 *Epigoni* [Successors], Iranian youths armed in Macedonian fashion and trained in phalanx discipline. All sources agree that the *Epigoni* arrived during Alexander's stay in Susa and aroused the jealousy and fear of the Macedonians by their brilliant display. Plutarch alone says that the institution was designed to promote a mixture and harmony; the vulgate sources see much more sinister motives. For Diodorus the formation was Alexander's reaction to the recalcitrance of his Macedonian troops ever since the Hyphasis mutiny (he speaks of the Ganges!). The king needed an *antitagma* for his Macedonian phalanx. Pierre Briant has recently elucidated the sense of *antitagma*; it was a counter-army. . . . Alexander intended the Persians not only to balance his Macedonian forces but also to be thrown against them if necessary.

Curtius describes the origins of this new counter-infantry, claiming that Alexander gave orders for the levy of 30,000 youths before he left Bactria in 327, intending them to be conveyed to him when trained, to act as hostages as well as soldiers. His order is presented as a security measure — a measure against the Iranians not the Macedonians. . . . Originally, then, Alexander's intention might have been to skim away the most outstanding youths of the central satrapies, train them in effective infantry tactics and then isolate them from their cultural background. As the morale and obedience of his Macedonians declined he saw the potential of his new infantry phalanx and deliberately used the new force to balance and intimidate his Macedonians. It was essential that the two infantry bodies were kept distinct — an obvious and permanent exception to any policy of fusion.

According to Justin there was a second body of *Epigoni*, the offspring of mixed marriages between Macedonian soldiers and Asiatic wives. Justin states that Alexander began to encourage these unions in 330, at the time when he first adopted Persian dress. Two motives are given — to reduce his troops' longing for domestic life in Macedonia and to create an army of mixed race whose only home was the camp. Justin is fuller than usual and not apparently garbled; and there is corroborative evidence. Arrian agrees that more than 10,000 mixed marriages had been contracted by the time of the celebrations at Susa and the veterans of Opis had produced a fair number of offspring by their native wives, enough for Alexander to retain them, promising to train them in Macedonian style and to reunite them with their fathers when they reached manhood. The evidence is consistent and indicates that Alexander had long- and short-term objectives. In the first place the legitimisation of his troops' liaisons with native women gave them an inducement to remain in Asia which was stronger than mere concubinage and politically desirable in 330, when there was agitation in the army to conclude the campaign and return to Macedonia. The ultimate aim, however, was to produce a corps of troops without roots in Europe or permanent home in Asia, the janissaries of the new Empire, whose loyalty would be to Alexander alone. The two bodies of *Epigoni* were alike in their close attachment to the court and their training in Macedonian discipline. In both cases Alexander was attempting to create a supranational army, but his motives were grounded in practical politics and military considerations were paramount.

So far the evidence has indicated that Alexander kept Iranians and Macedonians separated in both cavalry and infantry and that he used the two races to counterbalance each other. There is, however, one instance of a combined force of Persians and Macedonians. Shortly before Alexander's death Peucestas arrived in Babylon with a force of 20,000 Persians, reinforced with mountaineers from the Zagros and Elburz. The king commended this new force and assigned them to the Macedonian ranks. The details of this reorganisation are given, for once, and they are interesting. This new composite infantry was organised into files of sixteen, twelve Persians to four Macedonians. Each file was commanded by a Macedonian, backed by two other Macedonians in second and third place. The Persians then filled out the centre of the phalanx and a Macedonian brought up the rear. The four Macedonians were armed in traditional style (with the *sarisa* [pike]) and were given preferential rates of pay, whereas the Persians retained their native bows and javelins. The result was a curiously heterogeneous phalanx, packed with Persians untrained in Macedonian discipline. The Macedonians formed an élite, the first three ranks using *sarisae* and bearing the brunt of any attack. Even in the old phalanx there was hardly space for more than the first three ranks to use *sarisae* in couched position. In Polybius' day, when *sarisae* were longer, only the first five ranks were able to thrust with their weapons; the rest added weight and held their *sarisae* vertically as a screen against missiles. The Persians in the new phalanx added weight and numbers and no doubt they were intended to shoot arrows and javelins over the heads of the Macedonian ranks. . . .

It is strong *prima facie* evidence that Alexander's native Macedonian troops were in short supply by 323. There is every reason to believe that the main army was drained of Macedonians. . . . After Opis Alexander deliberately drained his infantry forces, sending with Craterus 6,000 of the veterans present at the Hellespont in 334 and 4,000 of the troops conveyed in later reinforcements. There is no statement how many remained, but one may assume that the fighting in India and the Gedrosian desert march took a heavy toll of life, and there is little trace of reinforcements. Only Curtius speaks of 8,000 *Graeci* [Greeks] sent to Sogdiana in 329–328 and 5,000 cavalry (*sic*) sent from Thrace in 326. There is no trace in the sources of Macedonian reinforcements and it seems that Antipater did not have the necessary manpower resources to cater to Alexander's demands. Diodorus says explicitly that Macedonia was drained of national troops in 323 because of the numbers of reinforcements sent to Asia, so that he could not cope with the initial crisis of the Lamian War. . . . [Alexander] was left with a nucleus of Macedonian veterans. He had ordered Antipater to bring prime troops from Macedonia to replace Craterus' army column but they could not be expected for some time after Craterus reached Macedon — and he was travelling with prudent slowness. But Alexander was about to embark on the Arabian expedition, and shortly before his death the advance orders for the departure of both land and naval forces had been given. There was no alternative but to make the best of his Macedonian veterans — to distribute them among the front-rank positions and fill up the phalanx in depth with Persian infantry. The mixture was patently forced upon Alexander by military necessity. Had the fresh levies from Macedon ever arrived, he would certainly have removed the Iranian rank and file and replaced them with the trained manpower from Macedon.

Nothing remains of the policy of fusion. As regards his military organisation Alexander was reacting to a series of problems. To begin with, his use of Iranians from the central satrapies was determined by his need for auxiliaries in the Indian campaign and the obvious desirability of removing crack fighting men from their native satrapies, where they would be fuel for any revolt against his regal authority. The next stage was to use his Iranian auxiliaries as a counterweight to his increasingly mutinous Macedonian troops, and finally, when the Macedonians were decimated and cowed, they were used as a pool of manpower to supplement the trained Macedonian cadres. There is nothing here remotely resembling a deliberate policy to fuse together the two peoples into a single army. If there is any policy it is *divide et impera.* We have seen Alexander at work at two levels. Firstly the continuous and traditional recalcitrance of his Iranian nobles forced him to proclaim his pretensions as the heir of the Achaemenids with increasing pomp and splendour and to make it increasingly obvious that his Greco-Macedonian nobles had in fact supplanted the Iranians as a ruling class. On the other hand the increasing disaffection of his Macedonian rank and file forced him to rely more on Iranian infantry and cavalry. If there is any consistent element it is Alexander's categorical claim to personal autocracy and the reciprocal demand for total obedience from his subjects at all levels of society. The resistance to that claim appeared in different forms and Alexander's response was accordingly different. There is little that can be said to approximate to careful premeditated policy; rather Alexander seems to have reacted promptly to the various challenges confronting him during his reign. The result is piecemeal and certainly less romantic than a visionary policy of fusion and conciliation but it is far truer to the evidence as it stands. . . .

Suggestions for Additional Reading

The immense scholarly literature on Alexander defies the restricted space of this section. The following is a selective guide for readers in English who would like to pursue the study of Alexander in greater depth.

The best general book on Alexander to date is A. B. Bosworth's *Conquest and Empire: The Reign of Alexander the Great* (Cambridge University Press, 1988). It combines an account of Alexander's career with discussions of specific problems associated with his reign. Peter Green's *Alexander of Macedon, 356–323 B.C.: A Historical Biography* (University of California Press, 1991) is a biography written in a lively style and includes some insightful and original observations, especially about Alexander's personality. J. R. Hamilton's *Alexander the Great* (Pittsburgh University Press, 1974) is a concise and straightforward account of the king. U. Wilcken's *Alexander the Great* (trans. G. C. Richards, W. W. Norton, 1967) was published originally in German in 1931 and represents one of the pre–World War II perceptions of Alexander in the influential German historiography of the king. An incisive review of Alexander's historiography can be found in E. Badian, "Alexander the Great, 1948–1967," *The Classical World* 65 (1971): 37–56, 77–83, and "Some Recent Interpretations of Alexander," in *Alexandre le Grand. Image et Réalité* (Entretiens Hardt, vol. 22, Vandoeuvre-Geneva: Fondation Hardt, 1976), 279–311. Badian concisely describes Alexander's campaign in *The Cambridge History of Iran*, vol. II (Cambridge University Press, 1985), 420–501, 897–903.

The fragments of the lost ancient works on Alexander were collected and commented upon by F. Jacoby, *Die Fragmente der Griechischen Historiker*, vols. IIB, IIBD (E. J. Brill, 1957–1969 [Berlin: 1927]). They were translated into English by C. A. Robinson Jr. in *The History of Alexander the Great*, vol. 1 (Brown University Press, 1953). L. Pearson's *The Lost Histories of Alexander the Great* (The American Philological Association, 1960) is an extensive examination of the fragments along the lines of traditional source criticism. Bosworth, one of Arrian's best readers and harshest critics, commented on the first three books of the *Anabasis* in *A Historical Commentary on Arrian's History of Alexander*, vol. 1 (Clarendon Press, 1980). Readers would benefit from his literary analysis of

Arrian in *From Arrian to Alexander* (Clarendon Press, 1988). J. R. Hamilton wrote a model commentary on Plutarch's *Alexander* in *Plutarch's Alexander: A Commentary* (Clarendon Press, 1969). The most important study of Curtius Rufus in English to date is J. E. Atkinson, *A Commentary on Q. Curtius Rufus' Historiae Alexandri Magni Books 3 & 4* (J. C. Gieben, 1980). N. G. L. Hammond, *Three Historians of Alexander the Great: The So-called Vulgate Authors, Diodorus, Justin and Curtius* (Cambridge University Press, 1983) presents Hammond's views of the other extant sources on Alexander. Translations into English of Arrian, Plutarch, Diodorus, and Curtius Rufus are published by Penguin Books and in the Loeb series of Harvard University Press. For Justin see *Justin, Cornelius Nepos and Eutropius,* trans. and ed. by J. S. Watson (G. Bell, 1875). An ancient fictional account of Alexander is *The Greek Alexander Romance,* trans. R. Stoneman (Penguin Books, 1991).

Interest in ancient Macedonia has increased in recent years. N. G. L. Hammond's *The Macedonian State: The Origins, Institutions and History* (Clarendon Press, 1989) and E. N. Borza's *In the Shadow of Olympus. The Emergence of Macedon* (Princeton University Press, 1990) are two studies that combine literary and archaeological evidence in analyzing the political and social history of Macedonia, thus illuminating Alexander's debt to his father and native land (see also Bar-Sharrar and Borza below). The Greek archaeologist M. Andronikos excavated the magnificent tombs in Vergina, Macedonia, and identified one of them as Philip II's; see his *Vergina: The Royal Tombs and the Ancient City* (Ekdotike Athenon, 1984). In "The Death of Philip II," *Phoenix* 17 (1963): 244–250, E. Badian suggests that Alexander was involved in his father's assassination.

For Alexander's relationship with the Greeks, V. Ehrenberg's *Alexander and the Greeks* (Basil Blackwell, 1938) is still useful. Badian discusses Alexander's treatment of the Greek city-states and the Greeks' perception of the Macedonians in "Alexander the Great and the Greeks of Asia," in *Ancient Society and Institutions* (Basil Blackwell, 1966), 37–68, and "Greeks and Macedonians," in B. Bar-Sharrar and E. N. Borza (eds.), *Macedonia and Greece in Late Classical and Early Hellenistic Times* (National Gallery of Art, 1982), 33–51.

Alexander's aims and plans are discussed by C. B. Welles in

"Alexander's Historical Achievements," *Greece & Rome* 12 (1965): 216–228, and by Bosworth in *From Arrian to Alexander*, 185–211. Relevant here, and to Part VIII, is Badian's rejection of Tarn's attempt to portray Alexander as a misunderstood visionary: "Alexander the Great and the Loneliness of Power," in *Studies in Greek and Roman History* (Basil Blackwell, 1964), 192–205.

Alexander and the Macedonian army are much praised by the prominent British military historian J. F. C. Fuller in *The Generalship of Alexander* (Da Capo Press, 1960 [Rutgers University Press, 1960]). M. M. Markle discusses in detail the weapons of the Macedonians and their employment in "Macedonian Arms and Tactics Under Alexander the Great," in Bar-Sharrar and Borza, 87–111. For the political aspects of Alexander's relationship with his army, see E. M. Anson, "The Evolution of the Macedonian Army Assembly (330–315 B.C.)," *Historia* 40 (1991): 230–247.

W. Heckel's *The Marshals of Alexander's Empire* (Routledge, 1992) is a very useful tool for anyone interested in the individual histories of commanders in Alexander's army; see also his "Factions and Macedonian Politics in the Reign of Alexander the Great," *Ancient Macedonia*, vol. 4 (Institute for Balkan Studies, 1986), 293–305. For the king and the nobility's relationship, N. G. L. Hammond's "Royal Pages, Personal Pages, and Boys Trained in the Macedonian Manner During the Period of the Temenid Monarchy," *Historia* 39 (1990): 261–290, is a study of Macedonian social history that has relevance to Part VII as well.

J. P. V. D. Balsdon, "The 'Divinity' of Alexander the Great," *Historia* 1 (1950): 363–388, argues that Alexander's request for *proskynesis* was an attempt to abide by Persian social customs rather than the expression of a personal wish to be deified. For Alexander, Callisthenes, and Anaxarchus, T. S. Brown's "Callisthenes and Alexander," *American Journal of Philology* 70 (1949): 225–248, is a sensible account; see also E. N. Borza, "Anaxarchus and Callisthenes: Academic Intrigue at Alexander's Court," in H. J. Dell (ed.) *Ancient Macedonian Studies in Honor of Charles F. Edson* (Institute for Balkan Studies, 1981), 73–86. Useful also is E. A. Fredricksmeyer's "Three Notes on Alexander's Deification," *American Journal of Ancient History* 4 (1979): 1–9.

Tarn's idea about Alexander's dream of a world of unity and brotherhood is elaborated in his *Alexander the Great: Sources and*

Studies, vol. 2 (Cambridge, London, New York, Melbourne, 1948), 399–450. It is convincingly refuted by Badian, "Alexander the Great and the Loneliness of Power" (above). J. R. Hamilton, "Alexander's Iranian Policy," in W. Will and J. Heinrichs (eds.), *Zu Alexander d. Gr.: Festschrift G. Wirth zum 60. Geburtstag am 9.12.86*, vol. 1 (Verlag Adolf M. Hakkart, 1987–1988), 467–486, is a response to Bosworth's study in Part VIII.

The following studies examine topics that are related to Alexander's reign but could not be included in this volume. *The Cambridge History of Iran*, vol. II (Cambridge University Press, 1985), describes the history of the Persian Empire before and after Alexander's conquest. On Alexander and his tutor Aristotle, see P. Merlan, "Isocrates, Aristotle, and Alexander the Great," *Historia* 3 (1954–1955): 60–81. The burning of Persepolis is discussed by E. Badian, "Agis III," *Hermes* 95 (1967): 170–192; *contra*: E. N. Borza, "Fire from Heaven," *Classical Philology* 67 (1972): 233–245, and see Badian's response in "Agis III: Revisions and Reflections," in I. Worthington (ed.), *Ventures into Greek History* (Clarendon Press, 1994), 258–292. F. L. Holt in *Alexander the Great and Bactria* (E. J. Brill, 1988) explores the disruptive impact of the conquest on the peoples of central Asia, and see also A. K. Narain, "Alexander in India," *Greece & Rome* 12 (1965): 155–165. E. Badian, "Harpalus," *Journal of Hellenic Studies* 81 (1961): 16–43, is a seminal study of Alexander's brutal treatment of high officials in the empire following his return from India. W. Heckel in *The Last Days and Testament of Alexander the Great* (Franz Steiner Verlag, 1988) discusses traditions surrounding the end of Alexander's reign. For Alexander in coinage and art, see, respectively, M. Thompson's "The Coinage of Philip II and Alexander III," in Bar-Sharrar and Borza (above), and E. von Schwartzenberg's "The Portraiture of Alexander," in *Alexandre le Grand* (above).